PATRICK SWAYZE
one last dance

Also by Wendy Leigh

Arnold: An Unauthorized Biography

One Lifetime Is Not Enough with Zsa Zsa Gabor

Liza, Born a Star

Prince Charming: The John F. Kennedy Jr. Story

Edward Windsor, Royal Enigma

*The Secret Letters of Marilyn Monroe
and Jacqueline Kennedy*

True Grace: The Life and Times of an American Princess

Life with My Sister Madonna with Christopher Ciccone

PATRICK SWAYZE

one last dance

WENDY LEIGH

SIMON SPOTLIGHT ENTERTAINMENT
NEW YORK   LONDON   TORONTO   SYDNEY

Simon Spotlight Entertainment
A Division of Simon & Schuster, Inc.
1230 Avenue of the Americas
New York, NY 10020

First Simon Spotlight Entertainment hardcover edition May 2009

SIMON SPOTLIGHT ENTERTAINMENT and colophon are trademarks of Simon & Schuster, Inc.

For information about special discounts for bulk purchases, please contact Simon & Schuster Special Sales at 1-866-506-1949 or business@simonandschuster.com.

The Simon & Schuster Speakers Bureau can bring authors to your live event. For more information or to book an event contact the Simon & Schuster Speakers Bureau at 1-866-248-3049 or visit our website at www.simonspeakers.com.

Manufactured in the United States of America

10 9 8 7 6 5 4 3 2 1

Library of Congress Cataloging-in-Publication Data is available

ISBN-13: 978-1-4391-4997-3
ISBN-10:   1-4391-4997-6

This book is dedicated to Sandy Williams-Martel,
a true woman of substance

CONTENTS

Prologue   **THE STAR**   1

One   **DEEP IN THE HEART OF TEXAS**   5

Two   **AN IMPRESSIONABLE AGE**   11

Three   **PRINCE CHARMING**   33

Four   **MY ANGEL**   41

Five   **EMERALD CITY**   61

Six   **TOP OF THE WORLD**   73

Seven   **DIRTY DANCING**   88

Eight   **SWAYZE MANIA**   108

Nine   **GHOST**   120

Ten   **BREAKING POINT**   135

Eleven   **THANKS FOR EVERYTHING**   146

Twelve   **DOWNWARD SPIRAL**   159

Thirteen   **FIGHTING BACK**   170

EPILOGUE   185

ACKNOWLEDGMENTS   187

SOURCE NOTES   193

prologue
THE STAR

8:07 a.m., Monday, August 18, 1952
Maternity and Children's Building
St. Joseph Hospital, Houston, Texas

The beautiful twenty-five-year-old girl was unconscious, her slanting dark blue eyes closed, her long, lustrous bronze-colored hair matted, her flawless olive skin covered in perspiration. Labor had begun unexpectedly and no one, least of all the girl herself, had been prepared for the agony she had just gone through. After all—like Scarlett O'Hara—she was of hardy Irish and Southern stock and this wasn't the first time she had given birth.

But this baby was different, this baby was six weeks premature, so premature in fact that even the pediatrician was caught by surprise and wasn't yet in the hospital.

The two nuns watching over the mother prayed silently that the pediatrician would make it in time and save the baby's life, but they gravely doubted it. The placenta had come loose from the uterine wall before the baby's head was delivered, thus depriving its brain of oxygen, and the baby was in danger of dying any second now.

They did everything possible to make the mother comfortable, but as for the baby, their only alternative was to pray that the poor mite would manage to breathe a few quick breaths rather than suffer such a cruel and untimely end.

Suddenly the maternity ward door swung open, and the hospital supervisor and surgical nurse strode in. Hospital supervisor Gladys Karnes (the former Gladys May Snell) was a champion swimmer, a woman of authority, a tough cookie not to be trifled with.

"We think we've lost the baby," one of the nuns said, her Irish brogue thick with emotion.

Gladys ignored her and reached into the mother and manually pulled the placenta away from her womb, freeing the baby to breathe for the very first time. As the two nuns wiped the mother's forehead, Gladys lifted the newborn baby into her strong arms and began rhythmically but gently slapping it on its back.

For a second the baby let out a small breath, then nothing. Gladys pressed her mouth to the baby's mouth and breathed air in, as much as she could, for as long as she could, infusing the tiny lungs with oxygen.

Then the pediatrician was by her side at last, caring for the baby, while the two nuns watched, mesmerized, not daring even to cry out "It's a boy" when they saw that it was.

He was less than fifteen inches long—five whole inches smaller than the average newborn baby—yet it was clear to the nuns, to Gladys, and to the pediatrician that he was struggling to breathe on his own, fighting to live, to survive.

To their relief, the baby boy was starting to breathe regularly. And it was almost uncanny that, with his rosy cheeks, long black eyelashes, and one blond wisp of hair in the middle of his forehead, he didn't look as if he had suffered any trauma whatsoever.

As the nuns gently passed him to his now-conscious mother, they were lost in wonder that he had survived and looked so perfect, so beautiful. "Your baby was born with a star on his head," one of the nuns said to the mother.

Exhausted as she was, and as emotional, Patsy Swayze understood perfectly. "Patrick had been born with a star on his head because he had survived one of the most traumatic births they had ever seen," she proudly declared years later, in her trademark throaty voice adding, "I'll never forget the words of that little Irish nun. But I knew what she meant . . . that Patrick was our little miracle, because he had survived such a difficult birth."

He was, indeed, born a survivor. Born to fight, born to win. He was also born to garner the untrammeled love, undivided attention, and unbounded admiration of the female sex. Not just because he would grow up handsome, charming, and unimpeachably masculine, but because the die was cast from the very first few minutes of his birth, when he was surrounded by three women who already loved him unconditionally: Gladys, the hospital supervisor, was his grandmother; the pediatrician was his great-aunt; and his mother, the strong-willed Texas beauty who, because he had almost died but didn't, would forever afterward love him with a love so passionate, so riddled with great expectations, that she would dominate his very existence.

And then there was that star . . .

one

DEEP IN THE HEART OF TEXAS

atrick Swayze was born in Texas, the second largest U.S. state—a state which, like him, is dramatically larger than life. But while he has always been universally regarded as the quintessential Texan, a close examination of his paternal roots tells quite another story.

While a large number of Texans boast Spanish, Mexican, or Indian ancestry, Patrick, in contrast, can trace his lineage back to England, where in 1619 his ancestor, John Swasey (sometimes known as "Sweezy"), was born in Bridgeport, Dorset. Christened at the church of St. Mary's, Bridgeport, in 1633, John Swasey sailed to Massachusetts on *The Recovery*. There he became a planter and, in 1640, purchased four acres of land in Salem, Essex County.

In May 1650, John Swasey married Katherine Kinge of Essex, England. Some genealogists claim that Swasey was one of the earliest Quakers, citing this as the reason for his refusing to take the oath of fidelity to the colony of New Haven. Whatever the grounds for his refusal, not taking the oath made him persona non grata in Salem. Consequently, in 1658 he and his wife moved to Southold, Suffolk County,

Long Island, New York. In 1706, at the age of eighty-six, he died in Acquefague, Suffolk County, leaving seven children behind.

One of those children, Joseph Swasey (born 1653), married Mary Betts and had six children with her. Samuel Swayze—later a judge—was born to Joseph and Mary in 1689 and was one of the first family members on record to use the modern-day spelling of the Swayze name.

In 1736, Samuel Swayze, his wife Penelope Horton, and their children moved from Long Island to Black River, Chester Township, Morris County, New Jersey, where they bought a parcel of land.

Samuel was a fervent Congregationalist, and in 1747 he and his fellow Congregationalists built their own meetinghouse with pews and galleries seating four hundred and worshipped there together. In 1753, Samuel Swayze Jr. (born in 1712) became the first pastor of the church, where he served as minister for the next twenty years.

In 1772, Samuel Swayze Jr. led a group of seventy-two families on a migration from Black River to the outskirts of Natchez, Adams County, Mississippi, where he formed a Congregationalist church. Soon he and his flock became known as the Jersey Settlers, who are today considered an integral and highly respected part of the history of the South.

Strangely enough, when Patrick made his big career breakthrough starring as Orry Main in *North and South*, part of the miniseries was filmed in Natchez. When Patrick received great acclaim for his acting in the miniseries, he gave masses of press interviews yet never mentioned that he is a direct descendant of the Reverend Samuel Swayze Jr., the most famous of all the Jersey Settlers, or brought up the coincidence of *North and South* being filmed in Natchez, the home of his ancestral forebears.

Nor did he ever broach the subject of his other celebrated relatives: *Stalag 17* star William Holden, his seventh and eighth cousin (because Reverend Samuel Swayze and his brother Richard married their own cousins, who were themselves sisters), and *Amadeus* actor Tom Hulce, another, more distant cousin.

Patrick's Texas roots on his father's side begin only with his great-grandfather, James Wesley Swayze, who originally lived in Franklin Parish, Louisiana, before moving to Texas. From then on, the Swayzes were true Texans, born and bred. Texas is the birthplace of Patrick's paternal grandfather, Jesse Elijah Swayze, and his maternal grandparents, Victor and Gladys Karnes—and his parents Jesse Wayne and Patsy Swayze, both regarded themselves as Texan to the core.

In many ways, Patrick was the embodiment of Southern pride. No matter how famous he would become, he never jettisoned his Southern values or his Southern manners. As a matter of fact, when he was on the threshold of becoming a star and his agent chided him for calling men "sir," he rounded on him indignantly and declared, "That's insanity," and in no uncertain terms informed him that he was brought up the Southern way and was proud of it. "You hold the door for women, you pull their chair. It's your job, it's not a macho thing."

Then, switching tacks, with a characteristic twinkle he added a caveat: "If you say 'sir' in a different context, it can be also very dangerous. 'Sir, you mess with me one more time and I break every bone in your body.'"

"There's a real power to Texans. Texas gives you a belief in yourself," he said with considerable pride on a 1986 visit back home. "There's a lot of emotion involved in being in Houston. This is my hometown! These are my roots!"

The TV series *Dallas* has ensured that as far as most of the world is concerned, Houston has been relegated to the second-best-known city in Texas. However, Houston is a far more international, multicultural city than Dallas. Apart from being the location of NASA's Lyndon B. Johnson Space Center, one of Houston's other major claims to fame is that it boasts the second largest concentration of theater seats in any downtown area in the United States.

Horses, too, are the business of Houston, and Patrick's paternal grandfather, Bud, was the foreman of the King Ranch—the largest horse- and cattle-breeding ranch in the Lone Star State, sprawling across six counties. When Patrick was a boy, his grandfather tied Patrick's wrists to a ram's horns and his feet to the ram's belly and let him go. "By the time I got off, I was close to unconscious," he recalled. "But I've always said since then, 'If it's got hair on it, I can ride it.'" His father too was a horseman, a Texas state champion cowboy, so it was hardly surprising that Patrick grew up to cherish horses in all their glory.

A love of horses was in his blood, and so too was dancing. His mother, Patsy, (born Patricia Yvonne Helen Karnes on February 7, 1927), was not only a gifted dancer herself but would also become one of the most influential dance teachers and choreographers of her generation.

His father, Jesse Wayne Swayze—nicknamed "Big Buddy"—was a tall, muscular, handsome man with jet black hair and blue eyes who bore some resemblance to Cary Grant yet retained the veneer of a tough macho Texan.

When Patsy and Big Buddy met in 1944, Patsy was seventeen and spirited, Big Buddy was eighteen and dashing. From the first, the passion that flared between them was inevitable. She was on the threshold of graduating from the Incarnate Word Academy of Houston, the oldest Catholic school in that city (a school which she would later credit as having taught her "that there is no such thing as failure"), and Big Buddy had enlisted in the navy. After learning that he was about to be shipped overseas, Patsy and Big Buddy were married in Missouri City, Texas, on August 6, 1944, just two weeks before Patsy's graduation day.

Their first child, Vicky, was born in 1949, followed by Patrick three years later. Like one out of every nine native Houstonians, including Kenny Rogers and Barbara Mandrell, he was born at the art deco–style St. Joseph Hospital, which was founded by the Catholic Sisters of Charity of the Incarnate Word in 1887. His brother Don was born in 1958 and Sean in 1962.

The Swayzes' first home in Garden Oak was adjacent to their

next home in the romantic-sounding Candlelight Wood area of Oak Forest, a large residential community in northwest Houston that was established in 1947, with most of the houses sold to World War II veterans for between $8,000 and $10,000. The Swayzes were to live there through most of Patrick's childhood, right into his late twenties. Almost rural in character, yet less than ten miles from the heart of Houston, Oak Forest, situated literally in the midst of a forest, was safe, suburban, even beautiful, and the Swayzes' two-storey Greek revival–style antebellum house on Del Norte was the ideal setting in which to raise a family.

However, even in the early pre-feminist fifties, powerhouse Patsy wasn't about to become a desperate housewife on a Houstonian Wisteria Lane.

Fate in the form of a car had run her down when she was a child and caused her to take up dancing as a form of physical therapy. Soon—through her formidable will, one which she would share with her eldest son, Patrick—she became a dedicated dancer prepared to suffer the grueling hours of practice and hard work in quest of the joy of devoting herself to her art, her raison d'être and her lifelong passion.

Initially she studied with Marcella Donovan Perry, the formidable ballerina and Broadway dancer who infused both style and discipline into her dancing. By the time Patrick was born, Patsy was already well established as Houston's premiere dance teacher and choreographer. A liberated woman far ahead of her time, she founded and directed the acclaimed Houston Jazz Ballet Company, helped to develop Houston's High School for the Performing and Visual Arts, choreographed countless musicals, and ran her own dance company and dance studio, where she taught ballet, tap, and jazz to generations of students, including Patrick.

"I kind of came out of the womb onstage. I can't recall a time in my life when I wasn't dancing," he has said. And while he wasn't exactly born in a trunk in the Princess Theater, Pocatello, Idaho, like Judy Garland's Esther Blodgett in *A Star Is Born*, as a babe in arms he was carried onstage during an operetta, already in show business before he could even walk or talk.

When he was only eight months old, his mother took him with her to her dance studio, where he'd hoist himself up in his playpen and dance in time to the music, along with her pupils. And, whenever possible, she took him with her to the theater where she was choreographing a show, and he'd either watch mesmerized or sleep contentedly on the theater seats.

At three he had his first ballet lesson with his mother. The group photograph of him in shorts and shirt show him already gleeful and happy, standing with perfect posture among the other tots in the class.

Even at that early age, Patrick's charisma was notable, as his pictures from that time testify. And out of Patsy's four children, "Patrick was the most outgoing," she said. At six he appeared in a children's production of *The Most Happy Fella*. Soon after, she dressed him in a sailor suit, put tap shoes on his little feet, and taught him how to give an accomplished performance singing and dancing to Shirley Temple's winsomely girlish hit, "On the Good Ship Lollipop."

Above all, through his childhood, teens, and right through high school and into his twenties, his life would revolve around classes and rehearsals at his mother's studio. There his hopes, dreams, ambitions, and the very basis of his character would be forged by Patsy, not only his mother but also his teacher, and set in stone.

two

AN IMPRESSIONABLE AGE

ife inside Patsy Swayze's studio on Judiway, and of course the phenomenon of Patsy herself, would have made the perfect case study for Malcolm Gladwell's groundbreaking *Outliers*, his analysis of the complex elements contributing to large-scale success in life. The high success rate of Patsy's students was such that during certain periods as many as three hundred of her pupils—who included Jaclyn Smith, Tommy Tune, Randy Quaid, and of course Patrick Swayze—were appearing in different shows on Broadway at one time. And those that weren't were running their own dance schools or dance companies throughout the world.

And it is clear that the extraordinarily high level of success of her students was primarily due to Patsy's iconoclastic teaching talent, philosophy, and innate grasp of child psychology.

Meld the Jesuits' "Give me a child until he's seven and I will give you the man" and the fictional Jean Brodie's "Give me a girl at an impressionable age and she's mine for life," and you will have a sense of Patsy Swayze's seismic impact on her young students and—above all—on her son Patrick, the performer and the man into which he would one day evolve.

Even five decades since they first started dancing with Patsy, mention her name to many of her former pupils and they veer between naked adoration, deep-dish fear, and sheer gratitude. One of her former students, Cookie Joe, who is now a celebrated Houstonian choreographer and teacher but was nine years old when she started training with Patsy, puts it this way: "She reminded me of Lauren Bacall, with her long wavy hair and her smoky voice." She was one of those rare breed of women who manage to be simultaneously glamorous and strikingly steely.

Far from being a girlie girl, Patsy was far more of a tomboy—muscular and athletic, with a strong well-defined body set off to its best advantage when she wore dance clothes or, away from the studio, bell-bottom jeans or her favorite black strapless vintage dress, which was reserved for important occasions and lent her the allure of a queenly mermaid.

Perhaps as a reminder to her young students—the majority of whom were girls ranging from two upward and into adulthood—of her illustrious past in tap, jazz, and ballet, along with her Hollywood-wattage allure, a velveteen portrait of her in a sequined belly-dancing outfit, a jewel stuck in the middle of her forehead, dominated the studio.

If Patsy was the queen bee reigning over her studio, Big Buddy reigned as king, albeit a benevolent one. "He took care of the organization at the studio and was looked up to by all the children. He was tall and towering and Patsy was gorgeous. Top of the wedding cake," enthused Danny Ward, Patrick's lifelong friend who went to Waltrip High School with him and also sometimes accompanied the dancers at the piano during studio rehearsals.

"A dance studio is like a family. And having Big Buddy there was like having a daddy around," Zetta Alderman recalled. She had started studying with Patsy when she was ten years old, and her mother, Dorothy Shook, was Patsy's best friend and reception-ist. "He would sit in the dance studio for hours, we would dance for hours and he would just watch us."

"Big Buddy was like a big cowboy, only he didn't wear a cowboy hat. You took one look at him and you knew that he could do any-thing and he knew how to do it," said Rick Odums, one of Patsy's former pupils and now a world-renowned choreographer who for the past thirty years has run Les Ballets Jazz Rick Odums, his company and school in Paris. "Big Buddy was mischievous and fun and very loving and kind," said Zetta Alderman, adding a note on the subject of the Tom Sawyer side of his expansive nature. "One time he got a bunch of rubber bands and, when Patsy wasn't looking, he popped us with rubber bands from across the room. It didn't hurt, he was just teasing us, but Patsy got so mad at him because he was disrupting the class.

"He was warm and bright and kind, and we all loved him. One time, he was carrying a glass plate, slipped, and sliced his arm really bad and was rushed to the hospital. All of us children in the studio were crying, devastated that he'd been injured."

When he wasn't in the studio, Big Buddy was at home caring for the children, and in some ways he was the classic Mr. Mom, an anomaly in the Texas of yore. Unafraid to carry out traditionally female tasks, Big Buddy often picked up the children from the dance studio, cooked for them, and supervised their homework.

While Patrick has described his father as "born and bred a red-neck," he also proudly pointed out that he could complete the *New York Times* crossword in fifteen minutes as well and that "My father was the kind of man that allowed his sensitivity to be there, and yet he was a man's man." Later he added, "My mother was the driven one, while he wore his heart on his sleeve. I took after my father."

"Little Buddy really has a lot of his dad in him—his wonderful, warm, loving caring side," Zetta Alderman concurred. "Big Buddy was a hero. The kids just bounced around him when he came in the door. And Patrick was Daddy's kid and loved and respected his father," said Cookie Joe. "His father was the rock, his mother was the fire," added Patrick's boyhood friend Larry Ward.

The studio children adored slumber parties at the Swayze home, with its informal, relaxed, often disorganized atmosphere, the walls decorated with dance pictures, and an eclectic and stimulating mix of Rachmaninoff, Billie Holiday, and the Beatles blaring away on the stereo.

The Swayzes, however, were not exactly the Partridge family, the Osmonds, or the Brady Bunch. "Patsy wasn't the type to make lunches and cook dinner," Cookie Joe said. "Patsy wasn't a housekeeper or a cook. The Swayze family wasn't a normal family," said Zetta Alderman. "I don't remember them going on vacation much, or doing a lot of family stuff together. Patsy, you see, had her alternative family, all of us at the studio."

She was a dance teacher right down to her very soul. "I love to watch people develop strong bodies and a sense of worth," she said. "I love watching the tiny ones—their balance, their coordination improve. I see coltish, little awkward bodies develop into ethereal beings. To see the child blossom, that's the thrill of teaching."

Intensely focused and utterly dedicated to her students and her craft, Patsy was the antithesis of Shaw's bon mot "Those who can, do. Those who can't, teach." Not only was she gifted at ballet, tap, and jazz dance, but she was also a champion swimmer, diver, gymnast, roller skater, and ice skater. In common with Big Buddy, she was a renaissance person in every sense of the word, and naturally Patrick would grow up to become a renaissance man.

As a teacher, Patsy had the power and ability to inspire toddlers and teenagers alike. "She was the most wonderful teacher in the world as far as creating artists. She made us fall in love with the arts and everything there was about performing arts and dance," said Zetta Alderman, who went on to work with John Travolta in *Urban Cowboy*, dance in the first international Touring Company of

A *Chorus Line*, and is now artistic director of her own dance school and company, Daza Studios/Indigo Dance, in Colorado.

Unlike most teachers—particularly in the South—Patsy didn't demand that her pupils address her as "Mrs. Swayze" or "Miss Patsy," but instructed them to call her "Patsy." In turn, she called them "honey" or "sweetie." Not that she was all sugar and candy. Far from it. Class would begin at a variety of times each day, and woe betide the student who came late or left early. As the students took their places at the barre, Patsy perched on a stool, a cigarette in one hand and a baton in the other, beating time to the music, often a Broadway show tune.

Gypsy was a favorite—both of Patsy and the students—and she'd choreograph some of the production numbers for them, yelling out at the lead, "Sing out, baby (inserting the girl's name)," just like Rosalind Russell as the quintessential stage mother Rose intent on pushing her daughter Gypsy to stardom.

"Patsy was very much like Mama Rose," says Cookie Joe. To the distress of even some of her most adoring students, at times, like Mama Rose, Patsy would be a screamer and often profane.

"She was very short tempered," Zetta Alderman remembered. "And it was very easy to do something the wrong way and have her get really angry, really fast. She did it because she wanted us to be the best. So our respect level for her was extremely high." "Boy, you didn't want to get her mad!" added her former student Paula Abbott (who now runs the prestigious APAC dance school in Houston) more succinctly.

Patsy may have rivaled Mama Rose in decibel levels, but unlike Mama Rose with Gypsy, she didn't push Patrick to become a star. At least no more than she did any of her other pupils. Exhorting her students to "Get in the front!" "Don't take second seat!" and "Get everyone else out of your way!" she was as targeted as an Exocet missile on teaching all of them to be aggressive, to compete and win when they were out in the cutthroat dance world far away from her cocoon, the little world she'd so painstakingly constructed in the studio.

"Patsy was big on teaching us to kick the highest, twirl the most, jump the highest. She instilled a competitive nature in all of us," Cookie Joe remembered.

Patrick was no exception. "He was probably the most competitive person I've ever met," his best friend from childhood, Larry Ward, said. "Being second was just not acceptable to him. He was extremely competitive and worked very hard to be the best he could be."

If he ever fell short of his goals, Patrick became visibly downhearted. Once in high school, after he didn't win a particular sporting event, instead of admitting it to his mother, he slipped home, found a first-place ribbon that he'd been awarded in the past, and presented it to his mother, telling her he had won it that day. Coming in second, he believed, was not good enough—not for him and certainly not for his mother.

"I wouldn't trade her for the world," Patrick said as an adult, adding, "because with her, nothing less than first place was acceptable."

Patsy was clearly the Obi-Wan Kenobi of Texas and dispensed her dancing Force to all her protégés with a fair amount of magic and passion. But neither her son nor any of her students would have, in good conscience, been able to apply the lyric from "Down on the Range"—"where never is heard a discouraging word"—to life inside her studio. "All of us felt so challenged by Patsy. We all knew that she loved us in her own way, but we all felt like we never quite measured up," Zetta Alderman recalled. "She would always go, 'That was very good, but . . .'"

A classic Patsy vignette: When Cookie Joe was ten years old, along with her fellow dance student Nikki D'Amico, who would grow up to become Patrick's first serious girlfriend and dance partner, Patsy dressed them and all the studio's other ten-year-olds in clown outfits and choreographed "Put on a Happy Face" for them.

Over three decades later, after learning that Patsy was to be honored at the 2004 Tommy Tune Awards in Houston, Cookie dressed her ten-year-old students in the identical clown outfits she and Nikki and all the other little girls had performed in all those years ago and choreographed them in the very same routine so they could perform it as a surprise for Patsy on the night.

It proved to be a heartwarming and respectful tribute to Patsy, from both Cookie and Nikki, who flew in specially for the event. "Patsy didn't know Nikki was going to be there, or me, or that I'd trained my ten-year-olds to do her old clown routine dressed in exactly the same way. It was a surprise for her," remembered Cookie. "After the show finished, I went over to Patsy and the first thing she said to me was, 'That was wrong. The first two counts of eight should have been———.' Afterwards she did thank me, but those were her first words. Then again . . . she was right."

Like Billy Elliot's parallel chain-smoking ballet teacher, Miss Wilkinson—as incarnated by Julie Walters—she refused to countenance the thought that dance was purely a female pursuit, nor would she brook any challenge to the contrary either from onlookers or from the boys themselves. "With the boys, you have to build a desire [to dance] a little more. And when they grow up, they want to show off their prowess, how high they can jump, how fast they can turn," she said sagely.

Even as a child, Patrick would possess a daredevil streak as wide as the Bering Strait, and it didn't need Sigmund Freud to surmise that in exercising it he was partially acting out his craving to demonstrate to his mother exactly how high he could jump, how fast he could turn. His daredevil propensity for risk was already in evidence when, at the age of nine, he cheerfully collected a dollar at a time from a group of workmen who were building a two-story house in the neighborhood and who paid him the money for jumping off the roof merely for their amusement.

Worse still, he and his brother would ride their bicycles down a sheer concrete embankment. "One boy had already been killed doing the same thing," Patsy recalled. "Every night I would go to bed and thank God he'd managed to live one more day."

Patrick rarely rested, or just relaxed and simply hung out like other kids, but because too much introspection was never Patsy's style, she didn't draw the obvious parallels between her son and herself. "He wanted to do everything," she said almost wonderingly. "A skater, a swimmer, involved in all the Little League sports, baseball, football. Ballet dancing every day, played the violin, sang in the school choir, was in school plays from junior high up. I guess you could call it hyper, but he had to be busy." He had to be busy partially because of his lively personality but also because she, his mother, had decreed he should be, because he was her doppelgänger, her creation, and because—above all—he wanted to please her and make her proud of him.

"She wanted all of us to achieve the same levels and hopefully surpass her. We weren't tall on having much free time in our household," he said. Later he expanded: "She is a very intense woman. She drove me hard, and I started out wanting to prove something to the world."

The ripple effect of Patsy's rigorous standards and the difficulty of living up to them clearly had such a strong effect on Patrick that as an adult in a brutally honest interview he said, "My mother was so intense and demanded so much. You never knew if she was going to praise you or hit you, and it took me quite a while to really learn to trust women—or men."

Harsh though his comment might have been, he did not make it out of malice. "Patrick was so openhearted and always wanted to tell the truth in interviews," recalled Lois Zetter, who, with Bob Le Mond, her partner in Le Mond/Zetter Management, managed Patrick for eleven years, from the early days of *Skatetown USA* until *Ghost*. "Sometimes Bob and I would cringe when he told journalists too much and was too honest about himself. But he was raised to tell the truth and he did."

Patrick was forever reaching out for his mother's approval, like one of those figures with outstretched hands set in alabaster in Keats's "Ode on a Grecian Urn." Patsy's impact on his psyche was immeasurable and was still obvious to a seasoned observer like the eminent director Roland Joffé, who, while making *City of Joy* in Calcutta in 1992 with him, observed, "I could see someone who is very rigorous with himself, who obviously had a tremendous amount of discipline as a dancer, probably very young had an enormous desire to achieve. But he was never going to fill the cup—that was set up from the early days. Someone had worked out how to put the carrot just out of reach, and it was going to stay out of reach forever."

"On certain levels, I felt ripped apart as a kid," Patrick confided to writer Stephanie Mansfield, who interviewed him for the February 1992 issue of *GQ* magazine. "I wanted to please my mother because she was so good at everything, and I wanted to be like her."

As his story will demonstrate, his wish came true on many levels. Even when he spent over five months making *The Beast* under the cruelest of circumstances, he took only one and a half days off due to his sickness.

In that, as in most things, he was following religiously in his mother's footsteps. "I can't remember Patsy missing dance class because she was sick, or for any other reason," remembered Paula Abbott. Patrick has often paid tribute to his mother's work ethic, which, he said, produced "an ability to work, a level of discipline in me that is like a pit bull terrier's."

The degree of self-confidence—whether inborn or developed by Patsy—he demonstrated in that remark was already present in his early childhood. After his very first day at school—at St. Rose of Lima Catholic School—he announced, "You know, Mom, I'm not only the smartest kid in that room, I'm also the best looking."

He was also "convinced that he could do anything as well as or better than anyone," Patsy said. "He was never one to want help," she went on. "It was always, 'No, Mom, I can do it myself.' And there was never any problem in Patrick achieving something. He always had absolute confidence in everything he did."

He was not, however, particularly academic. "Patrick was one of those students who get A's if they like a subject and just scrape by if they don't," Patsy explained, adding the stipulation, "I wanted my children to be interested in more than just academics. To me it was more important that they explore music, the arts, and sports. And I told them, 'Whatever you want to do is all right with us, but do it the best you can.' "

Patrick was a kind and loving little boy who—as an eight-year-old cub scout—on Mother's Day gifted her with a five-gallon ice cream carton that he had painted red and plastered with magazine pictures of his favorite subjects—horses, dogs, and Indians.

At nine he found a dead bullfrog on the roadside and, bursting with pride at his discovery, put it in his jeans' pocket and took it home, excited at the prospect of presenting it to his mother. But once there, he promptly forgot all about it. Later that night his mother, unaware of the bullfrog in the pocket, threw his jeans into the washing machine. When he learned what had become of his gift to her, he was distraught.

He was acutely sensitive and suffered from dreadful nightmares. "Ever since I was a little boy, I've been having dreams about a warrior," he revealed much later in life, explaining, "When I was really small, the warrior took the form of a monster and I would wake up screaming because I was so scared. The monster would come out of the fog and I would hide behind this tiny clump of trees at the end of my neighbor's house. But just as the warrior was about to kill me, I would wake up sweating. I used to be terrified to go to sleep because I didn't want the warrior to try and kill me again."

Yet—his sensitivity aside—he was all boy. "I've been an adventure king since I hit the planet," he said, harking back to his childhood when—dressed in a red loincloth—he played Tarzan, his brother Don played Boy, and together they swung through a network of vines and ropes through the five miles of trees around Oak Forest so fast that their feet never touched ground.

Big Buddy taught his eldest son to respect and love nature. On many a day father and son, Big Buddy in his jacket with his nickname emblazoned on the back and Patrick with his nickname Little Buddy on his, drove out to the Trinity River in the Big Thicket, portions of which had never been penetrated. There Big Buddy taught Patrick how to survive on the land and make salads with cattail roots, root tubers, and chicory, to sauté grub worms in bone marrow, and to snare and cook a rabbit.

He was as intent on proving himself to his father as to his mother. To his shame, his father once witnessed his defeat by his friend Larry Ward at a track meet. But instead of pandering to Patrick's chagrin at having lost, his father laughed and chalked up the experience as a life lesson which, he hoped, would teach his son a modicum of humility.

Unbeknownst to Big Buddy, before Patrick was even in his teens his peers had already taught him some harsh lessons of their own. As Patrick later explained, "Being a dancer just didn't work in redneck country. They assumed you were gay if you were a dancer. I was beat up over and over . . . I remember getting jumped in the back of the church. I feel like I fought all my life."

He studied ballet, played the violin, and, as far as his contemporaries were concerned, wasn't a real man at all. He was an outcast, a target for taunts, there to be humiliated, beaten, and bullied by rednecks who yelled "Twinkle Toes" and "Sissy" at him.

Pam Brumfield, who went to F. M. Black Junior High and then Waltrip High with Patrick, recalled, "Buddy was in the theater group and he also did ballet. The guys at school called him 'pansy' behind his back. I thought that was cruel and mean and unfair."

In the spirit of the little boy who was capable of performing "The Good Ship Lollipop" one moment and playing Tarzan the next, away from dance Patrick's other great passion was sports. He swore to win the respect of his oppressors, played football with a vengeance, and during one memorable high school game, scored every single touchdown.

But the taunting and the beatings continued. Taught by his

father to turn the other cheek and told, "If you ever start a fight, I'll kick your tail," the obedient Patrick always allowed the other guy to throw the first punch. Oppressed and exasperated, he turned to his mother for counsel. Her advice was to ignore the bullies because they simply didn't grasp the joy of dance and were jealous.

When she discovered that the bullying was still going on, she swung into action. At that time, before the move to Judiway, she had rented space in a dance studio on Richmond Avenue, next door to a martial arts studio. So she made a deal for all her students to receive free lessons there, bartering dance lessons in return.

Patrick took full advantage of the deal and began by learning judo, then aikido, tae kwon do, kempo, and kung fu, becoming expert in all those varieties of disciplines. He was now fully armed against any redneck who might want to mock him for studying dance. Nonetheless, the memory of all the beatings, all the bullying, burned itself into his soul. Later, he would recall, "I started walking around with a chip on my shoulder and looking for fights . . ."

When he was fourteen years old, after school one day, a group of boys jumped him and broke some of his ribs and his jaw. When he'd recovered, an incensed Patsy advised him to fight back at last, instructing him to "beat the snuff out of them." Unlike his tormentors, though, he believed in fighting fair, so he challenged them to a formal fight in the gym and proceeded to beat each and every one of them.

But that wasn't all. Part of Patrick Swayze's universal appeal, both as a star and a man, rests on the fact that he isn't all brawn but is also heart and mind as well. So when it came to driving home his point to the bullies once and for all, his cleverness came into play.

"He issued them a challenge," Zeta Alderman remembered. "He said, 'If you guys will come and take the whole ballet class and make it through to the end, then the girls will come and play touch football with you.' And the boys came to ballet class and they couldn't make it past the first fifteen minutes. They were passing out. And so, of course, we didn't have to go play touch football."

His mother's students, some of whom had known Patrick since they were little girls, all adored him unreservedly. If Patsy was the queen of the studio and Big Buddy the king, Patrick was the prince.

"To his face, we called him 'Little Buddy,' but behind his back we all called him 'The Body' because of his great build," Cookie Joe remembered. "But he wasn't at all vain. If he looked at himself in the mirror, it was only as a dancer does—critiquing himself, not admiring himself. He was swaggering, with a sincere confidence, but he was very good at making everyone feel comfortable. Whatever group he was in, he never stayed separate from anyone, he made everyone feel good."

In his spare time, Patrick was a lifeguard at the Olympic-size pool in the studio backyard. All summer long Patsy's students would start the day with a swim, take a dance class, rehearse, then go straight back into the pool again and swim.

"Little Buddy volunteered to teach me to dive," remembered Zetta. "He stood behind me on the diving board and said, 'Okay, I'm going to count and when I get to the third number, you're going to jump.' And we would get to that number, and I wouldn't go. And we would get to that number again, and I still wouldn't go." He lost patience with her and said she *had* to go. "I still wouldn't. Finally, he just pushed me off the diving board, and that's how I learned to swim!" she said.

Patrick was brotherly and kind, and the studio girls always cherished their moments with him. One summer evening, class finished early and he and Cookie Joe cleaned up the studio together. "We got done early. Buddy pulled out his guitar and started playing for me. We just sat there talking together," she said with a certain amount of nostalgia.

"He was very resilient and very versatile. He was really better than average at a lot of things, but didn't apply himself fully to any of them until he decided to become a classical dancer—then he became great."

Even the boys involved in the studio liked and admired him.

"He was a strong, strong character. A straight shooter and honest. There's no beating around the bush with this guy. And it was a bit unusual to see someone who is built like a football player able to dance the way he dances," said Danny Ward.

Patrick was so athletic that at fifteen he appeared in a trampoline act at Houston's AstroWorld amusement park. At Waltrip High School he became a star gymnast, running track, swimming, wrestling, boxing, and setting state records in diving, broad-jumping and track, and became a star running back for the school football team—the Waltrip Rams. Most of the girls at Waltrip felt warmly toward him. "He was kind of shy. Shy people know who shy people are," observed Debbie Contreras, who took math with him and noticed that he didn't particularly like the subject.

Fellow Waltrip student Brenda Kruemcke recalled her amusement at the Donald Duck noises he used to make in class—which he'd soon air publicly during a part of a professional engagement—and viewed him as "not really the typical jock."

He was popular among the girls, but not quite popular enough to be voted Mr. Waltrip by the entire school. Judy Britt, who campaigned for him, remembered that "In my year book, Patrick wrote, 'Well Judy, it sure has been good knowing you these years (but it sure is good to be leaving!). You're really a good friend and I like you a lot (even if I didn't win Mr. Waltrip).'"

Even though he ended with the words "just kidding," the defeat clearly rankled with him. Competitive and a workaholic in the making, even in his teens he worked nonstop, starting every day at three in the morning with his paper route and ending at his mother's studio, where he practiced ballet as late as midnight.

Predictably, though, Patrick still found time for romance. Even if he hadn't been tall, strong, and handsome, he still would have attracted girls in droves. After all, he was prince of Patsy's studio, and most of her young female students who had initially viewed Little Buddy as an ersatz big brother were now in the throes of developing other, more intense emotions for him.

At twelve he had his first kiss with pretty Mamie Scheidemantel, a girl of his own age whom he'd known since they were both
small children and who lived in the same neighborhood and attended Waltrip as well. "Buddy was very handsome, very sweet, and
we went behind the sheds at the school and he kissed me," she remembered. "He gave me his initial ring and said, 'Now we're going
steady.' So we had hamburgers together at Brannon's Chuck Wagon,
close to his mother's studio, and went skating together every Friday
and Saturday. It was a mutual crush, but we both thought we loved
each other."

The course of young love was almost derailed after he took a ride
in her sister's Studebaker Lark with classmate Pam Brumfield, who
was twelve to his thirteen. "I had a crush on him," Pam said. "He had
great-shaped hazel eyes, he smiled a lot and when he did, his eyes
would light up. I kissed him straight on the mouth, he blushed and
looked like he was in a state of shock, but he didn't return my kiss."

Perhaps Patrick was unwilling to be untrue to Mamie, but
most likely he had just begun dating his mother's star pupil, Nikki
D'Amico, in the process pleasing his mother immensely. "Patsy
loved Nikki and she was like Patsy's little girl. She was teeny and I
think Patsy's dream at that time was for Buddy and Nikki to end up
together," said Cookie Joe.

In the case of Nikki, and later Lisa, his mother's imprimatur
would represent the alpha and the omega of his dating trajectory.
Through most of his teens and right up until he started dating Lisa
in earnest, Nikki would remain a constant in his life. "Whoever he
dated, he always went back to Nikki in between times. They were
very close," said Mamie Scheidemantel.

Around the same time as his stolen first kiss with Mamie, he
simultaneously developed a major crush on one of Patsy's most talented dancers, a tall brunette named Jaclyn Smith. However, Jaclyn
was seven years older than he and would leave to pursue her career in Manhattan long before he was old enough to summon up the
courage to ask her for a date.

However, by the time he was fifteen, he and his friend Larry Ward looked mature enough to sneak into Houston's most sophisticated nightclubs. Then if they happened to spy a couple of ultra-beautiful women, they would position themselves strategically close to them and then engage in a loud, animated conversation about "their" yachts and "their" planes.

But even if their rather crass tactic paid off and they lucked out, Patsy had set a midnight curfew for Patrick, and even Larry trembled at the thought of inciting her ire. "One thing you didn't do was cross Patsy," he recalled. "When Patsy said be in at midnight, by golly, don't make it twelve-oh-one because she had this finger right here cocked and loaded. She'd pound it and Patrick's jaw would tighten."

Larry might have observed Patrick's jaw tighten when confronted by the specter of Patsy's temper rising, but now that Patrick was in the full flush of his teens, he was unafraid to stand up to her. "He inherited Patsy's quick temper, but he only ever lost it when he argued with her," said Cookie Joe.

"Patsy would tell us what exercises to do and how to do them, she'd put on the music, we would follow her instructions and she'd go down the row and tell us what we weren't doing right," Zetta remembered, adding "or rather, often yell it."

And while Patsy was utterly democratic yelling at the girls as much as at Patrick, there was one difference. "None of us would have ever dreamed of yelling back or arguing with her. Patrick was the only one who did. I never saw him out of control or angry with anyone except his mother. They fought about choreography in dance class. Patrick thought he was always right and always knew what was best, and so did Patsy," Zetta disclosed.

Like all heated arguments between two people who love each other but are too similar, too pig-headed, their battles generally fell into a pattern. "When she'd get to him and tell him what he hadn't done, he'd say, 'I *was* doing that.' She'd go, 'No you *weren't*. And don't you talk to me like that.' Then they'd take it into her office, because Patrick had much too much intelligence and class to fight with his mother in front of us. But I do think that sometimes he felt his manliness was undermined when she yelled at him," Zetta said.

However harsh a taskmistress Patsy may have been to Patrick and all her students, by the time he was sixteen her rigorous training methods were already starting to produce dividends.

Until now, Patrick Swayze's publicity invariably cites Prince Charming in Disney on Parade as his first major public appearance, but that was not the case. The truth is far less romantic, for on Christmas Day 1968 the musical fable *The Pied Piper of Astro World*, starring Kenny Rogers and the First Edition, Jim Henson, Leslie Gore, and Soupy Sales as the Pied Piper, was broadcast on national TV and featured the sixteen-year-old Patrick, clad in a bear costume, his face completely obscured from the audience. A quirky and inauspicious launch for his career, but still a start. And the following year, he did a turn as the ringmaster, again at Astro World.

But lest the impression of Patsy relentlessly driving her charges into the limelight eclipse all others, it is only fair to elaborate on equally important facets to her nature. And courage was one of them. For even in the midst of the racially prejudiced early sixties, and in Texas, she was not afraid to stand up to racism in its most blatant form.

"She believed that every child had a right to dance and to learn, so—knowing that she'd be penalized for it—she accepted us black children into her school," Rick Odums, who is African-American, testified. "When she took us on as students, some of those Texas ole boys just didn't want their little white daughters to dance with black boys. So Patsy lost those students just like she knew she would."

On one memorable evening, Rick witnessed a dramatic display of Patsy's principles in action. She had made an appointment at the studio with the female owner of a big Texas family firm who was primed to invest much-needed and substantial funds in her dance company, intending to hash out all the details with her.

"Patsy was running late, so she asked me and Rob, another black dancer, to open up for her," Rick remembered. "We were outside unlocking the doors when the limousine pulled up in front of the studio. But the woman never got out of her limousine, and just sat inside it, waiting for Patsy to arrive. When Patsy finally got there, she asked the woman why she hadn't come inside the studio and waited for her there. The woman shook her head and started, 'Well, you know, black boys . . . ' And Patsy replied, 'Okay. Go away then. I don't need your money,' " he said, his voice still trembling with emotion at the memory.

"She and Big Buddy accepted us completely, so did the rest of the family. All the boys became like my brothers. Patrick used to give me advice. In fact, the best advice he ever gave me was, 'If you want something, just go and do it.' And Patsy used to call me 'My black Buddy.' It was a compliment, as if I were her black son," Rick said.

In yet another indication of the Swayze family's liberalism, in 1969 the family sponsored a four-year-old Korean orphan via the Christian Children's Fund, which had informed them that the little girl was found abandoned in a park when she was only a year old, was partly deaf, and perhaps not overly intelligent.

Undeterred, Patsy and Big Buddy continued to sponsor her and to receive her photographs in return. Patsy always brought them into the studio and passed them around among her dancers, who would all cluster around excitedly, curious to see pictures of the thin, waif-like little Korean girl.

Deeply touched by the image of the fragile little girl, Big Buddy one day exclaimed that her eyes seemed to be gazing out from the photograph and imploring them to rescue her and become her family. Patsy agreed and said that because the little girl looked as if she were on the verge of terminal starvation, they should adopt her. Her name was Song Bo Ra, which in Korean means "beautiful velvet." Even the fund was unsure about her true age, judging her to be three when she might well have been older, but Patsy was unconcerned and immediately launched her campaign to adopt the little girl.

First she wrote to the Korean orphanage, making the request. Informed that Song Bo Ra was available for adoption but that the orphanage didn't facilitate foreign families seeking to adopt one of their children, Patsy ploughed on regardless. First she studied adoption law in the library, then wrote to the orphanage once more, repeating her request that she and Big Buddy be allowed to adopt Song Bo Ra.

At that time, any foreigner wanting to adopt a Korean child generally had to wait years before the adoption went through. Yet solely as a result of Patsy's persistence, it took just six months for the paperwork to be completed. Thereupon she dispatched it posthaste to the authorities, along with a stiff letter in which she announced that she wasn't prepared to wait two years to adopt Song Bo Ra but insisted that the adoption be ratified then and there. Bludgeoned into submission by Patsy's Sherman-style determination, the authorities crumbled, the adoption papers were instantly signed, and within a few months Song Bo Ra was en route for Houston via San Francisco.

"I saw this little girl coming down the plane stairs, with this little rice bowl haircut, looking very frightened and malnourished," remembers Cookie Joe, who, with Zetta Alderman and Paula Abbott, was part of a small deputation of ten- and eleven-year-old dance studio girls whom Patsy and Big Buddy took with them to the airport so they could join in welcoming Song Bo Ra to her new country and make her feel comfortable there.

She couldn't speak a word of English, bore a scar on her side from an injury, and had been separated from her sister back in Korea. Nonetheless, after she overcame her shyness and shock at being in such a different environment, she was happy she'd been adopted by her new American family.

"The Swayzes practically saved my life," Song Bo Ra said years later. The moment she arrived in Houston, they treated her like part of their family. Following in the well-worn footsteps of Vicky, Patrick, Don, and Sean before her, Song Bo Ra was first baptized and then—most unsurprisingly—Patsy enrolled her in dance lessons.

On one of Song Bo Ra's first nights at her new home, Patsy tucked her in bed, then read her a bedtime story. That story was *Bambi*, and the little girl was so enthralled that she announced that she didn't want to be called Song Bo Ra anymore, but Bambi. And so she was.

As Bambi grew older, it turned out that the orphanage had been wrong about her. She was not deaf, although she did have a chronic ear infection. Nor was she in any way stupid, because for most of her scholastic life she was an honors student. Moreover, to Patsy's delight, Bambi also proved to be a talented dancer.

From the first she adored her new brother Patrick. He called her "Princess," and she anointed him the Prince Charming of her dreams. "I remember watching Patrick dance when I was a young girl and I was totally in awe of him because he had such a presence," she remembered, adding, "He danced in such a strong, manly way. Then, when Patrick married Lisa, who had been one of my mother's students, they became my inspiration. It was magical to see them move. They looked fantastic together and still do.

"Patrick is so kind and considerate. The kind of big brother every girl dreams of." He was indeed kind and considerate, and dedicated himself to protecting her as well. "When I began going out with boys while I was still going to school, Patrick used to tell them, 'You'd better not mess with my little sister or I'll be right behind you,' " she said.

As she grew older, his protectiveness assumed a more paternal form. When she fell in love and planned to marry, he decreed that she couldn't unless he met and approved of her intended husband, Don.

"Patrick said Don would have to have his approval—and he meant it. He said, 'If you ever need help, or he hurts you, I'm here,' " she remembered.

Fortunately for Bambi, when Patrick met her fiancé, he did indeed approve of him, and the wedding took place with his blessings.

Patrick didn't restrict his well-honed and touchingly kind protective instincts to his family members alone. In 2004, more than three decades since he'd last seen Zetta, he learned she was married and asked to meet her husband. "He took my husband into a room, stayed in there with him for half an hour and, when he came out, said, 'I'm glad you married him.' Afterwards, my husband told me that Patrick had asked him a lot of questions, systematically checking him out to make sure I'd be safe and happy with him," she said.

Patrick's desire to protect and take care of a woman was partly inborn but was also a direct consequence of his classical dance training. "It's bred into male dancers to be protective of women," Rick Odums explained. "When you do a pas de deux with a woman and she's up in the air and comes flying into your arms, you're responsible for her. In lifting class, Patsy always used to tell the male dancers, 'If the girl you are dancing a pas de deux with ever falls, you better make sure you fall under her!'

"Buddy was my role model in that he was a male dancer who wasn't gay. And like me, he came from a football background, so we had a lot in common. He was this huge male dancer when I met him, so he inspired me even more. As a dancer, he was really an artist. He lived, breathed, and thought about dancing. As talented as he became as an actor, his original goal was really to dance."

At the same time Patrick was also toying with the prospect of becoming a professional football player. College scouts had observed his play, noting his speed, and it seemed very possible that he might be offered a football scholarship. Then fate took a hand. In the second-to-last game of his senior year, he suffered a severe injury to his left leg that threatened to put an end to his burning ambition to become either a professional football player or a professional dancer.

He was so badly injured that his knee underwent total reconstruction, leaving massive scar tissue in the wake of the operation. He was in severe danger of ending up crippled. But neither one of his parents refused to countenance the possibility and, every single morning before he left for school they wrapped scalding hot towels around his knee in order to break the scar tissue.

"I would scream while my father held me down, but I finally got back almost full use of the knee," he said afterward.

His mother's strict dance training had taught him to exercise control over his body and to battle pain, no matter what. "You just turn yourself into a master and commander when it comes to pain," he said. "My mother wanted me to be everything, and she trained me to have the ability to be everything in a physical way. The biggest thing I remember growing up is you don't look at pain and you don't look at fear and insecurity—you just do it. The approach is to apply will and drive over everything."

three
PRINCE CHARMING

hrough sheer will and determination, Patrick was soon dancing again.

"Buddy was a masculine dancer and he didn't let his injured knee stop him. He would jump like his knee wasn't injured and he wouldn't give it a rest," Rick Odums said in admiration.

Rick didn't witness just Patrick's fortitude in the face of pain and injury, he also witnessed the effect he had on virtually all the girls who attended the studio with him. "Buddy is a paradox. I mean he's this big gorgeous man and women threw themselves at him, but when he had his eyes on somebody, he kept them there. He was not a player," Rick said.

Patrick had never been a player or an embryonic Bill Hendrickson in the making, for even in his hot-blooded teens he was more of a serial dater than a full-blown seducer. "At least ten women have come into my dance studio and said, 'Oh, you grew up with the Swayzes. Patsy was my teacher! And I dated Buddy!'" Paula Abbott recalled in amusement.

Whether they dated or not, most of the studio girls' admiration and passion for him simmered away undiminished. "One of my first memories of Patrick is of him sitting around the pool surrounded by girls and lip-syncing to the song 'Gitarzan.' The girls all liked him even then," said Maggie McNair, the daughter of his close friends Rhita and Tom McNair, whom he had known since grade school.

"Patsy used to brag that girls called the house a lot asking for him. 'Those silly girls calling my boy at the house all the time . . .' She didn't like it, but she wanted to let us dance studio girls know about it all the same," Cookie Joe said, and added, "He was so full of class and so kind. Whenever he stopped dating a girl, there never seemed to be any broken hearts."

In April 1971, four months before his nineteenth birthday, he started dating Terri Harsch, who attended Waltrip with him, the daughter of a Southern Baptist deacon. She was an enthusiastic member of the Imperial Guard, the school's drum and bugle drill team. At the end of one particular day she found herself in the team's office when, all of a sudden, Patrick—"Buddy"—opened the door and asked her if she'd like to go to the beach with him that Saturday.

"I was shocked because we'd never talked before," Terri recalled. "We really didn't know each other at all, and at that stage in his life he was just a normal, All-American boy, no different from any other football player at Waltrip."

Unlike all his past girlfriends, she was not a dancer. Yet she looked uncannily like his future wife, Lisa, and was a beautiful, diminutive green-eyed blond. Like Patrick, she was an All-American teenager, yet in contrast she was devoid of any show business aspirations. Instead, she nurtured ambitions to become a teacher. Their relationship would last two and a half years, and as it first unfolded and right up until it ended, it was the most regular he had ever had in his whole life and ever would.

"On our first date we went to Galveston to the beach with another couple, and spent the day enjoying the sunshine and the sunset," Terri said. They dated over the next few weeks. Then in June, at the end of their school year, he wrote in her yearbook, "I love you" and signed it "Ducky." Terri didn't give him the nickname, but today says she thinks he liked calling himself that as a nod to his Donald Duck imitations, which all the class loved so much.

Patrick was so engaged by Terri that he invited her to be his prom night date, but to his shock and surprise she unself-consciously told him that she had never really learned to dance. "So before the prom, he decided he ought to try and teach me," she remembers with some amusement. "He tried to teach me in my backyard, and tried to do a lift with me, there and in the swimming pool. And I really related to the *Dirty Dancing* scene in which he and Jennifer go out to the lake and he tries to teach her to dance there."

Yet although Terri had "Johnny Castle" as her dance teacher for an indeterminate number of hours, by her own admission she never succeeded in learning to dance well. And even if she had, she had a long way to go before she rivaled the other girls who'd danced their way through his life up till now.

"He was amazed that I couldn't lift my leg and put it up beside my ear like every other girl at his mother's studio," she said. But her failure not to make the grade as a potential prima ballerina didn't disturb him too deeply. And even if it had, he was much too much of a gentleman to make his disappointment visible to her. Nor did it diminish his feelings for her.

Right after prom night, he took her to Lake Travis, where they water-skied together and spent time with her aunt at her lake house. Soon after, he wrote her a love letter, followed it up with more, and gave her a watch as a love token.

Terri Harsch was the typical girl-next-door, a God-fearing Gidget, and he called her "My Little Prudence," perhaps as a tribute to her cautious, religious nature. She, in turn, cleaved to him with such ardent devotion that she would even arise at the crack of dawn and accompany him on his paper route.

"We'd end up in a local convenience store and have a spicy sausage and 7-UP for breakfast. I think he burned so many calories dancing that he didn't have to monitor what he ate," she remembered. "We spent a lot of time watching TV at my house. Neither of us had a lot of extra money, so our times together were mainly 'hanging out.' We also went water skiing together.

"He was a part-time lifeguard at the pool behind his mother's studio on Judiway. I'd go and hang out at the swimming pool with him when he was on duty. He was pretty confident in whatever he took on. Whether it was gymnastics or water skiing, he thought he was the best at it and that's the way he came across.

"I met his father and I thought he was a very nice, down-to-earth man. Buddy always wanted to make him proud. His mother was also very nice to me, but I think she always knew deep down that because Buddy and I came from different worlds, we would never last."

Yet she was far too enamored of him to disdain his cultural universe, and if she couldn't dance with him like Nikki or the other studio girls, at least she could watch admiringly and applaud. Consequently, she proved to be an accomplished creative audience, a cheerleader who encouraged him in his ambitions.

"I was in awe of his talent and it amazed me how good he was at so many artistic endeavors. I never believed there was anything he couldn't do if he set his mind to it—and I was right," she said.

Fortunately, despite Patrick's artistic pursuits and bohemian background, her family didn't oppose her relationship with him. And Patrick valiantly did his best to conform to hers.

"One of my happiest memories of him was when he attended the Christmas Eve service at our church with us. He played the guitar and we all sang 'Silent Night' together. There was no other sound but him on the guitar accompanying our singing and that was lovely. My parents loved him, just like I did."

After graduation, he attended San Jacinto on a gymnastic scholarship and Terri enrolled in the University of Houston. However, after just one semester, he followed his mother's advice that her students should strive to attain further experience by auditioning as often as possible. He opted to audition for a place in the touring company of Disney on Parade, a show featuring dancers dancing dressed as some of Disney's best-loved characters.

Just before he was due to drive to the audition in Austin, his car developed engine trouble, so the ever-obliging Terri lent him her own dark green 1970s Chevrolet Malibu for the three- or more-hour ride there.

The audition went well and he was elated to be awarded a place in the company. Then on the drive home from Austin, disaster struck when he accidentally hit a deer and slightly damaged the side of the car.

"He came to my door that evening, said he had a problem, and asked my dad to come out to the car so he could show him the damage," Terri remembered. "He proceeded to open the trunk of the car and there was the dead deer! He had been concerned that my parents wouldn't believe his story, so he had brought home the evidence!

"We had no idea what to do with the deer, so we called my uncle, who lived in Friendswood, thirty-five miles south of Houston. He was a hunter, so we figured he'd know what to do. We drove to his house late that night, drove the car inside his garage, covered up all the windows, then my uncle, my dad, and Buddy gutted, then disposed of the carcass.

"I didn't watch, but I understand it was pretty rank by that time, so the smell was terrible. Buddy and I drove home, laughing because we thought we might get stopped by the police, they'd see blood coming from the trunk, and we'd really be in trouble, but thank goodness that didn't happen," she said.

Soon after, in May 1972, he left Houston to go on the road with Disney on Parade. "I knew he'd be away on tour all summer, but I didn't want to hold him back," she said. A week after he left, she found she already missed him, so she and her sister caught up with the tour in Dayton, Ohio. "I stood in front at the railing, waving. He didn't know I'd be there, so it was fun surprising him. I was happy to see him. He was playing the part of the cowboy in the finale of the grand parade and was in a cowboy outfit, with big furry chaps on."

At this stage in their romance, he'd already given her a ring they'd bought together at a flea market and which he'd had engraved with the initials "B.S."—for Buddy Swayze. Terri, as pragmatically as possible, given how she felt about him, always claimed that she viewed it as a friendship ring, although when pressed she admits that in those days she still hoped that they would be together forever.

Disney on Parade marked the first time that a commercial organization would capitalize on Patrick's radiantly masculine charisma. And a few weeks into the tour, while they were away on the road and he was still the dancing cowboy, on June 30, 1972, he auditioned and won the part of Prince Charming to Snow White in the show.

However, there was nothing remotely fairy-tale-ish, charming, or glamorous about touring with the Disney show. With a cast of sixty-five, the Disney on Parade company performed in arenas seating 18,000 and the show routines were often hard on the dancers.

Sam Kwasman, who danced in the show with Patrick, remembered: "We were all trained in ballet, tap, and jazz and danced ten to fourteen two-and-a-half-hour shows during the week—two on Fridays, three on Saturday, two on Sunday. We lived out of suitcases.

"There were thirty guys in the company and seven of us were straight. Buddy, of course, was one of the straight guys. He was a real gentle guy, silent but strong. The women loved him. They all wanted to date him, they all wanted to be with him," Sam said.

"We were at a club somewhere and this girl walked up to me and asked what my name was. I told her. Buddy rolled his eyes, and the girl said, 'Well, who's your friend?' She just wanted me to introduce her to Buddy, she just wanted to meet him."

Patrick was on hand when one of the show's leads, Roger Seward, irked by a malcontent who hadn't heeded his warnings and continued to mess with him, picked the man up, swung him in the air, and then pitched him headfirst into a trash can. "Buddy was really strong, but Roger Seward was stronger," Sam Kwasman said.

Witnessing Roger's superior strength, Patrick's strong competitive instincts came to the fore—and remained there. Ten years after Patrick first danced with Disney on Parade and witnessed Roger's Herculean achievement, he had a chance encounter with Sam. "His first question was, 'How's Roger? Is he still as strong as he used to be?' And I told him that he was," Sam recalled.

The competitive spirit that Patsy had etched deep into her son's heart and soul was still so strong that nearly twenty years after he first witnessed Roger Seward's impressive demonstration of superior strength, it still clearly rankled with him. "I met Buddy again in 1989," Roger remembered. "And the very first thing he said to me was, 'Hey, Roger, are you still as strong as you used to be?'

"I saw that he'd gotten more outgoing, more open over the years. When we were dancing together in Disney on Parade, he was kind of quiet. My wife, Valerie Smith, who was Snow White to his Prince Charming and danced with him on Saturdays, always liked him because he was more like a prince, and most other women felt the same way.

"I played the Big Bad Wolf and did a number with a girl named Betsy, who played Cruella de Vil. When Buddy got into the company and she found out he was straight, she latched on to him and kept him busy for a long time, though I think it was just a fling for him."

It probably was. He was still writing to Terri on a regular basis, although today she says, somewhat wistfully, "I suppose I was naive, but I thought I was the only one."

Meanwhile, his Disney on Parade career was proceeding apace. In "The Barnyard Dash" he played Colonel Sanders and so had the opportunity to enlarge upon his high-school Donald Duck imitation. "In Mexico City, he did Donald Duck in Spanish. He was very humble, very quiet, very courteous," Sam Kwasman said.

The grueling tour took the company all over the United States, Canada, and Central America. "The horror story there was doing the Russian tarantella number from *Fantasia*," Patrick remembered. "All that squatting and turning, eight shows a week, periodically hospitalizes you. The dancers would drop like flies on that show."

"The Tarantella sequence lasted twenty minutes," Sam confirmed. "The dance was exhausting. Buddy had a bad knee, and he had to get it worked on every day, otherwise he would stiffen up."

Despite the pain, despite the fact that Disney on Parade wasn't the ballet company of his dreams, soon he would be up there dancing with the best of them. But even that wouldn't be enough for him. One day he would put it: "I don't ever want to get satisfied. I want to always be looking for something better. That's called passion, and I live on passion."

four

MY ANGEL

*I*n the late summer of 1972, Patrick returned home from the Disney tour, and his arrival was the occasion for great excitement and celebration at the studio. Being away from Houston, touring America, had lent him added sophistication and enhanced his already striking masculinity.

He had never been averse to fanning his kaleidoscopic peacock feathers for the benefit of all his appreciative and admiring young female acolytes at Patsy's studio, now more than ever. Consequently, when he made his grand entrance into the studio after the Disney tour ended, he was dressed in full Tom Jones regalia—as he later described it, presumably referring to the Welsh singer, not to Henry Fielding's engaging rogue, though he probably radiated twice as much sex appeal as both the fictional and the real-life Mr. Jones.

Clad in an open-necked shirt with only laces covering his bare chest, thus displaying it to the best advantage, knee-high leather boots, tight jeans, and a big-buckled belt, it was surprising that a herald didn't precede him with a fanfare trumpeting that the prince was back.

Observing his grand entrance that first day at the studio, a beautiful, petite, ethereal blonde dancer new to the studio hung back in the shadows appraisingly. Though sources differ as to whether she

was fifteen or sixteen years old at the time, it was, however, indisput-
able that, young as she was, Lisa Niemi already possessed the face of
Raphael's Madonna and the sangfroid of a riverboat gambler. While,
as Lisa's mother later reported, "all the dancers were fussing over
Patrick, he was truly every young girl's Prince Charming," only Lisa
remained remote, hung back, and wordlessly observed the studio
girls clustered eagerly around him.

Surveying the scene, all the admiration swirling around Patrick,
his own princely, if modest, natural acceptance of the adulation he
excited, Lisa sized him up and decided "he was the all-American jock
and a Casanova whose head had to be shrunk to enter a doorway."

She was wrong about that. As she'd soon learn, he was far less
confident than she imagined. But that day, surrendering to her first
impression of him, strong-minded and opinionated, she told herself
that he needed a lesson. Besides, she certainly wasn't in the habit
of flirting, and never would have dreamed of chasing after any boy,
however handsome, even if he was the prince of the dance studio
and a handsome heartbreaker.

"Lisa said later that she saw all the girls chasing him so she decided to let him chase her," her mother, Karin Haapaniemi, later
disclosed.

Lisa Niemi didn't need to morph into Diana the huntress in order to captivate Patrick, for it wouldn't take long before he began to
pursue her and she knew it. By all accounts from fellow students who
attended Patsy's classes with her, she was an old soul with an intense
beauty and a gravitas far beyond her years. Moreover, when Patrick
witnessed her dancing her very first dance that day, "she blew everybody away. She had a natural gift," as he said.

Although he was unaware of it at the time, she was blessed with
another gift, a lethal weapon not of her own making but one which
would soon cause him to fall under her sway as quickly, easily, and
completely as if she were an alabaster Elphaba and had cast an un-
breakable spell over him, and, as it transpired, over his mother as
well.

"The very first time Lisa walked into the studio, Patsy fell in love with her on the spot. She adored her," Zetta Alderman said, adding, "It was very hard for all the rest of us because we had all been at the studio for years, working really hard, and then Lisa walked in and it was like she had this special thing with Patsy that none of us could even touch. None of us could even get near it. Not then, not ever."

"Patsy called Lisa 'my angel' because she danced like an angel and looked like an angel," Paula Abbott, who was in the same class as Lisa on her very first day at Patsy's, said. "You would never have known it was her first day. She had these legs that went on forever and ever and ever and she moved like water, she's that fluid. She has beautiful ballet technique, and I think that's one of the reasons Patsy loved her so much."

Lisa Anne Haapaniemi (whose last name is also the name of a rustic resort on the shores of Lake Haapajärvi, in Finland) was four years Patrick's junior, fine-boned, with large cornflower-blue eyes, and the only daughter out of five boys born to Finnish parents Edmond Haapaniemi, director of Red Cross safety services in Houston, and her mother, Karin, a registered nurse.

Yet despite the differences in their background, beneath the surface the similarities between her and Patrick were manifold. A natural-born athlete like Patrick, she was something of an infant prodigy, walked at eight months, learned to swim at three, and at the age of four became the youngest member of Houston's main synchronized swimming group, the Shamrock Corkettes.

Girls with brothers, unlike girls without them, are born with a marked advantage. Unlike brotherless girls, when girls with brothers grow up, start dating, and become women, they are already familiar with every facet of the male psyche, the male body, male passions, and male interests, and so it was with Lisa.

"I think being raised in a family of boys influenced her life a lot. She liked to keep up with her boisterous brothers. Consequently, she was a tomboy who could outrun any boy her age," her mother confirmed.

She was also knowledgeable about football, adept at carpentry, and—like Patrick—was also a daredevil, with a childhood tendency to take risks. Just as he had relished taking his life into his hands by jumping off buildings and playing Tarzan, as a child Lisa, as her mother put it, "tried 'flying' off a garage roof, among other daring deeds."

She and Patrick also had in common a marked duality of nature. Like him, she was a jock yet also passionately embraced artistic interests from very early on in her life. She was not even nine months old when her mother witnessed her rocking in time to the strains of a symphony orchestra playing on TV. At four she took her first dance class, and at seven she began to play the violin.

A renaissance woman, just as Patrick was a renaissance man, she loved reading, drawing, and painting, and wrote poetry as well; she adored pets, in particular her male kitten, which she inexplicably named Judy Garland.

Her ability to focus, her utter one-track mindedness, also rivaled Patrick's. "She was always very determined, very focused with everything she was interested in," her mother said.

Nonetheless, she was compelled to drop out of high school due to severe insomnia, which may well have hindered her progress, and she signed on at Houston's High School for the Performing Arts. She initially intended to study drama, but on her first day she got lost en route to the department. "I started out again to locate the Drama Department," she remembered, "and when, for the second time, I wound up at the Dance Department, I decided it was my fate to be a dancer!"

It was also fate that Patsy would be one of her dance teachers at the school, and it was just a matter of time before she took lessons at Patsy's studio as well. As the story goes, when Patrick first saw her there, he immediately made his move—a surprisingly saucy one—and pinched her bottom.

"We clicked off right away, but not necessarily in a good way," she said, afterward, adding, "I was introverted and had a mind of my own."

Soon after, he redeemed himself somewhat by politely inviting her to dance with him. The piece was a very sexual one. "I ended up on the floor and he's lying on top of me for what felt like about five minutes," Lisa later recalled.

Titillating as the moment might have been, in those first days at the end of the summer of 1972, after he returned home and the studio dancers hadn't yet cast Lisa as the Yoko Ono of Oak Forest, he focused on picking up where he'd left off before Disney.

First, he took a job as assistant manager for the Galleria Ice Pavilion skating rink in Westheimer, Houston, where he also gave skating lessons.

"Buddy was so great, he had the keys to the rink, and after the rink closed at midnight, he'd let a group of us Patsy dancers in so we could skate there," Zetta Alderman remembered. "Buddy and all of us would skate and skate until we were done. Then we'd rush up and down the Galleria and dance and play and do lifts up and down the halls."

Meanwhile, there was still the matter of his relationship with Terri Harsch, who believed that he remained as bound to her as she was to him. "Buddy and I were still committed, but I began to feel that we had drifted apart," Terri remembered. "We were seeing less of each other."

Nevertheless, Patrick remained close to her family and courteous to them, so that when her sister Karon married on November 11, 1972, he sang "One Hand, One Heart" from *West Side Story* and the Lord's Prayer at the ceremony.

Whether by design or accident, Patrick and Terri's romance was put on hold when, in the summer of 1973, a few months before his twenty-first birthday, he contracted to be guest artist with the Buffalo Ballet Company in western New York. When he was presented with the opportunity to start his professional dance career in earnest, he had very little conflict about leaving Houston and Terri and moving to Buffalo. From his early childhood, his mother had drilled him in the importance of setting goals and achieving them, whatever the cost. Besides, he was still very young, and there were plenty of other women, willing and available to him, worlds away from Texas.

He spent three months dancing with the Buffalo Ballet Company, partnered mostly by dancer Sandra Perez. Soon they were dating, and their relationship became so serious that, like Terri before her, Sandra introduced him to her family, who liked him very much.

After three months, he was so smitten by Sandra that he actually asked her father for her hand in marriage. Aware that Sandra was involved with someone else, then away at college, her father gave his consent but warned Patrick that she might not agree.

A few days later, as Sandra's father drove her and Patrick home from rehearsal, Patrick presented her with an eight-page love letter and an engagement ring. She was not surprised. "He was very romantic with writing poetry and love letters," she remembered years later. "But I was involved with someone else at college and Patrick was going to New York City in the fall. It just wouldn't have worked out."

He took her refusal in good spirits, and like all his former girlfriends, she was left with fond memories of him. "Patrick is really a lot like his character in *Dirty Dancing*," she observed. "He is a lot of fun, very good looking, an excellent dancer, an excellent partner; he's just charming. He's really a great guy."

His eagerness to propose marriage to Sandra Perez after so short an acquaintance probably says all that needs to be said about his emotional make-up, not just in his early twenties but for always. He was twenty-one, tall, strong, handsome, and—judging by the harem-size number of nubile dancers all wilting for the love of him, whose passion he didn't requite—he wasn't in the least bit polyamorous. And the moment he had become involved with a girl, he immediately assumed that marriage and monogamy were a foregone conclusion.

He had at one point talked marriage to Terri Harsch, who remembered, "He made a lot of plans and said, 'When we get married, we'll go camping on our honeymoon.' " Her heart sank because she wasn't an outdoors girl, but she was so intoxicated by him that she didn't protest.

Now that the Buffalo Ballet season was over and Patrick was back in Houston again, Terri found him changed. Witnessing him light up a cigarette, she was shocked, remembering how health conscious he had always been. Yet although he would spend years trying to kick the habit, no matter how hazardous smoking would later become to his health, he never could.

Sensing as well that his interest in her had diminished, in the hope that he would react by swearing his undying love and proposing to her, Terri, the Baptist deacon's daughter, capitulated to a hitherto recessive gene in her make-up that she may well have inherited from some distant poker-playing ancestor and attempted to bluff Patrick by offering to return his class ring to him. He called her bluff, and it was hardly surprising. After all, since the time he could walk, the female sex had pursued him as if they were homing pigeons in heat or tarantulas plotting to trap him within the gossamer threads of their spider's web charms, and he had become practiced at evading them all with finesse.

Instead of Terri's gamble paying off, Patrick gently but firmly made it clear to her that their relationship was over, and they broke up then and there. Sometime later, she arranged to see him at his mother's studio, just in case there was a chance their relationship might be resuscitated.

"We met outside the studio. We talked for a while, then he walked out of my life forever," Terri remembered. In the end, although she didn't know at the time, it came down to this: Much as he cared about Terri, Lisa was his mother's pick, her "angel," the princess she'd chosen as consort for her son. And no other woman would get a look in, as, for once, his mother's will and his own happily coincided.

"Lisa had a very wise head on her shoulders," he said. "I knew she was the smartest chick I'd ever met in my life." So he asked her out on a date.

He took her to a rodeo, driving her there in a Corvette lent to him by a friend, but, to his surprise she wasn't particularly impressed, either by the car or by him. "Love is supposed to start with bells ringing and go downhill from there. But it was the opposite for me," she said many years afterward.

Many a Houstonian mother would have willingly crawled over broken glass had that ensured that her daughter would be romanced by the eligible Buddy Swayze, but like her daughter, Karin Haapaniemi was no pushover.

"I wasn't sure I liked Patrick at first," she recalled. "With all the girls so crazy about him, I concluded he was something of a heartbreaker. And when he bought Lisa home late from their first date, I wasn't very nice about it. The next day he returned with roses and an apology. I said, 'Don't let that happen again!' It didn't."

Clearly, Mrs. Haapaniemi was strong, assertive, very much in the Patsy mode, and so of course was Lisa. He quickly learned that Lisa was also eminently capable of making him toe the line. "She didn't buy any of my nonsense. We spent half our dates in total silence as she wouldn't talk to me if she thought I was putting on an act. She was different from any other woman I'd known. I'd be playing Mr. Cool and she wouldn't have it. If I started my macho stuff, she'd cut me off fast," he ruefully recalled.

Even at this early stage, she was cracking the whip over him, metaphorically speaking. Accustomed as he was to his mother, who loved her husband, Big Buddy, very much, but was clearly the kind of woman who was more primed to blare out "The King is in his altogether" rather than drench him in honey, hearts, and flowers, Lisa's blunt self-assertiveness must have seemed extremely familiar and almost reassuring to Patsy Swayze's son. So was Lisa's marked lack of vanity. "I never met a girl like her, who wasn't just looking in the mirror," he said. For as beautiful as she may have been, with her long hair that tended to be limp rather than big and bouffant, she wasn't in the habit of primping, preening, or acting the feminine little woman.

"I was not the cheerleader type," she said succinctly. "I was never encouraged to learn how to curl my hair or put on lipstick."

Away from the dance studio, she wore bell-bottom jeans, very little makeup, and smoked. She was a brilliant dancer and also possessed another unique talent, one that he'd never encountered before: She was so flexible that "she could slap herself in the face with her legs."

For her part, she discovered that "as we stayed together, the bells rang louder," and she concluded that she was less magnetized by Patrick's Adonis-like body, his athleticism, and his masculine presence than by the heart of him. "I wasn't interested in his accomplishments," she explained, "but I always thought there was something inside of him that was pure gold.

"We were both kind of misunderstood people," she pointed out. "He had this terrible reputation as a Casanova, and I as this loose girl and a dope user, even though I wasn't. Still, I had such a strong sense that something was going to come of the two of us."

True love, as all lovers of romantic sagas, both high and low, from *Romeo and Juliet* to Barbara Cartland, well know, is only further enhanced by thorns encountered along the rose-petal-covered path of the lovers.

So it was that Lisa and Patrick's budding romance was thrown off course when he won a coveted scholarship to study at the prestigious Harkness Ballet Company in Manhattan. And not even the greatest love in the universe would have prevented him from accepting it.

Now that he had decided to pursue classical ballet in earnest, Patsy was overjoyed. "She was so proud of him," Cookie Joe recalled. "Behind his back, she used to brag about him and described him as 'my beautiful son' as in 'My beautiful son just did this . . .' "

Like some modern-day picaresque hero (think Barry Lyndon, think Dick Whittington), Patrick left Houston with Lisa's love and his mother's blessing.

The image of this twenty-one-year-old storybook hero gazing up at the dreaming skyscrapers of Manhattan and vowing that one day his Siegfried would set not only the city but the entire ballet world alight, is irresistible. It's an unpleasant fact of life, however, that even the most worthy of heroes don't necessarily always scale the castle walls at their first attempt, or indeed even come within dancing distance of one. So it was a matter of course that Patrick moved into a squalid basement apartment on West 70th Street, renting it for a sum so exorbitant that he was left with only about ten dollars a week for food.

"There was just a small living room, the kitchen was right in the living room, and there was a very, very small bedroom," said Rick Odums, who visited Patrick there. He added: "But what I remember most is that there was a bathroom without a door."

But no matter how humble his Manhattan abode, Patrick was moving toward achieving his dream of becoming a professional dancer, and that to him was all that mattered.

At first, his ambitions met with a few predictable setbacks. "In Houston, I was Mr. Kingpin," he said. "Then I came to New York and I was nuthin'. That was a big lesson to learn. So I studied very hard here."

The discipline involved in studying classical ballet was a far cry from his multidimensional dance training with Patsy. Yet however arduous the classical ballet classes, however grueling, Patrick steadfastly refused to be deterred. Years later, looking back, he asserted, "I'll always be a classical ballet dancer at heart. It was the greatest challenge I'd ever faced in my life."

Linda May-Randell, who was a trainee at Harkness at the same time as Patrick and danced with him there, remembers that he was more than equal to the challenge. "He made a big impression on me, as he stood out from the other dancers, partly because of his integrity because he was focused, hardworking, and also because he was masculine. He was not at all distracted by gossip or trivial things. He just worked hard."

He worked hard but earned a pittance. Life in the city wasn't remotely easy for him as he heroically struggled through all the traditional first-act vicissitudes. However, he stalwartly avoided becoming too downhearted by embarking on a routine of daily affirmations, in which he would religiously repeat to himself, "I'm a winner, my life works."

Although he had been brought up a Catholic, Buddhism also attracted him and in the future he would make *Zen and the Art of Archery* and *Zen and the Art of Motorcycle Maintenance* his Bibles, claiming he was, "trying to find out who I was and trying to like myself. I just went into this soul-searching period of my life that put me in a head I've never lost."

"I did the est training, TM, I got my mantra, was into Scientology . . . In martial arts it's called 'finding your chi'; in Buddhism it's called your 'Buddha nature,' your soul, your spirit, your god within you," he said.

With his ardent, questing nature, his hunger for self-improvement and, above all, what he would later term his obsessive-compulsive tendencies, he would throw himself into soul-searching as ardently as any white knight scouring the world for the Holy Grail.

Meanwhile, back in Houston, the studio girl dancers who adored him so much were missing him and wishing him well. "We were very excited for Buddy when he joined Harkness," remembered Cookie Joe. "And when he heard that—because his physique was so beautiful—they'd decided to use it as the model for the mural on the ceiling of the Harkness Theater, Patsy was very proud."

Lisa too must also have been proud. "She talked constantly about Patrick and the fact that they were writing and calling each other all the time," said one of the studio dancers, with an undertone that spoke of the almost universal jealousy Lisa seemed to have aroused among those girls who had coveted him. Now they classified her as an Eve Harrington who had eclipsed all of them and then turned Lorelei and bewitched their beloved Prince Charming with her siren song.

Meanwhile, as she responded to all the calls and letters in which he'd artlessly prattled on about the various New York women he was dating—or as he put it, "this lady and that one"—he grew increasingly fond of her. "Even if I dated other women, she'd always be in my mind," he said.

She was still on his mind and in his heart and his sentiments were clearly reciprocated when, in 1974, after she had graduated from high school, she announced her intention to study with the Harkness as well. "When I found out Lisa was coming to Manhattan, I was beside myself," he recalled. "I realized at that moment she was the one I wanted."

Patrick invited her to move into the small apartment with him. From that time on, there was no doubt that he and Lisa were now a couple, that their destinies were entwined, and that it was just a matter of time before their relationship deepened and became permanent.

Back in Houston, Patsy gave them her blessing. "I think it was perfect for Patsy that Buddy fell in love with a beautiful dancer and that they could dance through life together," Cookie Joe said.

As those who knew both Lisa and Patsy well agreed, there were striking similarities between both of them. "Patsy was very strong, and Lisa was very strong," said Zetta Alderman. "And Lisa's kind of like Patsy as well because she's also hard to read, and you never really know what she's thinking about you. They're very similar."

"Lisa does have Patsy's character. And the older Lisa gets, the more she even begins to look like Patsy to me," Rick Odums said recently.

The resemblance between his wife and his mother, both on a deep-seated level and superficially, hadn't escaped Patrick. "I tried to make Lisa my mother early on, but she wouldn't stand for it," he later confessed.

There were also deeper-rooted problems. In retrospect, perhaps as a result of the therapy he underwent after *Dirty Dancing*, he realized that "I mistrusted women and found it hard to let myself go." At the same time, he felt unworthy of Lisa's love, somehow prefiguring "She's Like the Wind," the song he cowrote, which was featured in *Dirty Dancing* and included the lyric about being "out of my league" and "I'm a fool to believe I've got anything she needs."

"I just felt at that time that I'm very, very lucky to have a woman who thinks I hung the moon, when I know I didn't," he said of their early relationship.

She understood and loved all of him, including his overriding insecurity that he was merely a machine with a body that performed at will but nothing much else. "I thought all I was was what I looked like and what I could do with my body. I didn't know if there was anything inside that anyone would care about," he admitted. As Lisa confirmed, "Every bit of validation he'd gotten in his life was because of that. He was extremely insecure that he was shallow and dumb, neither of which is true."

Patrick knew he had primarily devoted his academic career to sport, not intellectual pursuits, and had concentrated on his body, not his mind. In later years he would come to feel that in honing that perfect body he had also, in effect, created the equivalent of a Frankenstein's monster that was sometimes in danger of eclipsing the rest of his kaleidoscopic persona.

Patrick's insecurity about himself expressed itself in burning jealousy of any man who came within any distance of Lisa. "When someone looked at Lisa in a certain way . . . I felt it was an affront to me," he said. At times, his insecurity reached such a peak that he was afraid to let her out of his sight. As Lisa later confided, "He gave me a hard time if I wore something nice. He preferred me in a baggy shirt and overalls."

Patrick was insecure about himself and even more insecure about sex. The truth was that, despite the fact that he was strikingly handsome, had the body of a Greek god, and had dated numerous Texan girls, he had very little sexual experience.

He also was forced to grapple with his inborn sexual inhibitions. "I grew up with a lot of sexual hang-ups," he admitted, attributing them to his Catholic upbringing. "It took a long time for me to realize that there wasn't anything wrong with sex, you know." By the time he began living with Lisa, however, he was no longer a virgin, and claimed to journalist Lydia Slater that his first sexual experience was a disaster. "My father walked in halfway through!" he said.

As a result of that first, unsatisfactory encounter, he was cautious about his next, so that Lisa would be only the second woman he had ever had sex with. "I couldn't sleep around. I lied about it a lot in the locker room, but I didn't do it," he said before making the startling admission, "Lisa and I lived with each other and slept together for a year before we made love. I had to propose before we felt our relationship was serious enough to have sex with each other."

Propose he did, Lisa accepted, and they flew home to Houston, where—on June 12, 1975—the wedding ceremony took place in the backyard of her home; the reception was held in Patsy's studio, where they'd first met.

Beforehand, Lisa sewed her own wedding dress because she and Patrick were too broke to buy one, nor could they afford an engagement ring. But they didn't care. They were young, in love, beautiful, and blessed.

If he was unsure of himself as a man, Patrick had no doubt whatsoever about his ability as a dancer. His confidence was further boosted when he was invited to dance in the Joffrey Ballet's second company.

Founded by the dancer-choreographer Robert Joffrey and Gerard Arpino in 1956, the company first took form with an ensemble of six strong, iconoclastic dancers who performed original ballets all over the country. The Joffrey Ballet's approach was innovative and uniquely American. Who better than the All-American Patrick Swayze to be one of the dancers?

Soon, Lisa too joined Joffrey II, with both of them earning a small weekly salary of no more than $50. Subsisting on peanut butter sandwiches, dancing with the Joffrey most nights, and rehearsing during the day, they survived however they could. Given that Patrick and Lisa were already accomplished self-taught carpenters, they started a carpentry business, rushing from appointment to appointment, hoping against hope that someone would want to use their services.

Lisa—who had started sewing at the age of twelve—also took a part-time job working for a costume company sewing costumes and danced for a while with Manhattan's Contemporary Chamber Dance Group, which Rick Odums was directing. Then Patrick won the small part of Riff in a Westchester County stock production of *West Side Story*, in which, according to Rick Odums, who saw the show, he was "wonderful."

Unfortunately, though, stock didn't pay much money. Consequently, Patrick also worked part-time in a Hallmark card store. When photographer Ron Schubert informed him that he could make easy money by doing commercial modeling, Patrick, desperate for cash, agreed to pose for a campaign advertising a Manhattan men's boutique at 983 Third Avenue. One of the photographs from the shoot, which featured him dressed in only his underwear, appeared in the gay magazine *After Dark* during the seventies and was again republished in a tabloid sixteen years afterward, causing wishful rumors to palpitate among the gay community. But much as the gay world might have loved to have claimed him as one of their own, Patrick Swayze is neither bisexual nor gay. As he so pithily declared, he was always "as heterosexual as a bull moose."

Life in Manhattan held other, more lethal dangers for Patrick than being inveigled into posing for a revealing picture. Late one night he was traveling on the subway when two men mugged him and one of them pulled a knife on him. He swung into action. "I went insane. I took the knife away from him and hurt both of them real bad," he confessed. The two men ended up in the hospital, and although Patrick had been acting in self-defense, he afterward tormented himself that he had gone too far.

However, courage was in his blood and fighting off muggers was a family pattern. When his grandmother Gladys was advanced in years, she managed to fight off two muggers in a shopping mall parking lot. "They held her up and tried to grab her purse, but she wouldn't let go of it. She was an old lady, but they couldn't get her purse, so they ran away empty handed," said Rick Odums.

Patrick's own mythology was further enhanced when he began roaring around Manhattan on a motorbike in Marlon Brando *The Wild One* style, except that he didn't terrorize anyone, preferring instead to tempt fate by performing daredevil stunts on the New Jersey Turnpike.

He was reckless, brave, adventurous, and, in contrast to most dancers in the effete world of ballet, surprisingly strong. "I was the Godzilla of ballet," he once cracked. "I had nineteen-inch arms. I was unique in that I looked like a man on stage."

"He was a tough guy and a sensitive person," remembered Eliott Feld, who hired him to dance in his company in 1975 and who experienced the dichotomy that lay at the heart of him. "I found him very sensitive, almost overly so," Eliott said, also observing that Patrick was concerned as to whether or not he would be accepted in the company and make his mark there.

He had no reason to worry. Feld—like Patsy, a hard taskmaster whom Patrick once described as "a genius"—quickly promoted him to be one of his principal dancers.

Toward the end of October 1975, Rick Odums was in the audience at the New York Shakespeare Festival's Newman Theater, where Patrick was dancing with the company in *Excursions*, Feld's uniquely American ballet in the style of Agnes de Mille's *Rodeo*. "He was this motorcycle freak at the time, so he picked me up beforehand and had me on the back of his motorcycle, flying through Manhattan too fast. He was brilliant in the ballet, though, and afterward we had a long talk during which he explained to me what every movement in the ballet meant," Rick said.

Ballet was now Patrick's life and, he believed, his destiny. Soon ballet magazines were comparing him to the spectacularly athletic male dancers of Russia's Bolshoi. His success as a dancer seemed a foregone conclusion. Then fate intervened.

Patrick was poised to leave on a South American tour with the company, during which he would be dancing the lead in *Mazurka, Intermezzo and Concert*," when he developed an abscess in a tooth. Within days, it worked itself into a staph infection in his bloodstream and then finally settled in his previously injured and fragile left knee, the weakest part of his body, which a staph infection invariably seeks out. Doctors gave him the grave news that, unless the infection subsided within a week, his entire leg would have to be amputated from the hip. "I thought my world was destroyed," he said.

However, he heroically put on a brave face for his mother. "Patsy was devastated," remembered Paula Abbott. "But Patrick just kept saying, 'It's gonna be alright. It's gonna be fine.'" Then and in the future, his bravery, his pride, and his concern for those who loved him would remain paramount. There was no way in the world that he wanted his family to know how much he was suffering, and he would always be true to his noble intent at all costs, no matter how much he would suffer, no matter how much pain and anguish he would experience.

The dance studio girls waited for news. "All of us were terrified that he wouldn't dance again, but knowing Buddy, we knew that if he wasn't meant to be a classical dancer, he would pick up his bootstraps and do something different," Cookie Joe said, somewhat prophetically.

Patrick's knee was already fragile from his football injuries, with massive amounts of scar tissue around the joint, and although doctors ultimately managed to save it, the writing was on the wall: Although he was at the top of his game as a dancer, after ten hard years of mastering his craft, his body was no longer up to the physically grueling discipline of ballet anymore.

He knew from experience that if he learned to compensate for his injury by taking the pressure off his left leg he could dance again, albeit in a less-challenging arena. He had been singing and dancing in his mother's productions of Broadway shows ever since he was a small boy. So he made the difficult but logical decision that, rather than becoming America's answer to Rudolf Nureyev, he would conquer the Great White Way instead.

Apart from all his previous experience in musicals back home in Houston, in 1974 he had danced in the chorus in a production of *Music Man* at the Paper Mill Playhouse in Millburn, New Jersey—a traditional launching pad for the early careers of stars such as Carol Channing and Liza Minnelli. And in March 1975, he had taken a walk-on dancing part as a servant in the Broadway musical *Good-time Charley*, which opened at the Palace Theater on March 3, 1975, and starred Anne Reinking and Jennifer Grey's father, Joel Grey of *Cabaret* fame.

Patrick weathered the setback to his ambitions to scale the heights of classical ballet partly because of his supreme, unwavering belief in his own talent, and that he would hit the heights on Broadway. "Pitted against what he just innately had as a person, his desire, the entire world would just have to stand aside; that is going to happen for him. It was destined," Lisa declared.

Soon after making his life-changing decision, he got his big break, replacing John Travolta in the starring part of Danny Zuko in the Broadway production of *Grease*.

Now that their financial situation had improved considerably, he and Lisa moved out of the West 70th Street basement and into a more salubrious apartment at 305 West 74th Street.

Lisa attended many of the early *Grease* rehearsals with him and, according to director Tom Moore, gave Patrick tremendous moral support by just being there. "It was always touching for me to see them together. They were the perfect couple," he observed. "Patrick was an incredibly good-looking man with an incredibly sure sense of his body and the effect all of that might be having on an audience and that's irreplaceable."

Patrick was an overnight sensation in *Grease*. "To me, he was more Danny Zuko than John Travolta was," Zetta Alderman, who saw the show more than once, enthused. "He was just wonderful. He was very strong and had a great singing voice. I've never seen him do anything he wasn't good at."

"I think sex appeal comes from who you are," he said in connection with his *Grease* performance. "There were nights when I didn't think I could make it through the show, when I wasn't trying to be sexy and do pelvis grinds, and those were the nights I'd put on my best performance."

Yet despite the good reviews, the accolades he garnered from *Grease*, the parts still weren't pouring in. He attended audition after audition, but to no avail. However, rather than becoming discouraged or sinking into a depression, he was buttressed by his mother's maxims. "She taught me [life] ain't about coasting," he recalled long afterward. "That's what pulled me through looking for a job in offices with fifty clones all better looking than I was. You don't waste your time looking in the mirror; you bury your butt in acting classes."

He did just that and invested part of his *Grease* earnings in acting lessons for himself and for Lisa at Warren Robertson's Theater Workshop, where Diane Keaton, James Earl Jones, Christopher Walken, Jessica Lange, and Robert De Niro, among others, had studied his legendary technique of pushing actors to confront their own demons.

"People would lose it, being on that stage in the fetal position, screaming and sobbing," Patrick recalled, going on to explain, "Robertson's objective was to break the picture you had of yourself. His reasoning was that we have the shy person, the gay person, the quiet person, the angry person, the macho person, the intellectual person inside of each of us, and the objective is to be able to tap any one of them at will."

And there is more, far more. Based on the Stanislavski theory of using emotional memory in order to create a believable character, Method actors like Marlon Brando, Robert De Niro, and James Dean were taught to summon up a relevant past memory and give it to the character they were playing.

Warren Robertson had studied the craft at the Actors Studio at the same time as Marilyn Monroe, Jane Fonda, and Christopher Walken, and like them was taught by Lee Strasberg, the father of the American Method, whose credo was "the actor creates with his own flesh and blood." Thus it was that at this formative stage in his acting career Patrick would indirectly come under the sway of what was virtually a cult, the cult of Method acting, whereby an actor didn't merely play a character—he would submerge himself in that character, would become it.

He would go on to embrace Method acting as fanatically as any Christian the Messiah, any Muslim Allah, and any Buddhist the Buddha.

Nonetheless, in Robertson—who hailed from Archer, Texas—Patrick had found a kindred spirit who truly understood him. "Patrick's a tough guy," he said. "He's not mean, but he has emotional power, integrity and honor, and vulnerability."

Warren Robertson was one of the earliest to be captivated by Lisa and Patrick as a couple, as well. "They were like Tristan and Iseult," he enthused. "Too beautiful to believe. I used think they left New York at night and went out to the woods together."

Warren Robertson's acting classes would hold Patrick in good stead when—after eight months—*Grease* closed, and he and Lisa moved to Los Angeles with $1,500 they'd saved. He had his sights set on Hollywood stardom and resolved not to fail.

"Most people come to Hollywood, step off the plane and that's as far as they ever go. I was determined not to let that happen to me," he later declared.

For as far as he was concerned, only an act of God would stop him now from becoming a star.

five

EMERALD CITY

ifteen hundred dollars and an iron will to win don't generally keep the wolf from the door for very long in Hollywood, even though the money is in the possession of an aspiring actor as godlike, handsome, and well built as Patrick Swayze and an aspiring actress as hauntingly beautiful and ambitious as Lisa.

Just a few days after they first arrived in Hollywood, they made the traditional arriviste actors' pilgrimage to Grauman's Chinese Theater and gazed hungrily at all the footprints and handprints of the stars of yore and dreamed of one day making their own there. However, unlike the majority of all the other young and gorgeous aspiring actors who come to Tinseltown with stars in their eyes, Patrick and Lisa would not be condemned to spending years suffering in the latter-day valley of the locusts that is Los Angeles. Back home in Houston, Patsy had now morphed from Simon Legree on a bad day into a female Albus Dumbledore, with one wave of her magic wand producing the most fascinating illustration of six degrees of separation; when Patrick was young, Jaclyn Smith was one of Patsy's students. Patrick had had an unrequited crush on Jaclyn. Jaclyn's favorite dance partner was a fellow Texan named Bob Le Mond. With his business partner, Lois Zetter, Bob Le Mond went on to form

Le Mond/Zetter Management. John Travolta was one of their first clients, Mickey Rourke another, and now—thanks to the aforementioned cascade of coincidences—Le Mond/Zetter agreed to manage Patrick Swayze as well.

The news that he was represented in tandem with Travolta only served to signal his potential to *le tout* Hollywood. Consequently, just weeks after he first arrived in Los Angeles, Patrick was cast in the teen movie *Skatetown USA*, costarring with Scott Baio in the pivotal role of bad boy gang leader Ace, who, in a reign of terror, ruled over a local roller skating rink until dethroned by another skater. Patrick celebrated winning his first movie part by going to Hollywood Honda and treating himself and Lisa to a DOHC 750.

After his euphoria subsided, he came to the unpleasant realization that he didn't particularly like the script, grumbling that it was "teenybopper stuff." His discomfort was further enhanced by the fact that Patsy was predictably scathing about the part, pointedly inquiring if he truly wanted to "dance around on roller skates." But— dressed in tight black leather pants and vest, strutting his stuff in a spectacular roller-disco showdown—he still did his utmost as the archetypical but sexy bad boy.

With Lisa, he made an appearance at the October 1, 1979, premiere at Flippers Roller Rink in L.A., and the fans loved him, both away from the movie and in it.

Part Elvis before he ballooned into Liberace and part Brando in his prime, Patrick's on-screen persona had the critics instantly scrambling for their superlatives. And on one of the few occasions of his career—along with *Dirty Dancing*—they were in total agreement about the star wattage of his performance,

"Not since Valentino did his tango in *The Four Horsemen of the Apocalypse* has there been such a confident display of male sexuality. Patrick Swayze sizzles," enthused Kevin Thomas in the *Los Angeles Times*.

"As Ace, Patrick Swayze displays more talent than this production can conveniently handle. He has a lean, smoldering, potentially dangerous presence suggesting a cross between the young Jack Palance and Andrew Stevens . . . also seems to be a graceful athletic dancer. One of the highlights of the show is his torrid pas de deux with the equally assured April Allen," raved the *Washington Post* critic.

In less lyrical, but equally positive terms, Yardena Arar in the *Indiana Gazette* wrote: "Newcomer Patrick Swayze is the guy to look out for. Comparisons to John Travolta in *Saturday Night Fever* are entirely justified by Swayze's erotic gyrations on the dance floor."

"His performance in *Skatetown USA* was a precursor of the passion he would bring to further roles throughout his career," said his manager, Lois Zetter. Consequently, she and Bob Le Mond were somewhat taken aback when he flatly refused to sign a three-picture deal offered him by Columbia Pictures.

Only recently Patrick and Lisa had been struggling to make ends meet. Now he was walking away from a contract worth millions. But like Patsy—who was always so disinterested in money that she didn't care whether she had a class with two children in it or forty, but taught both classes with equal energy, enthusiasm, and dedication—Patrick was never motivated by money.

"I nearly starved after *Skatetown*," he said. "I turned down every offer. What was I going to do? Become a teenybopper star? It'd take me ten years to live that down. I literally lived off the orange trees and peanut butter."

In reality, although he never publicly addressed it, one of the primary reasons he didn't want to be tied down to any one studio or any one particular type of role at that time was his loyalty to Lisa. "He wanted to work with Lisa, and to find a movie with a great part in it for her," Lois Zetter said. "So he turned down the Columbia deal. Bob and I and his agents all thought he should have accepted it. He was both idealistic and stubborn."

Meanwhile, as Lisa was also trying to pursue acting in Hollywood, she and Patrick took the same acting class together, not always a pleasant experience for him. "It used to screw me up if she even had a kissing scene with someone else," he said. "In fact, for years, I used to be a jealous husband, worrying that Lisa might leave me for another guy."

Perhaps as a result of his rampant jealousy, he quickly found a way in which he and Lisa could spend more time together, as well as subsidize their lifestyle: They formed Nepotism Inc., a construction company in which they worked together.

Patrick had always enjoyed carpentry but had little training, so he set about educating himself. "People couldn't understand why I spent so much time in the bathroom or why I had all these books in there," he recalled with a laugh. "I was looking it all up—How to Make a Mortice and Tenon Joint."

Lisa was a natural at carpentry, and later on, when Patrick was called away in the middle of a job, she could sail through the rest of it with few problems. Assisted by Patrick's brothers and some of Lisa's five brothers who worked for Nepotism (hence the name), together they took on small, top-quality jobs for friends and family, building a recording studio entirely out of African Padauk and a super luxurious doghouse for some friends.

The business expanded further when Jaclyn Smith hired them to rebuild her kitchen, and in 1981 when they built all the sets for the movie *I'm Dancing as Fast as I Can*, starring Jill Clayburgh.

The apex of their carpentry business was rebuilding a Pennsylvania Dutch home west of Coldwater Canyon, whose size they tripled to 7,000 square feet comprising maid's quarters, eight-and-a-half bathrooms, a sauna, a steam shower, and a solar-heated pool.

In 1980, Patsy was hired to choreograph *Urban Cowboy*, starring John Travolta and Debra Winger, and she and Big Buddy moved to Los Angeles on a permanent basis. In the course of her involvement with the movie, they had discovered Simi Valley, an incorporated city in a hilly part of Ventura County in the greater Los Angeles area, and had felt at home there, not only because of the close proximity to Patrick and Lisa but also because the area was rural like

Texas, and Vicky, Donny, and Sean, who were still living at home, could keep horses there.

Patrick's first post–*Skatetown* role was a guest appearance as Private Gary Sturgis, a young soldier dying of leukemia, in an episode of M*A*S*H entitled "Blood Brother," which aired on April 6, 1981. The part was small, but Patrick has always said that it was one of his most cherished.

For the first—but certainly not the last—time in his career he plays a heroic, self-sacrificing character who is unaware that he is suffering from leukemia and whose concern is only for a dying friend whose life he wants to save by donating blood to him. It is left to Hawkeye (played by Alan Alda) to break the news to him that he can't. Patrick looks achingly young in the part, and his performance is heart rending.

Around the same time he played the role of John Ritter's baseball teammate in *Comeback Kid*, a TV movie-of-the week released on April 11, 1980.

By the end of the year, Patrick may well have come to regret having turned down the Columbia contract, as he was out of work for a relatively long stretch of time that ended only when he was cast against type as the leader of a group of thugs in *Return of the Rebels*, a CBS-TV production that aired at the end of October 1981.

Then he was cast in the recurring lead role of Bandit in *The Renegades*, an updated version of *The Mod Squad*, the first episode of which aired on March 4, 1982. The series had its fair requisite of action scenes, but much to his manager's chagrin he categorically refused to use a stunt double in any of them. "I tried to talk him out of doing his own stunts, but he was stubborn and wouldn't listen. In this regard, he was a macho man. He could do his own stunts and wanted to show he could do them," Lois Zetter said.

The series was canceled after just one month, but by that time his career was such that the demise of *The Renegades* didn't matter much anymore. On March 29, 1982, he began shooting *The Out-*

siders, Francis Ford Coppola's movie version of S. E. Hinton's best-selling young adult novel about disaffected teenage boys whose parents have abandoned them to lives of poverty in Tulsa's tough North West part of town.

Forming themselves into "the Greasers," the boys clash with a group of privileged, upper-middle-class kids known as "Socs" (short for "Socials"), who live on the affluent south side of town. A cross between *West Side Story* and *Rebel Without a Cause*, the movie was the Nile of motion pictures, with many of the hottest rising young male stars of the early eighties, Patrick among them, all converging in it.

Given fourth billing after the movie's leads Matt Dillon, Ralph Macchio, and C. Thomas Howell, Patrick was nonetheless billed above Rob Lowe, Emilio Estevez, and Tom Cruise. He played Darrel Curtis, elder brother to Ponyboy Curtis (C. Thomas Howell) and Soda Pop Curtis (Rob Lowe) and at thirty was much older than Howell and Lowe (who were seventeen and nineteen, respectively).

Refusing to be rattled by the competition, he approached his role from the Method perspective imbued in him by Warren Robertson. Francis Ford Coppola, however, was not won over by his approach. From the first, Patrick and the veteran director clashed over Patrick's propensity for intellectualizing his part, for asking too many questions. He asked so many that—although he explained to Coppola that in order to play his part, he needed to know more about the character he was playing—Coppola became exasperated with him.

Consequently, he turned on Patrick and declared that Patrick had a problem, a problem that arose from his previous profession as a dancer. "We both know that dancers are very wrapped up with what they look like; they live their lives looking in a mirror," Coppola said.

Patrick was incandescent with rage at the suggestion that his acting technique wasn't technique at all but mere vanity. Looking back, he says that the blanket assumption "drove me nuts. It was very, very scary," he said. "I thought my career was going to be over." He admitted afterward that he felt like killing Coppola, but with hindsight acknowledged that Coppola may have been right after all.

"I look back and I've actually thought of calling him," Patrick conceded, adding, "I should get the courage and tell him, 'Francis, listen man, I was a kid. I didn't agree with some of your techniques, but those techniques changed my life.' "

Producer Grey Frederickson was far more positive about Patrick than was Coppola. "That film was a lot of young kids all having a good time and he was part of the good time, but he was a little more grounded than a lot of the others. He was always gracious and wonderful and I don't think he had an enemy in the world."

His part in the movie, although key to the plot, is not major. As Darrel, he is the authoritative snarling elder brother to the more appealing younger brothers played by C. Thomas Howell and Rob Lowe. He starts out terrorizing them and appears to the audience to be a villain until his brother makes the comment to him that he used to be so close to him and his brothers before their parents' sudden death in a car accident.

Once Patrick's character is humanized and the audience understands that his rage isn't truly directed at his brothers but at the universe for having taken his parents away from them all, long before their time, we understand and sympathize with him.

After his brother Ponyboy helps save children trapped inside a burning church, Patrick's character thinks Ponyboy has died in the inferno. But when he arrives at the hospital and discovers that his brother survived the blaze after all, he completely unravels and the real man underneath the angry exterior shines through at last. Almost crying in relief, he hugs and kisses his brother. Through Patrick's emotional performance in this scene—whether as a result of Coppola's directing or his own ability to reach inside himself and bring forth his deepest emotions—the man and the moment become multidimensional in their impact.

From that point in the movie, Patrick is able to give full rein to the sensitive, feeling side of his nature, playing Darrel's love for his brother and his emotional vulnerability for all it's worth.

Then, during one of the last scenes in the movie, lest the audience overlook the other, equally potent weapon in his acting arsenal, Patrick engages in a mesmeric reverse striptease. He starts out in jeans, bare-chested, then—almost in slow motion—dons an extremely tight, black T-shirt and, in the process, reveals his ripped, muscled torso and well-developed pecs to their best advantage. As he slides the shirt over his body, the muscles practically burst through it and he lingeringly turns up the sleeves, pulls them down, then— almost lovingly—tucks the shirt into his jeans. The final coup de grace, when he puts one hand and then the other into his jeans, ostensibly to adjust his shirt, begs the question as to whether or not he is adjusting a part of his anatomy at the same time, thus bordering on the erotic.

In that short sequence, Patrick puts on a masterly show of peacock-style male vanity and at the same time highlights not only his perfect body, but also his overwhelming sexual magnetism. As handsome, young, and appealing the other male stars in the movie may have been, in this scene, at least, Patrick upstaged every last one of them.

Nonetheless, he formed a bond with them, in particular with Tom Cruise, with whom he became friends. Long afterward, Tom said of him, "I've always known Patrick to be a good man."

In his classic, forthright style, Patrick said at the time, "I still feel all the guys in *The Outsiders* are my brothers. Anybody ever mess with them, I'll break their face."

His much younger costar, C. Thomas Howell, aroused his fraternal feelings even more than his other costars. "Tommy and I share similar backgrounds. We're both cowboys . . . He's like a little brother to me. If anybody ever tried to touch that kid. I'd hurt him."

He may well have harbored similar inclinations toward the critics after *The Outsiders* was released on March 25, 1983, and they roundly lambasted it. "*The Outsiders* isn't conventionally bad," Vincent Canby wrote in the *New York Times*. "It is spectacularly out of touch, a laughably earnest attempt to impose heroic attitudes on some nice, small characters purloined from a 'young-adult' novel."

But perhaps in tribute to Patsy's Norman Schwarzkopf tactic of focusing on the far horizon and storming ahead, irrespective of any enemy artillery, bad reviews would never stop Patrick in his tracks, not even for a moment. Nor would he ever hit back at any of the criticisms or publicly counteract them in any way, though others close to him would.

"I thought that Patrick did wonderful work in *The Outsiders*" his manager, Lois Zetter, said indignantly at the time. Patrick, too, was happy with his own performance but not the final cut. "I felt good about it [his performance], but I was not happy with what went on screen. *The Outsiders* was a film about three brothers and it looked like Francis tried to turn it into a film about Matt Dillon," he said.

His handsome rival aside, Patrick had been in a Coppola movie and held his own against spectacular competition in terms of youth and talent. His career was on track now, and he was confident that, with the help of his managers and his agents, Arnold Rifkin and Nicole David, it was just a matter of time before his big break materialized.

Although the money wasn't exactly pouring in yet, he felt that he was edging closer to his ultimate dream of making enough money to buy a ranch for his father so that he could breed Egyptian Arabian horses there. However, that was not to be.

On the morning of November 9, 1982, Patrick's father, Big Buddy, awoke early, worked out on his garage punching bag, and then went for a hillside hike, with the family dogs tearing along beside him. Patsy hung back at the foot of the hill, looking up at Big Buddy, so alive, so handsome, throwing sticks for the dogs to catch. Although almost forty years had passed since they first met, neither her love nor her passion for him had subsided, and she found herself wishing fervently that she'd brought her camera with her so she could immortalize the moment. Seconds later, he suffered a massive heart attack.

Lisa was at home alone when she heard the news of Big Buddy's death. She immediately called the studio and, without giving a reason, left an urgent message for Patrick to come home at once. There she told him that his father was dead. "If anybody ever died again, I'm never going to be the one to deliver the news. I felt for a long time that he never forgave me," Lisa said.

Grief-stricken in the extreme, Patrick and his brothers and sisters—except Sean, who wasn't home yet—all gathered at their parents' home to comfort Patsy, who earlier that year had also lost both her mother, Gladys, and her father, Victor, who had died that May.

Mistakenly believing that his family had already gone ahead to the mortuary where his father was embalmed, Sean went there to join them. Consequently, he was the first to see Big Buddy's embalmed body, and was devastated by the sight that met him. The big, bluff, handsome Texan cowboy, the loving husband, the affectionate, paternal influence whom the little girls at the dance studio had always worshipped and adored, the father whom they all venerated, loved, and needed, now looked like another man completely. His face was caked with clownish white makeup, blobs of rouge were smeared all over his cheeks, and his hair was mussed beyond recognition.

Sean rushed home, took Patrick to one side, and whispered, "Buddy, you have to do something. Mom cannot see him like this. He's as hard as a rock." Patrick slipped away from the house without Patsy realizing it. The memory of what he found at the funeral home would eternally haunt him.

Due to Sean, he had come forewarned and prepared, ready with comb and hairspray to restore his father to a semblance of his former self. "I did my best to try and make him look like our dad before Mother saw him. It freaked me," he said. "But every time I tried to touch his body, I lost control of my motor functions . . . And then . . . I just passed out cold," he said.

When Patrick came to, he began screaming, "I love you. I want you to know that."

"It was too much, his dying then. I wanted to buy him a ranch to put him back to his roots. He never knew that was my intention," he said later.

He was beside himself with grief, and after the funeral became wracked by huge self-recriminations. "I inherited my father's knife. And right before we put him in the ground, I had the impulse that I wanted to go up and use it to carve his initials on his casket. And I didn't do it. And it haunts me like a ghost. But it just wasn't appropriate," he said.

Even if Patrick had deemed it appropriate to carve his father's initials on the coffin, his hand would have shook far too much for him to do it. His mind, his heart, his emotions, his entire being were completely shattered by his father's death.

In the aftermath, he continued to suffer greatly. "I found his grief continued on an unusually long time," Patsy said. "He became more introspective and quiet. He took on everybody's problems, everybody's burdens. I guess trying to replace his dad."

Big Buddy's final resting place was in a Simi Valley cemetery. Patsy's name is beside his on the marker bearing the yellow rose of their native Texas. And despite her comments on Patrick's prolonged mourning for his father, her own grief was considerable and she planted a Texas pine nearby his grave and visited it on most Sundays.

Fighting his pain at his father's death, Patrick began aping his excessive drinking, partly as a means of assuaging the agony, partly on more complicated grounds, which he would one day elucidate through therapy. "Every time my life got to a place where it was doing well, I would sabotage it because I felt I had to suffer or I couldn't truly call myself an artist," he concluded.

During his drinking bouts, he made the unwelcome discovery that he needed only one or two drinks to get wasted and that, in contrast to his father, who'd always been a gentle, nonconfrontational drunk, his own drinking ignited his rage, causing him to pick irrational fights with those unlucky enough to cross his path at the wrong moment.

Other times his rage would turn inward and he would become inordinately self-destructive. In his New York days, his joyriding on the New Jersey Turnpike, his hair-raising roaring through the streets of Manhattan, were merely the symptoms of his youthful exuberance, with a touch of theater thrown in for good measure, and were not motivated by self-destructiveness.

Now, though, "I turned into a lunatic," he later admitted. "Nobody—and that includes my wife, Lisa—could talk to me. I would go up on Mulholland Drive, where the guys race suicidal, and I ran blind curves—it was a death-wish kind of push-it-to-the-limit mentality. I was scared of myself then, scared that I was not going to come back, scared that I was going to ruin my relationship with Lisa. She'd try to say something to me and I'd put my fist through the wall . . ."

"His pain was so severe," Patsy acknowledged before issuing a warning note: "Nobody can tolerate drink in my family. He could never drink." She was right. But drink he did. And in the wake of his father's tragic death, drink became one of the leitmotifs of his existence, the Voldemort of his soul against which he would be compelled to battle on almost a daily basis. In the future he would make no secret of it.

six

TOP OF THE WORLD

*D*espite the private demons he was battling, Patrick's career was now speeding full steam ahead. His next part was as marine Kevin Scott in *Uncommon Valor*, starring Gene Hackman as Colonel Rhodes, a former marine colonel whose son and his buddies were captured in Laos, never to be seen again. The movie, a Rambo-esque saga of the rescue of MIAs from Laos, not only afforded Patrick the opportunity of observing a major star working on a film but also of a trip to both Hawaii and Thailand, where the movie was shot.

He had never traveled outside of the United States before, and the trip was a revelation for him. Apart from seeing the world, he made the jarring discovery that being without Lisa for any length of time was difficult for him. At this early stage of his career, he appeared to cope with their separation seamlessly, decorating his hotel room wall with her pictures. However, in the future being apart from her for any length of time would prove to be unbearable for him.

One of the most lacerating lessons any movie actor is forced to learn is the reality that the director has the final cut. And if Patrick hadn't yet digested that bitter pill during his experience with *The Outsiders*, he certainly did when he saw the final cut of *Uncommon Valor* when it was released on December 16, 1983.

Up front as always, he was not reticent about expressing that disappointment publicly and said, "We shot a better film than what turned out. They sold out for the action. They chose to cut things that sucked you into caring for those guys in a big way. It was real upsetting to me."

With his quixotic, optimistic nature, he would probably never fully learn the lesson, and would be surprised by the director's omnipotence over the final cut way into his career.

Less demanding and far more lightweight than *Uncommon Valor*, his next project was *Pigs vs. Freaks*, a TV movie shot in Oregon. It was released on July 6, 1984, and in it Patrick played Doug Zimmer, a Vietnam vet and rookie policeman, with great conviction.

In *Grandview, USA*, a full-length movie that hit the screen on August 3, 1984, Patrick played a successful demolition derby driver, but he also had a chance to draw on some of his dance background. He and Lisa choreographed two dance numbers for the film, and he also cowrote the song "She's Like the Wind." The song never made it into the final cut. At the time he must have been infuriated and frustrated by the outcome of his hard work and talent, but in the future the exclusion of "She's Like the Wind" from the movie would prove to be a blessing.

In November 1984, Patrick and Lisa's most cherished project, the stage play *Without a Word*, a somewhat autobiographical story of three dancers that they had written for themselves to perform, was produced at the Beverly Hills Playhouse. The play's crowning glory was their pas de deux. "You could have fainted from the sexual tension between them. It was the hottest thing," said Lois Zetter, who was in the audience.

Gene Kelly came to see *Without a Word* and was enthusiastic, as were the critics, which, Patrick and Lisa hoped, boded well for a transfer to Broadway. As far as he was concerned, Hollywood hadn't lived up to its promise, and he was starting to feel burned out. His insecurities were surfacing again, this time around in terms of his professional abilities. He felt he wasn't good enough and yearned to work with actors like Robert De Niro, Harrison Ford, and Dustin Hoffman and cutting-edge directors like Martin Scorsese.

Instead, he felt he was becoming type-cast as a teen idol and that his worst professional nightmare had come true. "The only hope I had was to go back to class and try to progress as an actor and grow as a man," he decided.

To that end, he signed up for acting classes with famed teacher Milton Katselas, who had taught Gene Hackman, George Clooney, Alec Baldwin, Tom Selleck, Michelle Pfeiffer, and many others and whose philosophy was not dissimilar from Warren Robertson's, so that he would once more be exposed to the doctrine of Method acting.

At that critical juncture, his career suddenly accelerated when he was cast as the lead in John Milius's passionately felt war movie *Red Dawn*. Coincidentally, part of the movie would be shot in Las Vegas, New Mexico, where—in 2000—Patrick and Lisa would buy their seventeen thousand-acre ranch.

Directed by Milius, the hugely machismatic director who made *Conan, the Barbarian* and *The Wind and the Lion*, and who was credited as providing the original inspiration and script for *Apocalypse Now*, the movie was slated to explore war in all its horror. Once again, Patrick would be working with C. Thomas Howell, who took second billing to him, as did Charlie Sheen. Sixth billing went to actress Jennifer Grey, Joel's daughter, in the small part of Toni. Patrick and Charlie became fast friends. However, he and Jennifer did not. They would have a brief scene together—her deathbed scene, in which Patrick kisses her forehead tenderly just as she is about to lose consciousness for the very last time. Jennifer's part was peripheral to the movie, and she and Patrick did not form a friendship of any sort during shooting.

However, the movie would prove to be a landmark of sorts for Patrick. There is an ancient Chinese proverb that says, "When the pupil is ready, the teacher appears," and in John Milius, Patrick was to encounter a maverick who was to demonstrate to him exactly how to put Method acting into practice.

In the midst of shooting the scene in which his father is taken away to a concentration camp and he has to part from him, Patrick suddenly and inexplicably froze up. Milius shot the scene a few times, but Patrick seemed almost paralyzed and was unable to project the appropriate emotions. Until then, Milius had clearly studied him and arrived at the correct conclusion that he would always respond to a gauntlet thrown at his feet, and that a challenge would galvanize him.

Consequently, when Milius suggested they rehearse the scene one more time in the hope that Patrick would be able to produce the requisite emotion, he added, "You'll never feel good about yourself if you don't do it." Patrick squared his shoulders and braced himself to begin rehearsing the scene.

Then, in an undiluted moment of Method directing, not to mention a fair amount of trickery, when Patrick began the farewell scene, Milius turned on the camera without Patrick knowing it. Then he came over to him and whispered into his ear. "This time Patrick, before you leave, tell your father you love him."

During his father's lifetime, Patrick had never told him that he loved him, and after he died, he regretted it bitterly. As he spoke those words to his on-screen father (played by Harry Dean Stanton), the floodgates opened and every fiber of his being shook with emotion. Meanwhile, Milius recorded every second on film.

Milius had given Patrick an object lesson on how to employ Method acting to enhance his performance. From that time onward, whenever Patrick had to play an emotional scene in a movie, he would think back to his father's death in order to induce that emotion. Yet whenever he did, he felt guilty. "I hated myself for a time after he died," he confessed with characteristic transparency. "I felt like I was spitting on him, and I still do. Especially when you picture your father in that coffin and you touch his face and he's solid as a rock."

When *Red Dawn* was released on August 10, 1984, it was a sur-prise hit, taking $18.5 million in the first ten days, but Patrick's pow-erful performance didn't garner the rave reviews he merited. Janet Maslin in the *New York Times* lumped him in with C. Thomas How-ell and Lea Thompson as "adequate but less than memorable."

Lackluster reviews aside, at least Patrick had now established himself as a leading man. In his next movie, *Youngblood*, shot on location in Toronto, he played second fiddle to Rob Lowe in the title role. Essentially, the movie was little more than a vehicle for Lowe, who played Dean Youngblood, a hockey player on the Hamilton Mustangs whose teammates think he is too pretty and haze him un-mercifully. Given Patrick's experience of being bullied by rednecks, Lowe's part must have resonated with him.

As the polished professional player who befriends Youngblood, a novice at the sport, the role required a proficient player to double for him, but as always Patrick insisted on doing his own stunts and wouldn't have it any other way.

After all, his reason for accepting the part was predicated on the dual drives forever pulsating within him, drives that were as inexo-rable as if they were powering a Lamborghini or a 747: the drive to master a new sport and the drive to joust with danger. No matter how dangerous the stunt, no matter how difficult, in the future he would always insist on doing his own stunts, partly because he was a risk-taker who could never resist a challenge and partly perhaps because on a more subliminal level he was still trying to demonstrate to all those bullies from his past that he was more of a man than they would ever be.

So over a two-and-a-half-month period he trained at a Los Angeles rink with Eric Nesterenko, a former star for the Chicago Blackhawks, who was also playing the part of Patrick's father in the movie.

Thus primed, when *Youngblood* started shooting in the Toronto Hamilton area with many real hockey players in the supporting cast, Patrick issued a challenge. "I did something silly," he later admitted.

"I told them . . . 'Don't treat me like a Hollywood actor. Go for it.'
And they did. They almost broke my neck."

Yet however much Patrick reveled in the challenge and thrived
on surviving the trial of strength, *Youngblood* was yet another movie
in a string of coming-of-age teen-appeal movies. It didn't stretch his
acting abilities or burnish his Hollywood profile.

At this juncture in his career, his managers, Lois Zetter and Bob
Le Mond, made the somewhat unusual and seemingly regressive decision that he consider dedicating the next fifteen months of his life
to making a TV series, not a movie, and that he audition for the part
of Orry Main in *North and South*.

Starting with *Roots* in 1977, through *Lillie* in 1978, to *Winds of
War* in 1983, the seventies and eighties were the decades of the blockbuster miniseries, and *North and South* was projected to become the
daddy of them all. Based on John Jakes's blockbuster seven hundred
plus-page Civil War novel and optioned by producer David Wolper
of *Roots* fame, *North and South* had been adapted into a twenty-four-
hour $70 million ABC miniseries, with the first twelve hours to be
aired in November 1985 and the second part the following May.

North and South had all the elements—action, romance, the
South, and Orry Main a brave, romantic, passionate hero, who be-
comes a Confederate officer, finds himself in conflict with his com-
patriots, and along the way meets the love of his life, loses her to
another man, and then wins her back when it's almost too late—
which appealed to Patrick's deepest nature.

North and South was an ersatz *Gone With the Wind*. Orry Main
could best be described as a cross between Ashley Wilkes—a Southern gentleman, honorable, soulful—and the swashbuckling, virile,
masculine Rhett Butler. In reality, Ashley and Rhett, fictional characters as they are, actually personified both sides of Patrick himself,
and his managers knew it. While other managers might have coun-
seled Patrick against accepting a part in a miniseries rather than
waiting for the next movie to come around, Le Mond and Zetter had
spent months studying him, evolving a career strategy for him.

"During the early years of representing him, we got to know Patrick the man and finally came up with three words which we felt described him, three qualities we thought should always be present in all the roles we advised him to take," Lois Zetter said. "Off-screen, Patrick is heroic, idealistic, and gentlemanly. Whether it was a Civil War character, a bad guy from the wrong side of the tracks, or a Wall Street executive, those three words had to be part and parcel of any and every character we recommended he play, simply because they reflected the real Patrick."

However, before he could live out his romantic readiness in the part of Orry, there was the matter of him winning it, no small feat, given that he was up against many other actors wanting the leading part in this, the biggest miniseries in Hollywood history.

Even before he came within yards of *North and South*'s David Wolper, in Patrick's mind he'd already gotten the part, and it was already a done deal.

"I knew there was no one else who could do Orry Main because when I read that script, I knew I was Orry Main," he said with his usual self-confidence. "I'm a romantic fool to a fault. I think I was born in another time and reincarnated in this one."

The moment Patrick strode into the audition, like some miniseries Messiah, all broad shoulders and masculine swagger, coproducer Chuck McClain knew that he'd found his Orry Main. "We were looking for a strong male lead who was macho without being obnoxious about it," he said. "Patrick tested for the part at the very last minute. We just looked at him that day and said, 'Wow!'"

Producer Paul Freeman was even more glowing about Patrick's potential as Orry Main. "He has an uncanny natural ability that comes from his gut. [Playing Orry] will break Patrick out and make him hotter than a pistol."

Patrick's first appearance as Orry Main in *North and South* displays him in all his glory, galloping on his steed up a tree-lined avenue toward the family home, Mount Royal Plantation, his hair flowing in the wind. His family clearly love and adore him, he is kind

to the slaves, lovingly bids his family farewell, and during his peril-
ous journey to West Point saves the life of a damsel in distress—and
all this in the first hour of the miniseries.

Not even the most heroic of biblical or Shakespearean heroes,
not Russell Crowe in *Gladiator* or Charlton Heston in *The Ten Com-
mandments*, has ever been so well served in projecting their heroic
persona to the public so dizzyingly effectively, so swiftly, and so last-
ingly.

Le Mond/Zetter had shrewdly understood that Patrick would
win legions of fans during the series: The characters of Orry Main
and Patrick Swazye were both heroic, gentlemanly, and idealistic,
and so both would be inextricably intertwined in the minds of the
public forever. Patrick would work the same magic again twice in
the future: with Johnny Castle and with Sam Wheat.

Consequently, because of his own personal brand of alchemy
as an actor and the strategizing of his canny management, Patrick
Swayze would always be Orry Main for millions of his fans throughout the world. Or Johnny Castle. Or Sam Wheat. Or whichever one
of those heroes chimed best with their romantic fantasies.

While he was innately confident in filming all the action scenes,
he was slightly intimidated by the grandeur of Boone Hall, the old
plantation outside Charleston, South Carolina, that doubled for
Mount Royal, the Main mansion. "I rode down that double line of
oaks in a limo and said, 'Who is gonna believe I own all this?' " he
later remembered.

However, once he had donned Orry's clothes, he started to relax.
"It's exciting when you put on the costumes because that's like the final touch. In no way was I self-conscious then. It's like I was empow-
ered. You look in a mirror, and there's this guy, Orry Main," he said.

His costar, the spectacular British beauty Lesley-Anne Down,
who had catapulted to fame in *Upstairs Downstairs*, also underwent a
similar transformation.

David Wolper recalled in his memoirs, *Producer*, that after Patrick arrived early for the first script reading, he announced, " 'Patrick, you're going to freak out when you see how beautiful Lesley-Anne Down is.' She walked in a few minutes later wearing old clothes, no makeup, her hair disheveled, looking like a mess."

Appalled, Patrick said, "That's what you call beautiful, Wolper? You got to be kidding me." David Wolper reassured him, "Wait until you see her made up."

On the first day of shooting, as David Wolper remembered, "I was sitting with Swayze when Lesley-Anne Down walked out of her dressing room, her makeup in place, her hair perfect, wearing this long dress with a low bodice."

Patrick took one look at her and—to his credit—turned to Wolper and said, "I apologize," and later went further and dubbed Lesley-Anne "eye candy—she was that luscious." She returned that compliment in kind, enthusing that he was charismatic.

Many rising stars, when confronted by the not-always-pleasant specter of bigger stars they once worshipped in their youth, performing with them in living color, often affect a nonchalant air. Not so Patrick. While Elizabeth Taylor, Jimmy Stewart, Olivia de Havilland, Robert Mitchum, and his friend and all-time idol Gene Kelly were all cast in *North and South*, and he, Patrick Swayze, would be playing the lead, he remained endearingly humble. "Just the opportunity to get to meet these human beings, much less work with them in front of a camera and have them look me in the eye and take me seriously—me, Buddy Swayze!—that's staggering," he said at the time.

Patrick met Elizabeth Taylor when they were on location in Charleston, where she was shooting her scenes as a brothel madam. "I couldn't take my eyes off her," he said. "I was very nervous. But that smile of hers put me right at ease. She wished me good luck and shook my hand. God, that was great."

Meeting Elizabeth was only part of it. Meeting Jimmy Stewart was even more overwhelming for him. "My knees turned to butter and I couldn't remember one word of what I was supposed to say. I felt like a little kid . . ." he said.

"If you can talk with crowds and keep your virtue, or walk with kings—nor lose the common touch," Kipling's lines from his poem *If*, have always embodied Patrick both on and off the set. He wasn't charming and polite just to stars and not to other people.

Extra Judy Watts played a maid in *North and South*, and her part called for her to carry a tray of hors d'oeuvres on set. During filming, she slipped and her tray was sent flying through the air. "The next thing I knew, Patrick Swayze was on the ground and I was laying on top of him," she reported.

"The director screamed, 'Cut, Cut,' and then started yelling at people to 'Get her off him. Get her off.' They lifted him up and left me sprawling on the ground."

Ignoring everyone fussing over him, who were desperate to know if he was hurt, brushing his clothes off, catering to him, the gentlemanly Patrick instead helped Judy up and asked her if she was okay, concerned only about her well-being and not his own.

His part as Orry Main was mammoth and it was hardly surprising that, according to costar Lewis Smith (Charles Main), Patrick was sometimes exhausted. "He's either sleeping—and an atomic bomb going off wouldn't wake him," Lewis claimed, before going on, "or he's out being crazy. But he's very loyal . . . into defending people, possessions, territories."

He was also shy, in a blushing boyish way, particularly at the prospect of filming his first love scene, which was to be with Lesley-Anne Down. "I never realized how scared I would be," he confessed, adding, "It's a very, very scary thing to do such an intimate love scene. It's so personal that in a way you almost feel like a prostitute. A lot of people think it's the woman who has the most frightening time but, believe me, it's really just as frightening for the man."

Lesley-Anne Down was sympathetic and quickly put him at his ease. "Lesley made it easy because she was professional. She knew I was scared, so she helped me out," he said. She helped to such a degree that Lisa was duly impressed by his prowess during the love scene and said, "When it really started cooking, I thought, 'All right! Baby, you really nailed that one.' "

Love scenes would never be easy for him to film, not then and not for the rest of his career. "I believe there was some Southern boy prudishness in him, but I don't know if he was really aware of it," Lois Zetter later noted.

Down the line, he would evolve a unique way of coping as best he could. "I learnt to turn myself off when I was on location," he later admitted in one of those interviews that made his managers cringe at his frankness. "I poured all my sexual energy intro my work and made myself into an icicle . . . That's why in love scenes with Lesley-Anne Down in *North and South*, or Jennifer in *Dirty Dancing* the women feel safe with me. It's fairly obvious to them that my cookies have simply turned to ice. That I freeze a certain part of my body."

Later in his career, he came to feel that his unique love scene strategy had succeeded to such a degree that he began to worry that his ability to sublimate his sexuality might one day impact negatively on his marriage. "I'm so terrified that if I go on doing it for much longer I'll ruin my sex drive altogether," he said with characteristic honesty, adding, "All of a sudden I get back with my wife and it's not easy to just flick a light switch and turn it back on."

Then, in a moment of artless bragging reminiscent of the little boy who came home from his first day at school and announced to his mother that he was the handsomest and cleverest boy there, he added the punch line, "Though once I do, I more than make up for it—and she knows it!"

Their love and their marriage was now unfolding in a new and special setting: the intimate love nest they bought in 1985. Nestled in the foothills of the San Gabriel Mountains, overlooked by the Los Angeles National Park, the ranch stood on five acres of land. Built in the 1930s and—they later discovered—once a Mafia hideout, the ranch was the antithesis of Hollywood and everything it represented. "I needed to get away from the Hollywood scene," Patrick later declared. "That's why I didn't go buy a home in Beverly Hills."

The moment they first set eyes on the decaying ranch, Patrick and Lisa felt it was meant for them. Moreover, the property—just two small cabins connected by a walkway—featured beautiful pine floors, impressive wooden ceilings, two massive fireplaces, a pair of ornate Italian drinking fountains on the grounds, and a gigantic stone barbecue pit.

"What we saw was the potential for what the ranch could be. The place was trashed and everyone thought we were crazy (but they couldn't see what we could see!)," Patrick later enthused.

At first, though, the land surrounding the ranch would prove to be an immense challenge to them, infested as it was with weeds and covered with dead trees and used car parts. They made an offer, the seller accepted it, and they moved into a small bedroom there and cooked their meals on a camping gas cooker while they set to work on renovations.

They spent weeks hauling away dead trees and debris so that the land could be cleared. Along the way, they enlisted the help of friends and family. "They had these sabers out and they were slashing and parrying. They had made it into a fencing lesson," Lisa recalled with some amusement. In the same vein, they threw what they termed "rock parties," meaning that they invited a group of friends and family over, got them to pick up rocks strewed all over the grounds, and as a trade-off made a barbecue afterward.

They expanded the property by joining the two cabins, knocked down walls, tore out paneling, and transformed the ranch completely. Once the work was finished, they named it Rancho Bizarro. Not because of any kinky connotations but because, as Patrick elaborated, "it's bizarre. Our lifestyles are a little strange. It's like a mishmash of animals and things. You lose complete privacy in your life with this stardom stuff, so you wind up having to replace that with something, which is very weird for me. So we created a life on our ranch that is almost a city within itself." It was so far off the beaten track that the only outward trappings advertising that a movie star lived here was a large electronic gate with closed-circuit television cameras next to it.

Through the years, Patrick and Lisa repeatedly expanded the ranch, adding cedar beams and cathedral ceilings, tripling the square footage, carving a rustic sixty-foot swimming pool out of a hill, and adding on a basement recording studio, a mirrored dance studio, a solarium-style dining area overlooking jacarandas and coral trees, and a pale lilac master bedroom suite with a fireplace and a vast bathroom, of which Patrick cracked, "Our bathroom is bigger than our first New York apartment."

Harking back to those early days in New York when he'd first tried his hand at carpentry, Patrick built much of the Santa Fe–style furniture himself in the workshop he had set up for that purpose on the ranch. He and Lisa decorated the house with American Indian art. The two of them did the planting and landscaping themselves, and the ranch grew rich with vegetation and fruit trees bursting with apricots, figs, pomegranates, and persimmons.

At the heart of the ranch was Lisa's own private domain, a guest house called Little Bizarro, which stood in the middle of the property. "Woe be unto anyone who disturbs Lisa working in Little Bizarro," Patrick warned. "When she's in there, that's her time. She was very smart—she didn't run the phone line out to her place."

Horses and animals—including chickens, peacocks, two Rhodesian ridgebacks, and two standard poodles—dominated the ranch. It boasted a fenced-in ring in which to exercise the horses, a pinewood barn with sixteen stalls, a bunk room, and an office—which tellingly was not decorated with movie posters but with ribbons they had won in horse shows through the years.

Training horses would prove to be one of the most important, soothing elements in his life, providing a welcome escape from all the vicissitudes of making movies. "It takes my mind off it for a minute," he explained. "A young powerful stallion forces you to be right in the moment, right now, or he'll kill you. Training a young powerful horse is the most humbling experience I've ever found."

The ranch would become a haven, a fortress, and a refuge for Patrick and Lisa. "Living outside L.A. is a blessing, because when we come into town, it's like visiting the monkeys in the zoo," he once said. "For me, the ranch means survival, hanging on to 'Buddy' . . . staying a nice guy. Life doesn't work for an actor if he brings it all to acting."

His happiness at Rancho Bizarro, however, was diminished by his sorrow that his father hadn't lived to enjoy it, or better still to run it. "Everything he wanted for me, everything he dreamed about, he never got to know," he later told Barbara Walters.

Down the line, he and Lisa would buy an additional five thousand-square-foot waterside ranch in Lake Arrowhead, California. With five bedrooms, the ranch also had a master bedroom with a steam-sauna room, a gym, a family room with a large deck, and a living room with thirty-foot-high ceilings. They sold it in 1997 for $2 million and invested the proceeds in a new ranch in Las Vegas, New Mexico.

All that—the property, the riches, the prosperity—was ahead of them. And it all began with *North and South*. For, as it transpired, *North and South* would transform Patrick Swayze into a household name at last.

The first part of the miniseries was broadcast on November 3, 1985. An audience of millions upon millions tuned into the entire miniseries and, in Patrick's words, "fell in love with that character [Orry], men and women alike. They saw him, as I did, as a man of honor."

Critics dubbed him a heartthrob, fan mail poured in, and—for a flavor of the outpourings of adulation for Patrick—even jaded celebrity interviewer Fred Robbins went into paroxysms of purple prose, describing Patrick as having, "the muscular build of a young Brando, the sensitivity of a Montgomery Clift and eyes as blue as lapis lazuli."

Patrick was a bona fide star now. Not Brando, nor Clift, nor Pacino nor De Niro, but a star in the noble, romantic, swashbuckling Errol Flynn and Stewart Granger clean-cut heartthrob tradition, and armies of his fans acted accordingly.

"It was terrible at first," he later said. "It really bugged me. It made me feel like a piece of meat. Then something happened to make me understand it all. A girl was standing behind me [during a promotional tour], touching me, massaging my back, whispering things in my ear that you just wouldn't believe. Finally, I turned around and said, 'Don't touch me again.' I put my hand on her arm and looked straight at her when I said it, and the look in her eyes changed totally."

"I think she felt like she had a very important relationship with Orry Main—and I think she didn't know what to do with those feelings, so she turned them into sex. That's when I realized that [as an actor] I am really in a position to affect people in a big way."

Soon he would affect even more people than he could ever have dreamed, more strongly, more deeply, more profoundly, through his performance in a small film that he and all the actors firmly believed would go straight to video, *Dirty Dancing*, the film that would everlastingly secure Patrick Swayze's status as a global icon.

seven
DIRTY DANCING

*A*fter *North and South*, Patrick made two movies that would be completed before he made *Dirty Dancing* but released afterward, thus confusing and slightly alienating some of the fans.

The first was *Steel Dawn*, a futuristic movie set in a post-nuclear world in which he played Nomad, a mysterious warrior. According to Lois Zetter he took the part primarily because Lisa would be co-starring as his love interest, and it had always been his dearest wish for them to work together.

They traveled to the Kalahari Desert location, where they were prepared for the conditions to be primitive. "We expected to sleep in a sand dune, but instead they had incredible German food. We had a thatched cottage on a lagoon, and there were thousands of flamingos right outside our front door," Patrick remembered.

Although the movie was eminently forgettable, it marked Patrick and Lisa's first on-screen love scene, featuring an extremely passionate kiss during which their attraction was palpable.

In the future he would make on-camera love to leading ladies Kelly Lynch and Demi Moore, but Lisa—as sure as she was of his love for her—would never express any jealousy and would always endeavor to help him give the best performance possible.

"Lisa tells me whether I am any good or not," Patrick once divulged. "If I'm not delivering the goods in a love scene, she'll say: 'Listen, Buddy, that didn't turn me on in any way. Get your act together and start smoldering.'"

In her role as Kasha, Lisa was strong, proud, and suitably somber. Patrick, his hair long and blond, gave a credible performance as Nomad, although fans and critics alike would later dismiss the movie out of hand when it was released just three months after *Dirty Dancing*.

The second movie he made before *Dirty Dancing*, which was released afterward, would also perplex and irritate a public infatuated with his Johnny Castle persona, particularly because in that movie, *Tiger Warsaw*, he played the part of a violent, sociopathic drug addict of the same name. On camera, he sported a beard, sang briefly, and had a tender moment when he kissed a little tattoo on his girlfriend's stomach. Overall, though, the tenor of the movie was dark in the extreme.

"*Tiger Warsaw* is the most hardcore, emotionally demanding film I've ever done," he said. "But the further you go into acting, the scarier it gets. That's what makes my role in *Tiger Warsaw* the most fulfilling of any I've done, but also the most destructive for me personally." Then, in an admission of his own self-destructive tendencies, he said, "I wish somebody could tell me how you turn the light switch on and off; I would love to learn that secret. I'd gotten better at least looking like I'd dropped the character when the job was finished."

Drink was the outlet for his excessiveness, and his danger point, particularly when he was on location in Pennsylvania, without Lisa by his side to curb him. With classic honesty he confessed to journalist Sharon Feinstein, "While I'm making films I get very hyper because my brain is racing all over the place. I survive on two hours sleep a night, and I sit in my hotel room drinking beer and vodka, which can't be good for anyone.

"I'm an excessive person in every way and I have to fight to control my drinking. But endless hotel rooms can start to feel like a stream of prisons and it hurts less with a bit of booze to cheer you up," he said.

Inevitably, the death of a loved one often triggers heavy drinking bouts in incipient alcoholics, and Patrick was no different. On August 9, 1986, his manager, Bob Le Mond, died of cancer at just fifty-one years old. Patrick, who was always famously loyal to his agents and managers, was devastated by Le Mond's passing. His tragic death was also reminiscent of his father's passing and reverberated all the more because of it.

One night, in a bar, he was joined by a drunken old man who presented him with a key chain made from a coin. The initials "J.W." and the words "Republic Pictures" were embossed on the coin. "It was John Wayne's dressing-room key from his days making Westerns at Republic Pictures," Patrick said. Then he speculated about how the old man got hold of the key ring or knew that John Wayne was his idol. "All he said to me was, 'You're the only guy who can replace John Wayne, so you should have it,' " Patrick remembered.

He was flattered. However, much as he admired John Wayne, the perfect cowboy hero, his own career ambitions stretched much further.

By 1986 he had spent the last seven years of his career diligently toiling away in Hollywood, fighting tooth and nail to escape classification as either a latter-day Troy Donahue or a sleeker, less pumped-up Schwarzenegger, or even an ersatz John Wayne, and he certainly didn't want to be Fred Astaire or Gene Kelly. Moreover, he was so rigidly resolved not to hitch his shooting star to a musical that he decreed that his résumé must not detail his dance training.

In short, what he really wanted was a call from Laurence Olivier begging him to play Petrucio, or Trevor Nunn desperate to cast him as Titus Andronicus, and wouldn't he have been masterly giving Kate her comeuppance or treading the boards in a toga?

After *Dirty Dancing* was released, millions of women throughout the world swooned over Patrick Swayze's Johnny Castle, all firmly convinced that he was playing himself or that the part had been written specifically for him and only him.

That was not the case. Actor Billy Zane was the original choice to play Johnny Castle. *Dirty Dancing*'s creator, Eleanor Bergstein, had written the part a full twenty years before she had ever met Patrick; the semiautobiographical script and Johnny Castle himself were a figment of her somewhat fevered imagination.

Like Baby, Eleanor was a doctor's daughter and had a sister, and the whole family often summered at Grossinger's Hotel in the Catskill Mountains, New York State. Eleanor was the perfect well-bred Jewish princess, but back home in Manhattan she led a secret life as "a teenage mambo queen, a little nymphet," and would some-times slip away and "dirty dance" in raunchy rock-and-roll clubs downtown. And like Johnny, she once taught ballroom dancing at the Arthur Murray Dance Studio.

Eleanor had first pitched her *Dirty Dancing* concept to MGM in 1984, whereupon producer Linda Gottlieb signed on board to produce it. *He Makes Me Feel Like Dancin'* director Emile Ardolini was hired to direct, and Kenny Ortega—who had trained with Gene Kelly—came on board as choreographer. However, two years after her initial pitch to MGM, the movie still hadn't been made, sim-ply because she still hadn't been able to find the right actor to play Johnny.

Eleanor was adamant that she didn't want "Johnny to have love-me eyes like Travolta. I want Johnny to have very hooded eyes that can be dangerous so it's very brave of Baby to say, 'Dance with me.'" Eleanor had chanced on Patrick's picture, and just as J. K. Rowling saw her Harry Potter made flesh in Daniel Radcliffe and Helen Field-ing her Bridget Jones in Renée Zellweger, Eleanor Bergstein now knew that in Patrick Swayze she'd met her hero, Johnny Castle, in living color in all his handsome, chiseled, smoldering, hot-blooded storybook glory. Now all she had to do was convince him to accept the part.

So instead of Sir Peter Hall telexing his agents with the urgent offer of a season at the National, or Ingmar Bergman begging him to play a role in his upcoming masterpiece, here was a relatively untried screenwriter named Eleanor Bergstein, with only two movies, *Let It Be Me* and *It's My Turn*, to her credit, virtually at his feet, telling him that she couldn't make her movie without him, exhorting him to appear in her low-budget, small-time production, playing a down-market character who went by the name of Johnny Castle, who was not a rocket scientist or a molecular biologist, but horror of horrors (and apologies to ABBA), was a dancing king! And not one of the ilk of Fred Astaire or Gene Kelley, or even Patsy Swayze, but who was taught how to dance at the McDonald's of dance studios, Arthur Murray. Despite the intensity of her pitch, and even after taking a positive meeting with Emile Ardolino, he had serious misgivings about playing a dancer, and, as the son of Patsy Swayze, one of America's foremost choreographers, decreed that unless he first met and approved of choreographer Kenny Ortega, he wasn't going to play Johnny.

Aware that Patrick was due to fly from New York to L.A., and determined to snare him for the movie, Ardolino booked Kenny a seat next to Patrick on the same flight and instructed him to convince Patrick to accept the part of Johnny.

Toward the end of the flight, "Patrick pointed his finger at me . . . and he said, 'I'm going to do this movie, Ortega, don't let me down. This is a really important time in my life. Right now, these choices that I'm making in my life right now are really important. I'm excited by what you have to say, what Emilio and Eleanor have to say. Come through for me, don't let me down,'" Kenny remembered.

After listening intently to Kenny's assurances, Patrick capitulated. Thrilled as she was that he'd accepted the part, Eleanor wasn't fully aware of just how big a star Patrick truly was, particularly in the South, where female audiences in particular had adored him in *North and South*.

However, when she and Patrick changed planes at Charlottesville Airport en route to the *Dirty Dancing* location, just as they were about to board their plane, she suddenly announced that she wanted to stop and buy a hot dog from one of the terminal vendors.

Instead of volunteering to get it for her, Patrick just carried on walking in the direction of the gate, telling her, "Let's just get on the plane." Surprised that the normally gentlemanly, considerate Patrick wasn't taking any notice of her request, Eleanor became more strident and repeated, " '*Patrick*, I want a hot dog,' " but he ignored her and said, "Come on, Eleanor, let's get on the plane!"

On the verge of exasperation, she decided to get the hot dog herself anyway and told Patrick to board the plane ahead of her; she'd join him once she'd finished her hot dog.

"The second we stopped walking, we were instantly surrounded by what seemed liked thousands of women, just clawing at Patrick and giving him their phone numbers," she remembered. One of those women pushed forward, telling him that he would be perfect for her sister, Bonnie, and gave him her own number, saying that was the only way in which he could get in touch with Bonnie.

"We got on the plane," Eleanor remembered. "And Patrick started taking all these phone numbers out of his pocket and started tearing them up."

Eleanor, riveted by the woman who wanted her sister Bonnie to meet him, asked, "What about Bonnie's sister?" His reaction surprised her, "He said, 'What?' It was clear he never even heard her. He just tuned it out. Fascinating," she said.

With a small $5 million budget, the producers had found that they couldn't afford to shoot in the Catskills, where the story was set. Instead, toward the end of August 1986, rehearsals for *Dirty Dancing* began at the Mountain Lake Resort in Giles County, Virginia, located four thousand feet up in the Allegheny Mountains, and which—along with Grove Park Inn, North Carolina—would double for the fictitious Catskills resort of Kellerman's.

Actress Jennifer Grey had badly wanted the leading part in *Flashdance* and tested for it several times, but she finally lost the role to Jennifer Beals. Now she was determined to win the part of Baby in *Dirty Dancing* instead.

Nonetheless, she was still nervous and, according to producer Linda Gottlieb, brought her father, Joel Grey, along with her to the audition for moral support.

"Joel had to literally push her through our door," Linda recalled to *Chicago Sun-Times* journalist Cindy Pearlman. "Then Jennifer seemed to muster up some courage and say, 'I know I'm not supposed to say this, but I'd be terrific in this role.'"

Her self-confidence now sufficiently buoyed, and dressed in a leotard and sneakers, she put on a Jackson Five tape and did a wild, spontaneous dance to it.

"I pretended it was the seventies and I was at Studio 54 making a commotion," she remembered. Although Baby was ten years younger than Jennifer, her bravura audition proved that she was an accomplished actress who could play the part to perfection, and it was hers.

She was thrilled at first, then she learned the identity of her co-star, the actor playing Johnny Castle. "When Jennifer heard that Patrick was playing the part, she was not a happy camper," *Dirty Dancing* producer Linda Gottlieb said in an interview for *Access Hollywood*. But if there had been any problems between Patrick and Jennifer during the making of *Red Dawn*, now that rehearsals began they were all forgotten. "We had done *Red Dawn*, together, so we had known each other quite well," Jennifer said. "I remember us dancing together and it was all of a sudden very easy."

The ever-sensitive Patrick intuited that beneath her veneer of self-confidence Jennifer wasn't quite as sure of herself as she seemed. "I think Jennifer Grey was nervous," he later recalled. "She's much smaller than I am and I think she was worried about her dancing." Later he would pay her the supreme compliment, "She really jumped into this stuff and came out with a sensuality in her dancing that has just staggered everybody." After two weeks of rehearsal, the forty-three-day shoot began on September 5. As the budget was tight, the entire cast and crew stayed at Mountain Lake as well, and the resort would become a kind of summer camp for them. Often, Patrick, cast, and costars would stay up for most of the night working on the following day's script. "It was such a wonderful collaboration; I still get chills thinking about it," he said.

Early on they shot the first scene, in which Baby watches, mesmerized, as Patrick and Cynthia Rhodes (playing his first dance partner, Penny) dance together. Cynthia, a seasoned dancer, was immediately impressed by his dancing. "He's a great leader," she said. "He's technically trained and danced with the Joffrey Ballet."

Patrick and Cynthia were both such brilliant dancers that the director and producers were afraid that their dancing would throw the movie off balance. "Everybody kept telling me to tone it down, that we were too hot together, and it was going to overpower my later scenes with Jennifer," Patrick remembered. He knew what everyone wanted, but sure of his artistic vision, his own abilities, he fought back, insisting that the hotter his dance with Cynthia, the more the audience would wonder why they weren't romantically involved, but to no avail.

But he was now no longer the wide-eyed greenhorn of *The Outsiders* or *Uncommon Valor*, with little power over the production. He was the star of *North and South*, and now the star of *Dirty Dancing* as well, with the success of the entire movie resting primarily on his square, manly shoulders.

Aware of his own power, he made a stand. "I refused to shoot it unless they did it my way, because I knew what I planned to do later with Jennifer would blow the relationship with Cynthia away. So I fought and fought for that, but I really didn't have to fight too hard because everyone was willing to at least hear me out," he said.

On September 23 the scene was filmed in which Patrick teaches Jennifer to dance across a log. In a decision that was utterly alien to Patrick, she chose to have a stunt double for that particular scene, while he stuck to his guns and didn't.

In the first of many on-location disasters that would befall him throughout the years, his stubborn refusal to use a stunt double on *Dirty Dancing*, would have serious consequences during the log scene, when his pride literally came before a fall.

As Linda Gottlieb remembered, "He hits the rubber mats spread below and, as everyone rushes over, picks himself up, seemingly unhurt, and says, 'Let's continue.' He does several more takes, falls several more times, and always insists he is fine."

Forever the stoic, this time Patrick had pushed his body too far. The following morning he awoke with a swollen and painful knee—which, to mix metaphors, was of course his ever-present Achilles heel, his left one. An exasperated Linda Gottlieb, silently cursing Patrick's obstinate refusal of a stunt double, drove him to the hospital. There he gritted his teeth while—at his request—the doctor drained 80 ccs of fluid intermingled with blood from his knee. Afterward, the orthopedist gave him a strict warning to avoid any strain on his knee.

But like the seasoned professional he'd been since he was three years old and Patsy taught him his first plié, he knew the show had to go on, no matter what. And twenty-four hours later he was back dancing with, as Linda put it, "all his usual charm and energy. I can only imagine the pain he [was] feeling."

The following day it was Jennifer's turn to suffer a mishap, when, while filming a scene in Johnny's cabin, she was stung twice by wasps. On investigation, it turned out that the entire cabin was wasp infested and had to be fumigated.

Dirty Dancing's director, Emilio Ardolino, favored improvisation, which chimed with Patrick's past experience as an actor. As a result, the scene in which Baby and Johnny crawl toward each other during a dance lesson wasn't in the original script but was something they did spontaneously during a warm-up. Ardolini liked it so much that he had them re-create it on camera.

They had started the shoot in sweltering temperatures, but now it was mid-October and they had moved on to their second location in Lake Lure, North Carolina. John Mojjis, owner of the fifty-room

Lake Lure Inn, which he'd bought in 1983 and had only just finished renovating and where Patrick stayed in Room 205, was a keen observer of cast and crew during the shoot.

He noticed that Patrick never went anywhere without his big black dog and how he was happiest when Lisa came up for a visit, and went on to allege that Patrick was pretty uptight during filming and sometimes snapped at his coworkers, but he would immediately apologize afterward.

There were problems, too, in filming the exterior scenes. Fall had come early, and the leaves had turned. Given that *Dirty Dancing* was set in the summer, the set decorators were enlisted to spray paint the leaves green.

In the last days of shooting, as Jennifer and Patrick prepared to shoot the lake scene, the temperature dropped to 40 degrees. Both of them stripped down to the minimal, then they plunged into the ice cold water. By the end of the scene, their lips had turned blue and they were in danger of catching pneumonia.

The cold wasn't the only hazard they faced during that particular scene. "My knee was filled with fluid and killing me," Patrick later ruefully recalled. "Suddenly, I have to dance with Jennifer and look like I'm the happiest guy in the world when I probably belong on crutches."

Although Patrick has always been far too gentlemanly to raise the subject in interviews, his knee wasn't the only thing bothering him during this and many other of his scenes with Jennifer. "I remember Patrick Swayze complaining that Jennifer was just too nervous and emotional," Linda Gottlieb recalled to Cindy Pearlman. "She would burst into tears at the drop of a hat.

"This duo that had such terrific chemistry on screen didn't get on and would frequently fight, frequently argue off screen . . . Patrick and Jennifer hated each other. Jennifer didn't want to do any of the love scenes. She would stand there saying, 'I don't like the way he kisses.' "

In despair, Linda said, "Just close your eyes, Jennifer, and for

God's sake pretend it's Matthew [her then boyfriend, Matthew Broderick] when you're kissing Patrick."

However, Patrick's manager, Lois Zetter, has a different recollection of his on-set relationship with Jennifer and remembers it being cordial. "They got on well, except that it was hard on him that she wasn't a professional dancer and had no experience. Which was difficult for him as he had a bad knee and had to dance twice as hard to compensate for her inexperience."

"I remember he was very thoughtful around Jennifer Grey because at that point it was still early in her career," said George Baetz, *Dirty Dancing*'s sound recordist. "He was a very considerate person, which is unusual on a film set, and he was really nice to Jennifer between takes. He worked really hard and did his own stunts. He played the guitar and liked Buddy Holly a lot, as well. We used to talk about hobbies and he was into cars and liked the Chevy 57 we had on set. He was really into it. He was very easy going, very professional, joked a lot, was well-prepared for his scenes and was enjoyable to be around."

Although he was patient and kind to Jennifer, his dearest wish had been that Lisa costar in the movie with him, not as Baby, but as Penny.

Instead, Lisa's only involvement with the movie would be the visits she made to the set—visits Patrick longed for. "He was very, very dedicated to his wife. He always talked about her and he loved her very much," recalled *Dirty Dancing* production supervisor Eileen Eichenstein. "I really enjoyed working with him. He has such determination. I loved the fact that he wasn't one-dimensional, that he had lots of interests and hobbies. He had so much individuality. I once asked him what would happen if he didn't have his career and he said, 'Well, you know, I have other things that I love.' "

The movie wrapped on October 27, 1986, but the climactic scene, in which Patrick declares "Nobody puts Baby in the corner," had been shot much earlier. Then, and forever after, he loathed the line. "That was one of the hardest lines I ever tried to pull off in my life. I tried everything in my power to get it out of the movie," he said.

He would live to rue the day he lost the battle to cut the line from the script. Like "Make my day," "Show me the money," "I'll be back," "I'm gonna make you an offer you can't refuse," "I want to be a part of your life," "Frankly, my dear, I don't give a damn," and "There's no place like home," the line would cleave to him like a succubus; like Judy Garland forever condemned to sing "Over the Rainbow" and Sinatra to sing "My Way," the line would dog him forever afterward. The line stayed in, but—thankfully for Patrick—so did the one moment in which he allowed his dancing talent to shine to its full extent at last.

"I got away with one moment, very technical, at the end, when I come off the stage, do a double pirouette, then go down on one knee. That's the one time I got to throw in something that required real technical proficiency," he said.

Until then, his role in *Dirty Dancing* was tantamount to riding Secretariat or Sea Biscuit, only hobbled.

"From a dancer's point of view, *Dirty Dancing* was a very frustrating experience," he said. "Fighting my ego was the most difficult thing because I'm a much better dancer than Johnny Castle is. Johnny was trained at Arthur Murray, not Joffrey. My level of training went far beyond his. But in order to be true to the character, I couldn't allow myself to be too technically proficient."

John Mojjis witnessed the double pirouette scene being filmed and noted afterward that before Patrick made the jump—wary of injuring his bad knee—he insisted that a pile of mattresses be laid on the floor for him to land on. Nonetheless, it took Patrick, the quintessential perfectionist, more than twenty-five tries to get the jump exactly the way he wanted it.

Before the movie was released, he was optimistic about its success. "I think people can relate to the film because everybody dreams that somebody can look into his lonely world and see past the exterior," he said, adding, "I had a feeling *Dirty Dancing* might be special.

It was either going to be very milquetoast silly or really get to people. Although, at the time it came out, I tried not to care one way or the other. I had set myself up to be hurt so many times with films that didn't do anything."

Dirty Dancing opened on Monday, August 17, 1987. From that time on, Patrick's life would never be the same again. From the first moment he swaggers onto the screen, a black leather jacket slung over his right shoulder, he is the bad boy straight out of every red-blooded woman's dreams—part Elvis, part Brando, part James Dean, the leader of the pack.

His first scornful words—"Got that, guys?"—directed at Neil Kellerman, the hotel owner's obnoxious son who has just given the staff a patronizing lecture on not mingling with the guests, establish both his dominance and his defiance. And when Kellerman lashes out and calls him a "wise ass," Patrick as Johnny demonstrates his self-control by remaining impassive while a muscle in his neck visibly twitches with coiled anger, suggesting that he is clearly capable of socking someone if he wants to, but *only* if he wants to, and not because he's provoked. He's in control of his own emotions and that's intensely sexy.

And when he and Cynthia Rhodes as Penny make their entrance into the staff quarters, all the staff step back—much as if he is a god parting the waters—and cheer him, and his heroic status is established.

When he first meets Baby, he snarls, "What is she doing here?" then dances with her, Prince Charming taking pity on the poor little match girl.

In the next scene, dancing with Vivienne, as he snakes his way around the dance floor with her like a blue-collar Rubirosa in his prime, he plays the gigolo to perfection.

Then, in a complete change of pace, he is gentle and protective of Penny, cradling her in his arms, "OK, Johnny is here, I'm never gonna let anything happen to you."

When he teaches Baby to dance, he is patient, kind, and devastatingly sexy. His eyes may be hooded, as Eleanor Bergstein intended, but they never mask his emotion.

He's a Byronic hero, a working-class heartthrob, a new man, a dragon slayer, yet has enough of the little boy in him for every woman in the audience to want to mother him. He's a bad boy, but not so bad that he seems untamable.

His body glistens with sexuality in the dance scenes, yet he isn't a classic hunk, a poor man's Arnie. He's the romantic hero of every woman's dreams, masculine but not cruel, dominant but not destructive, sexual but not unbridled, kind but not weak. You know that he would protect you if you were lost in the jungle with him, save you if you were shipwrecked, and love you forever if you wanted to be loved.

Like all the great mythological heroes—when he bursts into the theater and insists on dancing the last dance of the season as always—he is a decisive man of action, yet one who has undergone a radical transformation.

And there is something uniquely American in Patrick's portrayal of Johnny Castle, something innocent, something pure, which exudes the quality of a cowboy, a dreamer, a lover, and a poet. Just like Patrick, and all part and parcel of his everlasting appeal.

The audiences adored the movie and it became the hit of the summer, the sensation of the decade, breaking box-office records galore. In less than a year, the movie grossed over $100 million. Sales from the soundtrack—which featured "She's Like the Wind," the song which Patrick cowrote with Stacy Widelitz and recorded—hit $62 million with 4 million copies sold and the *Dirty Dancing* album stayed on top of the *Billboard* charts for nine weeks.

After the premiere, at the sixties-themed party at Roseland, dressed in a conservative gray suit, Patrick listened to the throb of the mambo and the beat of the Motown oldies and said with regret, "I'd like to go back to the hotel and get on my jeans and really do some dirty dancing!"

There's an old Spanish proverb that says, "Take what you want in life and pay." *Dirty Dancing* would make him rich, famous, and successful beyond his wildest dreams, but the price would be high. And although he didn't know it that evening, his days of dancing at clubs, free and untroubled by fans, were already well and truly behind him.

Even the most cynical of movie reviewers praised Patrick's performance in the movie. "He's no slouch off the dance floor, when he has to show the fear behind Johnny's swagger," wrote *Newsweek*, continuing, "The dance lessons scenes between Swayze and Grey have a real emotional charge; the entire relationship unfolds in arched backs, his thrusts, the graze of a hand on a rib cage. No words needed."

Only Patsy, ever critical, ever acerbic, was not particularly impressed by his dancing in the movie. "My mom called me up and said, 'Patrick, I know you can do better than that,' " he recalled. But as he firmly pointed out to her, Johnny was a Catskills dance instructor, trained by Arthur Murray and not Patsy Swayze.

Fortunately, the Hollywood foreign press wasn't as critical of Patrick as his mother had been and nominated him for a Golden Globe for the Best Performance by an Actor in a Motion Picture-Comedy or Musical. Unfortunately for Patrick, he and the other nominee, William Hurt (for *Broadcast News,*), were beaten by Robin Williams, who won for *Good Morning, Vietnam*.

But he had been honored by his peers and to Patrick that was all that mattered. His fans, of course, continued to adore him, to venerate him as the epitome of masculinity, a sex symbol eclipsing all others. Women loved *Dirty Dancing*, so much that they saw it as often as one hundred times, in the movies, not on video—always and only because of Patrick.

Swayze mania was now in full throttle and he was mobbed wherever he went. When he made an appearance at a Sam Goody record store, five thousand screaming fans were on hand, desperate to catch just a glimpse of him.

"I guess I'm just this catalyst for their release of emotion. I look at it this way: What other opportunity in life does anybody get to stand there and scream at the top of their lungs, you know?" he said, in an attempt to rationalize the phenomenon.

The fan fever continued unabated when—with Lisa and Lois Zetter—on September 3, 1987, he flew to London to promote *Dirty Dancing*. There they stayed at the Athenaeum on Piccadilly, dined at San Lorenzo and Langan's. While Patrick did publicity, Lisa and Lois shopped, blissfully unaware of the storm that would break over them two days later when they moved on to Berlin.

"I'd seen the fans around Travolta and how they really seemed to need to touch him, so I was prepared for all the fan mania around Patrick as well," Lois said. Consequently, she requested bodyguards be on hand to protect them the moment they deplaned in Berlin, only to discover on arrival that precisely two had been hired.

"It seemed like eight million fans were there to meet us at the airport, all screaming, all wanting Patrick's autograph. I tried to get him out of the airport as fast as possible, but instead of ducking into the waiting limo, he yelled, 'O.K., be calm and I'll sign your autographs,' " she said.

"So he stood there, signing autograph after autograph, always writing something special, something personal for each fan, while I kept saying, 'Patrick, there are millions of people here and you can't sign every one of their autographs, let's go.' But he wouldn't listen. 'They all came here specially to see me and I have to pay attention to all of them,' he said, and I thought it was crazy."

"After about an hour and a half, he stood up and yelled, 'We're going back to the Intercontinental, but if you want to come over, I'll sign all your autographs.' We got to the hotel and more than a hundred people followed us, all wanting his autograph. Some fans had even brought along as many as six pieces of paper so they could get autographs for all their friends as well. By now, all the hotel guards were around us, and I did all I could to protect him, but Patrick stayed up all night until he'd signed the very last autograph," Lois said.

Day after day, the fan letters poured in for him, not just from younger fans but from older women as well, offering him what he described as "all kinds of things. Some of them even say they want to leave their husbands for me."

It isn't easy being the spouse or the consort of a global icon. Priscilla Presley sometimes retreated inside Graceland, Mrs. Tom Jones mostly remained secluded in their Beverly Hills mansion, Prince Phillip walks three paces behind the Queen of England, Heather Mills-McCartney founded her own charity when she was married to Paul, and Guy Ritchie skulked in the background while Madonna luxuriated in the limelight and adulation.

Lisa was now in the nightmarish position of having to cope with the tidal wave of female attention that came in the wake of Patrick's stardom, with love-struck women literally knocking her off his arm in their haste to get to him.

"There have been times when I have actually been shoved out of the way. I think I would have to be a complete martyr not to resent it. What it says to me is that I don't matter," she said. "All these people would lean over me and throw their coats over my head as they reached for Patrick. Day in, day out, everyone is pushing you out of the way and, after a while, all you hear is a tape saying, 'Lady, you're nothing.' "

Reduced from beautiful young rising ballet star to mere nonentity trapped in the white heat of Patrick's supernova aura, she was compelled to play Robin to his Batman, Watson to his Holmes, forever trailing in his gilded wake.

In a masterly display of understatement, she said of his fans, "I'm not crazy about it when they start getting touchy with him, and he's not crazy about it either. He was signing a bunch of autographs for thirteen- and fourteen-year-old girls and they were actually rubbing his bottom, kind of getting a feel in.

"It never occurred to me this would have as much effect on my life as on him," she said. "When we go places the little girls go crazy, the fans mob him, people push scripts at him, and I have to smile all the time. After a couple of weeks I found myself getting real irritable. I discovered the same kind of pressure was on me."

Patrick had always been an intensely chivalrous and protective man, a latter-day Sir Lancelot, forever willing and able to defend his Guinevere, and always fought bitterly to force everyone around him to treat Lisa with the respect he felt she deserved. Even at the very start of his career, when he was making *The Outsiders*, he fearlessly stuck out his neck for her.

Casting director Janet Hirshenson recalled in her book, *A Star Is Found: Our Adventures in Casting Some of Hollywood's Biggest Movies*, which she wrote with Jane Jenkins, that during the filming of *The Outsiders*, when her husband Michael visited her on the set at dinnertime, Michael and Lisa got in line for the catering truck. Suddenly an assistant director declared, "These other people can't be on this line. This food is just for people who are actually working on the movie." "Patrick Swayze laid into the guy," Janet said.

One of the more positive consequences of *Dirty Dancing* for him was that a young girl named Kristy Harvey, who had been born with Down syndrome, had reacted positively to *Dirty Dancing* and in particular to Patrick as Johnny Castle. Delighted, her teachers incorporated Johnny into her lessons. Patrick found out and—in one of the highlights of her life—he took the time to meet her. "Things turned around with the Kristy Harvey thing," he said. "That's when I realized you really can give something back by the characters that you play."

In general, however, his life was completely decimated by the tsunami of mass adoration that flooded over him in the wake of *Dirty Dancing*. And amid all the adulation, it was hardly surprising that—forever the Method actor, now condemned to play the part of Patrick Swayze, the Hollywood icon of masculinity, for all eternity—he began to live the role in all its darkest and most dramatic extremes.

"I used to have nightmares of Freddie Prinze, Janis Joplin, James Dean, and Marilyn Monroe, because I could see similarities," he said, with the subtext that he was afraid that he too would die young.

Like Marilyn Monroe, Jimmy Dean, Janis Joplin, Freddie Prinze, and all the other beautiful and damned entertainers whose lives ended in suicide or addiction, he also sometimes suffered from low self-esteem, which caused him to think that he didn't deserve all the attention. "I don't feel famous. I feel like I'm the same jerk I've always been! People say you're special, but that's not true," he said, later describing himself as a "driven individual, wrapped up in suffering and paying my dues. Because of what I look like and what I could do with my body, I wasn't sure there was anything inside of me."

On a deep level, he felt he was unworthy and then, and through the years, perhaps unconsciously set out to sabotage himself by drinking too much, risking his life in death-defying stunts, and proving himself.

Even if he and Lisa were together, they were no longer able to leave the house without him being mobbed. They used to love going out dancing, but, as Patrick said, "Even if it's a cool place, where you're not being mobbed, the minute you get up to go to the bathroom you can hear every head in the room spin around. *He's gonna dance!* It's weird. Sometimes I think I can smell people watching me."

The press, too, was now a constant thorn in his side, but he dealt with it with as much grace as he could. "You deal with the fact that the way you zip up your zipper in the bathroom could wind up in the newspapers. It just goes with the territory," he said philosophically.

For a while he kicked against all the adulation and tried to live as normal a life as possible, refusing to accept that he couldn't go out anymore without bodyguards. "I'd go out, and sure enough, it would turn into, 'Come on, dance with my girlfriend, man!' 'No, I really don't want to.' 'What's wrong—she ain't good enough for you?' "

On November 6, 1987, *Steel Dawn* was released, both shocking and somewhat disappointing Patrick's adoring public, not to mention the critics. Since the film came so closely on the gilded heels of *Dirty Dancing*, many of Patrick's fans were appalled by it. The movie opened and closed within two weeks, taking in a paltry $526,000, only to be resurrected on video but still not to any great acclaim.

His life on the ranch with Lisa, their dogs, and horses remained more important to him than Hollywood and all it entailed. During the first week of May 1988 he visited Ventura Farms Ranch in Thousand Oaks, California, to preview Arabian horses being auctioned at "The Sale of the Century," to benefit AIDS research.

On May 11, 1988, Barbara Walters's special featuring Patrick was aired on ABC. During the interview—filmed at Rancho Bizarro—Patrick gave Barbara a mambo lesson. "I think he's one of the most likeable kids I've ever met . . . He's adorable, sweet and honest," she later enthused.

Thanks to the rapport she and Patrick built up, his touching emotional honesty during the subsequent broadcast would be evident for all the world to see. He confided to Barbara: "Lisa literally is my creative partner. It feels like there is a real power between us, a real chemistry—like we're soul mates." Then, in a more confessional mode, he said, "There's an intense passion between us because our fights are huge. But our love is huge." Barbara was so taken by the phrase that, after the show, she sent Patrick and Lisa a pillow with the words "Our fights are huge, but our love is huge" stitched on it.

She had also invited Patsy to appear on the special as well, but—perhaps not wanting to steal Patrick's thunder even briefly—she declined. When Barbara asked him about his mother, he paid her the compliment of saying that she had taught him discipline. "But it was in a good way; that you can't waltz through life and you can't expect things to be handed to you on a silver platter. You've got to go out and work for it to be deserving of it."

Then, in the middle of the interview, Barbara suddenly asked him about the death of his father. He was unprepared for the question and then and there, with the cameras rolling, he broke down and cried. "I loved that man," he said, wiping his eyes. "He gave me my passion. I'm going to make that man proud of me until the day I die."

eight
SWAYZE MANIA

*T*housands of women throughout the world were madly in love with him, scripts poured in daily, directors begged him to work with them, and he was now the hottest star in Hollywood.

From the start of his career, however, he was determined to strike a cornucopia of notes in his performances. Turning down a lucrative three-picture deal after his teen idol success in *Skatetown USA* was the first of a long series of brave, if not foolhardy, moves he had made in his career.

His life's obsession would from then on involve him playing a kind of theatrical sleight of hand with audience and critics alike. He would start out by giving his all, creating a particular character to perfection, and then engrave on the public that particular image of himself as indelibly as George Washington's face is engraved on a quarter.

Just as the public and critics had accepted him at face value, he would execute a dramatic volte face and smash that image into smithereens. Like some latter-day Merlin, he would magic himself into another role, another image, irrespective of the fact that in each sea change he would also confuse, infuriate, and sometimes alienate his loyal fans.

His career tactics were partly predicated on the Warren Robertson–engendered philosophy that an actor has many people inside of him and should play a variety of parts so as to give expression to each and every one of them.

After his global success as a romantic idol in *Dirty Dancing*, it would have been logical for him to follow up with a similar role in the same genre; however, he chose not to. "He opted for some terrible movies after *Dirty Dancing*. They weren't my choice, but I couldn't talk him out of appearing in them," said Lois Zetter, who was now managing him alone since the passing of Bob Le Mond. She was not in favor of his choice of the follow-up movie to *Dirty Dancing*, nor many of the subsequent parts he would take.

In an attempt not to be typecast as Johnny, he opted to play a hillbilly country boy/turned cop set on avenging his brother in the action thriller *Next of Kin*, shot in August 1988 in Chicago and in Hazard, Kentucky.

He yearned to escape his Johnny Castle image off-screen as well as on, but on location in Chicago he was yet again confronted by predatory fans. After it was reported in the local press that he'd been dancing at the club Gatz 223, throngs of women swarmed all over the club, with one declaring that if he came back she was going to rip his clothes off.

After another woman confessed that if she saw him at the club, "I would come up to him and say, 'I'm not trying to hit on you. I want to see how you move. That's all I want.' " He wryly concluded, "Guess I won't be goin' back there."

However, such was the level of hysteria surrounding his presence in Chicago that he wasn't safe even in his hotel suite. Although the hotel management tried to protect him by cautioning the employees not to approach him or they would be instantly fired, they failed to insulate him completely.

"Word didn't get to the maids fast enough," he later recalled. "I was buck naked in the bathroom and one of them knocked on the door and asked for an autograph. I should have given her one. I should have stepped out and said, 'Here's an autograph you're never going to forget, woman!' "

At least he had retained his sense of humor. One night at 3 a.m. he was even able to evade his fans altogether. After riding around town on his motorbike, he braved a visit to Kingston Mines, a blues club, where, to his vast relief, no one troubled him.

"It blew me away, man," he said. "I didn't want to leave my bike, so I stood out in a hall, drinkin' a beer, listening to the music. Wonderful thing was, everybody recognized me and nobody f—— with me."

Patrick had fun off-camera with his costars, fellow Texan Bill Paxton, who would become the star of *Big Love*, Liam Neeson, and Helen Hunt. Neeson would become a good and loyal friend to Patrick, and seeing Patrick and Lisa together, Neeson later enthused, "A few times, Patrick and Lisa would be chatting about his early Broadway days when he was a dancer, and he'd suddenly start dancing—it was just like a piece of poetry. They'd just get up, and the two of them would dance. It was very beautiful, very moving."

Paxton remembered being on location at the Holiday Inn in Hazard, Kentucky. During a break in filming, they sat around the pool drinking beer. "There was nothing much else to do," Bill recalled. "Somehow we started chasing Helen around the pool . . . So anyway, she dives in the water with her clothes on to elude us. And we say, 'No, dive shallow,' because the thing was like a wading pool. But she went in right on her head, and we had to take her to the hospital."

In yet another testament to Patrick's star wattage, in a situation symptomatic of the way in which the world was closing in on him, he was compelled to stay in the car outside the hospital in case he'd be mobbed yet again and just wait there for news on Helen's health. Fortunately, she was discharged relatively unscathed.

Back at the seventy-room Holiday Inn, Swayze Mania roared on unabated. Alpha Burton, hostess and cashier, revealed that "We had to get several extra security guards. The traffic flow had been tremendous. We had girls out here till twelve the other night be-cause they heard Patrick was in the lounge and they wanted to get a glimpse of him. One lady even jumped in the pool the other day—fully clothed—just to get Patrick's attention. He just got out of the chair and calmly walked to his room."

Against all odds, he fought to live a normal life while on loca-tion, somewhat naïvely driving his white Lamborghini around town, and eating shrimp, potato chips, and soup at Circle T, the local res-taurant in Hazard. "He was wearing a gray sweatshirt with sleeves cut out and jogging pants, and his hair was wavy and longer than it was in *Dirty Dancing*," recalled Debbie Melton, who worked at the restaurant. "He was really friendly and talkative and took pictures and signed autographs."

Unfortunately for Patrick, the only thing worth noting about *Next of Kin* is that he sported a ponytail in it, and critics didn't think a great deal of the movie.

That same year, 1988, Patsy opened a dance studio in Simi Valley and trained Geena Davis for her dance in *Thelma and Lou-ise*, coached and choreographed Emma Thompson and Kenneth Branagh for their 1940s-style dance in *Dead Again*, and also coached David Hasselhoff for the Austrian segment of his Knight Rider tour.

Secure in her identity as Patrick Swayze's mother, Patsy lined the walls of her dance studio with pictures of Patrick. Ever the wily ama-teur child psychologist, adept at handling her young pupils, when-ever she was confronted by little boys who found dancing a trial, she was prone to point at Patrick's pictures up on the wall. "The boys adore him. Whenever they do something wrong, I tell them he's looking at them, and they straighten right up," she said.

Patrick and Lisa, of course, still remained her star pupils, not that she ever meted out any special treatment to them. "I've taught Patrick since he could walk," she noted with justifiable pride. "He doesn't like to study with anyone else. Because I am his mom, I am the only one who will really correct him. When you're a star, people tend to say, 'You're wonderful! You're great!' But I tell him straight, 'That's terrible, do it again.' "

As a valentine from Lois Zetter to Patrick and his family, she set up a deal for Patsy to make an hour-long video shot in her studio, featuring her coaching a group of young people who were about to enter a dance contest. Under Patsy's direction Patrick and Lisa demonstrated the art of dirty dancing. The video, "Swayze Dancing," released in 1988, remains a fascinating record of Patsy's teaching methods and a touchingly beautiful one of Lisa and Patrick dancing together in their prime.

Next, he accepted a $1 million offer to star in *Road House*, in which he would play the role of Dalton, the king of bouncers, called in to clean up a grungy bar—The Double Deuce—in a Missouri town.

His motivation for taking the part again dovetailed with his mother's acute analysis of the male sex, "when they grow up, they want to show off their prowess, how high they can jump, how fast they can turn," for, as he explained, "I've got all these martial-arts skills and I'm trained on the level of a stuntman, and I want to be able to put those skills on film. That's one reason I did *Road House*. I wanted people one time to see all that stuff."

Shooting on *Road House* began in mid-1988 in California's Santa Clarita Valley and was produced by Joel Silver. At Patrick's request, Lois Zetter's fifty-two-year-old husband, Walter Unterseher, went on location with him.

"Since his father's death, Patrick was always searching for a father figure. Walt was a cowboy, a biker, an auto mechanic, and fit the bill perfectly," said Lois.

"Patrick came to our wedding and was very happy that I'd married a cowboy he could get along with. He adored Walter. And after Bob Le Mond died, I was being a kind of mother to the clients and Walt a kind of father. So Patrick wanted to hang around with him, and asked him to be an extra in *Road House*.

"On the first day on location he spotted Walt standing in line for food with the other extras, and said, 'Oh, no, Walt. C'mon in here,' and from then on he took Walt with him to eat every day just to make sure Walt got fed well."

"Patrick was a nice young boy, with a lot of zip and zing in him," Walter recalled. "He seemed to be fairly level-headed, but he could be rougher when he needed to be. He was no pushover. And he was constantly pursued by women, but he got rid of them very politely and wouldn't say anything to offend them in any way."

Apart from the fact that Patrick sported a massive mane of hair—and later sighed, "that hair was the bane of my existence"— the movie was a long round of violence, including a scene in which his character is knifed but calmly stitches up his own arm afterward and another when he stabs a man in the throat.

For some light relief, Dalton—a philosophizing bouncer—has a love affair with a doctor played by Kelly Lynch. Lisa recommended her for the role. "She thought there would be good chemistry between Patrick and me," Kelly said.

As it was, Kelly so resembled Lisa that she looked like she could have been Lisa's little sister. Kelly, in turn, was enchanted by her close proximity to Patrick and Lisa. "They love each other and it's apparent," she would say in the future. "Their partnership is for life. Like any great marriage, they seem to move together as one person. They're like a single organism."

Lisa even helped choreograph the love scene between Patrick and Kelly. He recalled, "She told me: 'You have to imagine that you are so desperate for each other that you don't even have time to take anything off. You just undo your pants and let Kelly lift her dress and take her next to a wall or something.' Now that was a very sexy thought—and we decided to go for it." Hence the scene in which he backs Kelly up against a fireplace wall and makes love to her then and there.

Looking back, he said, "I wish it could have been in a little bit better taste with all that stuff up against the wall, though. I don't think it was necessary for all those pumps up against the wall."

"I've had more people come up to me and say, 'God almighty, that must have hurt, slamming her up against that fireplace,' " he said. Those solicitous fans needn't have worried, as Kelly wore padding during the scene, which protected her from injury. Off and on-screen, she was entranced by him. "He's strong, but he has grace and agility. He's not just this big thug throwing his muscles around out there," she said.

"He's a real down-to-earth guy. He treats everyone the same, whether it's actors or gaffers [technical workers]. He's a man's man, but still sensitive, with a great sense of humor. He makes you feel good."

"I loved Patrick, and I respect him as an actor. There's no doubt he's a real human being and that comes across on the screen," his costar Sam Elliott added.

His other *Road House* costar, Ben Gazzara, also echoed Sam Elliott's enthusiasm for Patrick, calling him, "a good kid who works very hard and who takes his craft seriously. I hate people who put out only seventy, eighty, ninety percent. He puts out one hundred percent."

He certainly did. One of the focal points of the movie was a massive fight with Marshall Teague, playing Jimmy, the villain. Patrick was trained for the fight by Benny Urquidez, who started out training him to kickbox by just spending a whole week hanging out a Patrick's house, observing him. "He looked like a cat while he is moving," said Benny. "I said, 'That's how I'm going to train him, I'm going to train him like a cat.' "

Training Patrick that way, with music playing in the background, produced wonderful results and he exceeded Benny's expectations in mastering kickboxing to such a degree that Benny even suggested that Patrick start competing in kickboxing events, a suggestion probably not appreciated by the movie's insurance company.

Patrick was shirtless during the climactic fight scene with Marshall—shot over five nights for up to six hours a night in forty-two-degree temperatures—and went on to pay the price for what some might term his vanity.

"Fighting on the river with no shirt on . . . was the dumbest thing, as it meant that I didn't have the luxury of pads on," he admitted, explaining, "What took the longest time on the set was covering all my bruises, my forearms, my ribcage, constantly black and blue."

In a comment that must have been music to Patrick's ears, Teague declared afterward, "I didn't worry about Patrick getting hurt. He performed as an athlete and as an actor, and was in tremendous shape. He's a real cowboy."

After the fight Patrick's knee swelled up yet again and doctors drained it, while he endured the pain without uttering a single complaint. He believed in the movie, believed in his performance, and felt that any discomfort he suffered would ultimately be justified.

Along the way he also did a stunt that required him to make a twenty-foot drop from a rooftop onto a truck bed. As a result he hurt his back, but as was his wont, he shrugged off the pain. "I've had so many injuries," he said, "I'm not going to let it stop me. You just get good at turning off that light switch in your brain to turn off pain and just see it as sensation—at least long enough to deliver the goods."

Perhaps because of the pain, he was still drinking, but not so much when Lisa visited the Fresno location, occasions when a cast member noticed that he was more subdued.

He was caught up in making *Road House*—which he saw as a classic western-style action movie and took extremely seriously—but continued to be undercut by crazed fans. Once or twice filming was interrupted because large groups of women, set on stalking him, materialized at the location.

After he and Sam Elliott judged a bikini contest at Tequila Pete's, a popular Fresno night spot, and Patrick took to the dance floor, the club was inundated with calls from obsessive fans wanting to know when he'd be coming back. And when he and Lisa went to dinner at Peppino's Italian Cusine in Fresno, where he ate scampi Italiana and she ate veal marsala, on the following day the restaurant was beleaguered by customers hoping he'd come in again.

Even extras on the set were overcome by Swayze Mania. While they were shooting in the Anaheim nightclub Bandstand, two hundred extras—many of whom had applied for the job in response to radio ads—doubled as club guests.

As one of them, Nicky Sterig, remembered, a female extra playing a waitress walked by. "She couldn't take her eyes off of Patrick. Well, she tripped and spilled her drinks . . . on me. Patrick handed me a napkin to dry myself off. I told him it was his fault, but he didn't laugh."

He could hardly have been blamed for not being in a laughing mood. Fans were increasingly more and more unbridled in their worship of him, screaming out their love for him whenever he came close. "I can't believe all the screaming women," he said with a sigh.

He still endeavored to retain his good manners when dealing with fans, even though they thought nothing of striding up to his restaurant table while he was in the midst of lunch or dinner and demanding his autograph.

He did his best to oblige, but his natural politeness was stretched to the limit while making *Road House*. As they were filming on a rugged stretch of private land, a pickup packed with middle-aged women appeared on the horizon and roared toward his trailer. They didn't gain admittance, but the experience must have been particularly unnerving to the man who, as a boy, used to be racked by his nightmare of being stalked by a monstrous warrior.

Another time, he was filming the seminal moonlight riverside fight with Teague when a raft sailed by carrying a group of lovestruck women. He was not in the least flattered by their attention. "It was actually messin' with my insides pretty bad," he admitted. "Women throw themselves at my feet all the time, some of them the most beautiful women you could ever wish to meet. Older ladies are the worst. They put their hands right on my butt. Then I hear them say, 'I did it Myrtle, I did it!' "

During one terrifying night on location in Fresno, the name of his hotel—The Piccadilly Inn—was leaked to the press, word traveled fast, and an enterprising fan managed to unearth his room number. According to Patrick, three hundred women stampeded down the hotel corridor, set on getting their hands on him. "If I'd stayed in that room, I'd probably be dead by now," he said. "They wanted any part of me they could get hold of. Just as they smashed down my door, I dived off the balcony from the third floor. I landed in the shallow end of the swimming pool."

Patrick Swayze was now considered to be the hottest star in movies; legions of women desired him and threw all inhibitions to the wind in their quest to get as close to him as possible and to touch him. He was so traumatized by all the attention his fame had brought him that he turned to therapy for help and understanding. "I've been in everything," he later confessed. "I tried this therapist and that therapist." Although he later credited Lisa as his shrink, excavating his psyche with professional therapists proved to be both painful and enlightening for him.

At that time in his life, Oscar Wilde's maxim "There are two tragedies in life; one is not getting what you want. The other is getting it" may well have resonated with him. For as he put it, "A real emptiness went through me after *Dirty Dancing*. Before the movie, I had allowed my dreams to be finite, and then, all of a sudden, I had achieved my dreams. I thought there was nothing left to accomplish."

Road House was released on May 19, 1989. After the premiere he and his younger brother, Don, challenged each other to a car race to his home. They were on the freeway, with Don on his motorcycle speeding along at 70 mph and Patrick in his new Mercedes racing ahead.

"He comes by doing 110, showing off his new car. Next thing you know, I'm going by him doing 140, just like he's standing still. I left my brother behind that time," said Don, who had always worshipped Patrick unreservedly and had stood in the wings cheering when he gave his earliest theatrical performances, but still couldn't suppress his glee at beating his movie star brother.

Losing the race may well have been an omen for Patrick; the subsequent reviews of *Road House* wouldn't help the movie win at the box office either. Many of the critics were perplexed and annoyed that he had followed up *Dirty Dancing* with such a violent movie and disliked *Road House* on its own grounds.

"Patrick Swayze has the most laughable role since Tom Cruise juggled a few liquor bottles and danced to 'The Hippy Hippy Shakes,' in *Cocktail*," Janet Maslin wrote in the *New York Times*, going on to quip, "Next to Dalton, Johnny Castle in *Dirty Dancing* seems like Hamlet."

Patrick was irritated by the bad reviews and debilitated by the constant attention from crazed fans, and hit the bottle even harder. Nonetheless, he was still his mother's creation, her work ethic was etched on his soul, and no matter how bad he felt, he wasn't even momentarily tempted to back out of a professional commitment.

Consequently, during the first week in June 1989, he and Lisa traveled to London where, on June 13, they attended the London premiere of *License to Kill* at the Odeon Leicester Square.

As the crowds surged toward them, he and Lisa stuck closely to each other while bodyguards kept them both out of harm's way. But once inside the movie theater, when Lisa slipped away to go to the bathroom, Patrick was suddenly surrounded by braying crowds.

"Everyone was grabbing me and I couldn't stand it. I felt trapped and alone," he said. "There was nobody around and nobody could help me. I felt incredibly embarrassed because the people waiting to be congratulated on their film were just standing there. It freaked me out."

Back in their hotel suite, the full impact of his ordeal struck him forcibly. He started drinking heavily. When he was younger, it took three beers and he was blasted, but with the pressures of stardom he had escalated to sprees of four six-packs at a time.

Afterward, he could only remember a little of what happened

next that night in London. "I destroyed the room. I punched holes in the walls, broke out all the windows, broke some furniture," he blurted out with his habitual honesty.

Lisa stood by, horrified. "He smashed windows. Furniture was broken. He went crazy," she said afterward. Sometime during the night, she walked out and left him.

Much later, Patrick confessed, "That's what slapped me in the face and said, 'Wait a minute! There's got to be a way to hold this stuff that's happening in my life in a positive way.' Like directing that wild man in a clean way."

Down the line, in a June 1992 interview with *Playboy* writer Lawrence Linderman, he made the startling confession that alcohol had not been his only addiction. "Cocaine put me into a living hell. I'd lock myself into a room because I couldn't be with people. Everybody else would do their coke and have a good time; I could not do it. This lasted maybe six months, spread out over a few years," he said, adding, "I did it mostly when I was on location. But coke and speed and downers didn't work for me—I hated to be out of control and unable to put words together."

In another, parallel confession—made this time to writer Melina Gerosa in a May 1998 *Ladies' Home Journal* interview—he described what might well have been cocaine-induced behavior.

"One time I got so angry and so frustrated and so confused that I went out the back door with a .357 Magnum and woke up an entire territory. The police showed up, just to make sure that I didn't kill someone. Understandably, Lisa was petrified. "I was running away because I thought he was trying to shoot me," she said.

He knew he could thank his lucky stars that she still loved him, still stuck by him. And that clearly a divine providence was watching over him, for just weeks after his London rampage he was able to throw himself into work so wholeheartedly that his passion for the movie he was making eclipsed even "that wild man." That movie was called *Ghost*, and he began shooting it on July 24, 1989, in Manhattan.

nine
GHOST

Whether or not Patrick had learned anything from his London crisis, he was acutely aware that he was rescued from his descent into darkness by the advent of *Ghost*.

"I really think it was a blessing for me that the movie came into my life," he once said.

Lisa read the *Ghost* script first. *It's a Wonderful Life* was among Patrick's favorite movies and she immediately knew that he would love *Ghost* as well. Then there was the effect the script had on her. "It made me cry," she said. "But I didn't want to influence his opinion. He read it and came walking in afterward with tears in his eyes and said, 'Why didn't you tell me?'"

He was mesmerized. He knew that the male lead—Sam Wheat (a securities broker who, after his murder, remains earthbound so he can rescue his wife from certain death)—spent the majority of the movie as a ghost and was not a fully rounded character. The part had been turned down by a stream of Hollywood actors, including Bruce Willis, Tom Cruise, Tom Hanks, Paul Hogan, and Harrison Ford.

Throughout his career, Patrick would ricochet between making dismal career choices, selecting some movies merely because they afforded him the opportunity to hone his athletic prowess or to demonstrate it to the public, and making inspired choices like *Ghost*, instinctively understanding that the part of Sam Wheat was tailor-made for him.

There was also a more personal reason for his determination to star in the movie. "*Ghost* was about living your life for the moment, because that's all you've got. If you don't communicate with the people you love, you set yourself up for incredible pain if you lose them," he said. "The reason I did *Ghost* was that it gave me the chance to believe that maybe I will get to tell my daddy I love him again."

Patrick was brought up a Catholic, but after having explored Buddhism and a variety of New Age disciplines, he also firmly believed in reincarnation, believed that he had already lived three lives, and had gone so far as to actually hire a psychic to channel them for him.

Strangely enough—given his childhood dreams of being stalked by a warrior—he discovered that in two of his past lives he really had been a warrior. He claimed that through channeling he was able to experience one of his prior lives and described what happened when he did. "There's a sense of foreboding and a dark shape that keeps coming at me. This warrior is looking to do battle, but the foe is not physical. I keep going down this trail to a clearing. There is a woman. It is about saving her."

He and Lisa also passionately believed in the power of white light. "Lisa and I both use our imagination to surround ourselves with white light and think of being perfectly safe," he said. "It is very powerful positive thinking."

He believed ardently in the theme of life after death. As he explained, "I am convinced that people who are dead can come back and visit loved ones. Death is a beginning, not an ending."

Patrick was passionate about *Ghost* and determined to star in it. Through his agents he conveyed his interest to *Airplane* director Jerry Zucker, who, in a dizzying change of genre, was now directing *Ghost*.

According to casting director Janet Hirshenson, who believed that Patrick was perfect to play Sam, "Jerry thought Patrick was a really nice guy—everybody did. But he wasn't sure if Patrick was the One."

Zucker envisioned the character of Sam as a young, smooth yuppie and, as far as he was concerned, Patrick was a cowboy, too rough-hewn. *Road House* had been recently released, and before finally rejecting him Zucker wanted to see Patrick on-screen. *Ghost*'s writer and associate producer, Bruce Joel Rubin, came with him and later recalled, "When we walked out, Jerry said, 'Over my dead body . . . ' "

Instead, Jerry decided Kevin Kline would be right for the part, and on learning that Kevin was out of town filming, booked a conference call with him a day or two later.

Janet Hershenson, however, was still convinced that Patrick was right for Sam.

As she remembered, "Jerry didn't want to be in the position of rejecting Patrick, whom he liked very much as a human being, even if he wasn't so sure about him as Sam the Banker. So I promised that if Jerry hated Patrick, I would take the blame."

With that proviso in place, Zucker reluctantly allowed Patrick to read for the part after all. "Okay, so we've got Patrick coming in to audition for Jerry and producer Lisa Weinstein—not the biggest Patrick Swayze fan on the planet, I have to say. Then, one hour later, we've got Kevin calling from Seattle for a phone meeting," Janet said.

Before the reading, Patrick learned through the grapevine that he was definitely not the favorite for the part, but with his characteristic optimism he ignored the odds. "I took it as a challenge even though it looked pretty hopeless because this man was taking a pretty hard position about me," he recalled. "It sort of freed me up to go in there and be completely honest."

"He knew exactly what the circumstances were, and to his credit, he didn't let it get to him. He just worked his way through every one of the script's big romantic scenes, and in one of the greatest moments of my acting career, I read with him," Janet said.

When they got to the climactic scene in which Sam finally says

"I love you," and Molly says "Ditto"—Janet looked up, and Lisa Weinstein, who had been one of the biggest voices opposed to casting Patrick, had tears streaming down her cheeks.

Jerry Zucker, too, who was utterly overwhelmed by Patrick's performance, cried, "Wow!" and leaped out of his seat, exclaiming, "That was beautiful. Patrick, you have the job."

"I saw a side of Patrick that I never knew existed. Patrick has enormous heart. He had much more range then I'd seen before," Zucker said afterward, adding, "There's no one who can deliver a heartfelt line like Patrick."

"I started realizing this could be one of those roles of a lifetime," Patrick said years later. "I needed to do it for my soul."

After Meg Ryan turned down the part of Molly, and Molly Ringwald and Nicole Kidman also auditioned for it without success, Demi Moore won the part. However, close to the start of shooting, the pivotal character of Oda Mae Brown, the psychic, still hadn't been cast. Initially the producers leaned toward either Tina Turner or Oprah Winfrey, but Patrick had other ideas and wasn't afraid to express them.

Whoopi Goldberg remembered, "He knew I was right for this part. You know, we had never met. But he liked what I did and he knew I was right and there was some resistance . . ." In the end, Patrick managed to persuade Jerry to consider Whoopi, and together they flew to Alabama, where she was shooting *The Long Walk Home*, to discuss the possibilities.

"Whoopi and I had an incredible rapport during the visit," Patrick recalled, "and after I left, I called her just to let her know that over my dead body would anybody else do that role." A grateful Whoopi later elaborated, "Patrick said, 'I'm not doing it unless she does it.' He fought, stomped, kicked, and screamed to make sure I got the part and I won an Oscar because of Patrick Swayze."

"I love being with Patrick," she went on. "He's easy to be around, great to be with. Not in the biblical sense, of course. But it did cross my mind."

Patrick and Whoopi had tremendous chemistry both on-screen and off, and he would sometimes joke that if he were not married to Lisa, he would have married Whoopi instead.

Their rapport aside, she did, however, find the first scenes in the movie in which Oda Mae is talking to Sam, but he remains invisible to her, difficult, because although Patrick was right in front of her, she had to give the impression that she couldn't see him.

"Not looking at Patrick was very hard and sort of crazy-making," Whoopi remembered. "Every once in a while we would be doing a scene and everything would seem to be going okay when suddenly Jerry would call cut."

"I would ask him what the problem was, and he would tell me I was looking at Patrick. I would tell him, 'No, I'm not.' So we would shoot the scene again, and I would be looking all around trying not to look at Patrick."

"Patrick and Demi are different types of actors than I am. They need more space and quiet between scenes. But I like a lot of noise and bad jokes," she said.

Despite the fact that Patrick and Demi shared the identical approach to acting, there wasn't much chemistry between them, although gossip hinted that her then-husband, Bruce Willis, was afraid there was too much.

Learning of the rumors that Bruce was threatened by his love scenes with his wife, Patrick categorically denied them, stepped up to the plate, and said, "That was so far from the truth, the stuff about Bruce getting jealous and showing up on the set and causing problems. Bruce was there a lot—holding his baby in his arms while Demi and I did a scene. The truth is, he was very supportive and very helpful to me as well."

Demi, in turn, was also kind and supportive of him as well and afterward asserted, "Patrick really had one of the more difficult jobs. He was dealing with emotion that doesn't relate to anything that most of us know in our world. He's sensitive and has a vulnerability that's right out there. And he also looks great with his shirt off . . .

He has a very sweet, gentle, kind heart, and those Southern manners, but he's also got a very rugged, animalistic physique."

Meanwhile, Zucker had moved from not wanting Patrick to play the part of Sam at all to learning to trust his creative judgment. Patrick was so passionate about perfecting his part that many times he'd stay up all night rewriting it. "I'd go home and write new dialogue and action for myself and then bring it to the set the next day for Bruce and Jerry's approval," he remembered. "They liked what I was coming up with at night so well, they'd say, 'Oh, Patrick, your instincts are incredible. Just keep doing what you're doing.' Then, in the next breath they'd say, 'Patrick, you're looking awful. You gotta get some sleep.'"

As usual, he endeared himself to the cast and crew. "One of my jobs was walking Patrick to the set. I remember thinking that he didn't have to talk to me because I was just a kid," production assistant Winston Quitasol remembered. "When I told him that *Ghost* was my first movie, he said, 'It's a tough industry, but it's a fun industry. Just stick it out because sometimes it can be brutal.' He was larger than life, but he was also down-to-earth, friendly, and kind."

"He was very prepared, always ready to do his job, and always expected the same of everybody else," recalled Charles Bukey, first company grip on *Ghost*, who also felt Patrick was pleasant and kind.

Initially, Zucker planned to use body doubles for the love scene between Patrick and Demi, but neither of them would hear of it. According to Zucker, Patrick said, "he felt it was so sensuous and so romantic that it said more than naked stand-in actors."

While Patrick could have sizzled in Mickey Rourke's part in *9½ Weeks*, Michael Douglas's role in *Basic Instinct* or Richard Gere's in *American Gigolo*, he would never have been tempted into playing any of them.

"We had a policy of no full frontal nudity for both our actors and our actresses, with the very rare exception of an important role in a big film with a really well-known to us director. And the main thing we taught our clients was 'no vulgarity,'" Lois Zetter said.

In this arena at least, Patrick listened to his managers. Then there was the issue of the shyness that would have always prevented him from taking part in an explicit soft-porn sex scene. And since the days of *North and South*, he had found filming even the most romantic love scenes difficult.

He and Lisa rehearsed the *Ghost* love scene together beforehand in an attempt to circumvent his embarrassment.

"It's weird to know that some people in the audience are thinking, 'Okay, let's watch how Patrick Swayze does it!' " he said, then admitted he was afraid that if he failed to fly the flag, audiences would carp, "That boy can act or dance, but he's hung like a field mouse."

"Patrick's face turned bright red when we would even talk about the [love] scene," Demi laughingly recalled afterward.

When he did manage to overcome his embarrassment, he voiced his feelings about the love scene and discovered that she felt the same. "It was exciting to me that Demi was as passionate as I was to make love scenes about two human beings connecting with their eyes and their hearts," he said.

Although their *Ghost* love scene would become one of the most celebrated ever made, Patrick and Demi were unaware of it at the time. "We had no idea that was going to turn into the most famous love scene in history," he said. "We were just actors trying to do the best job in the world."

One of their greatest challenges was to give the impression that he and Demi had been together for a long time and knew each other extremely well. "The whole thing was so awkward. It was, I swear, so embarrassing. I told Patrick that I thought we were back in high school," Demi said.

The scene begins at two in the morning when Molly, unable to sleep, is sculpting a pot, Sam interrupts her, straddles the chair behind her, covers her hands with his own, and together they crush and remold a phallic-looking column of clay.

At the outset the pottery scene wasn't particularly erotic to shoot for either Demi, Patrick, or any of the cast and crew on the set, many

PATRICK SWAYZE: *one last dance* 127

of whom were splashed all over with clay that flew off the wheel at an alarming rate.

Ever the romantic and a true Method actor, Patrick didn't care. "Getting all that mud stuff all over my arms—that was pretty sexy. Definitely got my juices going," he said.

Originally the pottery wheel and the dancing scene were intended to be two separate scenes. But instead of stopping at the end of the pottery scene, a shirtless Patrick and Demi segued straight into dancing an erotically charged dance together to the strains of the Righteous Brothers' "Unchained Melody."

"It was one of those times in both of our careers when something happened and both of us came alive," Patrick said. "The electricity between them dancing following the pottery scene was so electric that Jerry said we don't need the love making, this is the love scene," Bruce Joel Rubin reported.

Afterward, Patrick admitted that during the scene, in order to summon up his passion, he thought of Lisa, of "that core feeling about the person you love. It's there all the time. All you gotta do is call it up."

Lisa was often on the set, and, like most people who saw her and Patrick together, Jerry Zucker found their relationship to be heartwarming and inspiring and observed, "When they're together, they're all loving—but a lot of people are like that. What's more telling is how much Patrick talks about Lisa when she's not around. He credits her for his success."

Patrick believed profoundly in *Ghost*, and even before the July 13, 1990, release date, he declared, "*Ghost* will be a big word-of-mouth movie. It's really the audience that pulls the strings, so I don't even want to hear advance reviews. But the grapevine is that it'll be a big hit this summer."

Of all of Patrick's movies, *Ghost* was one of his favorites. "It's a movie I'm proud of because it has good things to say to the human race," he said.

On a private level, he and Lisa were trying hard to have a child

together, and she wore a white pure crystal in her belly button because she believed that could enhance her fertility.

In October 1989, during the shooting of *Ghost*, she and Patrick
received the good news that she was pregnant. On Valentine's Day
of the following year, Lisa went to her doctor's office for an ultrasound and Patrick went with her. Afterward, Patrick was called into
the office, where the ultrasound picture was displayed on a monitor.
The baby was dead.

They were both heartbroken. And when he called his mother to
give her the sad news, he was crying. "He told me he and Lisa had
their own little ritual of saying good-bye," Patsy recalled. "He said he
walked outside and looked out over the hills and saw a shooting star.
He said, 'I just know that was my baby saying good-bye to me.' "

Lisa was equally shattered by the loss of their child and—a year
and a half later—said, "I felt like I had lost a person—a person I was
never going to get to know." Yet at the same time, taking a leaf out of
Patrick's positive approach to life, she took comfort in the thought
that losing the baby had "put me in touch with how much I cared. It
woke me up to the love I felt for the child, Patrick, and other things
in my life."

Perhaps as a form of therapy, she and Patrick now threw themselves into work with a vengeance, with Lisa embarking on the biggest break of her career, playing the part of policewoman Carla Frost
in *Super Force*, a futuristic sci-fi TV series filmed in Miami and set in
2020, for which she went on to make twenty-three episodes.

While she was away on location, she and Patrick spent more
time apart since the days when they first met and he attended Harkness Ballet school in New York while she remained back in Houston.
But just as they had coped then by calling and writing, now they
talked on the phone every single night for often as long as three
hours at a time.

"No matter where we are in the world, we make a point of talking at least once a day. We never let two or three weeks pass without

seeing each other—even if it means flying all night for only twelve hours together," Lisa revealed.

In June 1990, perhaps in anticipation that *Ghost* would become a big box-office success, they formed their own production company, calling it "Troph" after the high-school nickname he was given in recognition of all his athletic trophies, and he went on to sign a deal with Twentieth Century Fox.

After the July 13, 1990, release of *Ghost*, as he had always predicted, the movie did indeed become the hit of the summer, beating even *Pretty Woman* at the box office and ending up as 1990's number one movie, grossing $180.6 million in just 115 days.

Moreover, the Hollywood Foreign Press Association honored him by nominating him for Best Performance by an Actor in a Motion Picture Musical or Comedy. He was up against Gérard Depardieu in *Green Card*, Johnny Depp in *Edward Scissorhands*, Macaulay Culkin in *Home Alone*, and Richard Gere in *Pretty Woman*. However, the Golden Globe went to Gérard Depardieu, who received it on January 19, 1991, at the Beverly Hills Hilton.

Patrick may not have won the award, but thanks to *Ghost* he was back on top again, on the A-list, a major Hollywood player in serious contention for parts in all the major films that were about to be made. He had money, power, and now unlimited clout in Hollywood. What he would do with it remained to be seen.

It is said that an adult's culinary appetites are predicated on the relationship he had with food as a child. In Patrick's case, his mother didn't cook much, preferring instead to snack on apples and yogurt, even at Denny's or the International House of Pancakes, where she and the studio girls would often end the day after class. Patrick himself didn't need to watch his weight much but disliked starting the day with breakfast, and usually just had coffee instead. Now, though, following in the footsteps of De Niro, who already owned New York's Tribeca Grill, and preceding Kevin Costner, Johnny Depp, and Arnold Schwarzenegger, all of whom would open restaurants in the future, Patrick plowed some of the profits of *Ghost* into his own restaurant on Manhattan's Third Avenue, which, perhaps as a nod to his wild bike rides of yore, he named Mulholland Drive Café.

Although Patrick didn't specify how much time he would be spending at the restaurant, his coowner, Bobby Ochs, shrewdly promised, "When he is in town, he will come by," and fans flocked to Mulholland Drive Café, where they supped on roasted baby chicken at $9.50, hamburgers at $5.50, or warm chicken salad at $8.50.

Next he signed to make *Point Break*, opting to play the supporting role of Bodhi, a scruffy surfer turned bank robber, with Keanu Reeves and Gary Busey playing the leading parts of two FBI agents investigating him.

Yet again, Patrick had made a surprising choice of movies. But, drawing an analogy from his childhood, if starring in the romantic *Ghost* was the equivalent to performing "On the Good Ship Lollipop," then the high-octane action movie *Point Break* was the equivalent of playing Tarzan in the forest.

However, after *Ghost* his legions of fans were probably hoping that he'd play another romantic character in his next movie. But Patrick had always marched to the beat of his own personal drummer and this time around wanted to star in a movie that was fun for him to make.

His manager, Lois Zetter, was once again disappointed in his choice of movie and didn't mince words in voicing her conviction. "I would tell him why he shouldn't take certain parts, but he wouldn't listen. And I just couldn't sit there and agree with him if I didn't," she said, adding, "He didn't like me very much at that stage."

"I think one of the reasons he left my management company in the end was that I was too much like Patsy. And, if anything, he wanted a father, not a mother."

Whether subconsciously or not, Patsy's influence still lingered, driving him to risk his life by doing his own stunts, pitting himself against the elements, proving over and over that he was the best, that—metaphorically speaking—he could still kick higher, twirl faster, better than anyone else and demonstrate, "Look, Ma! No hands!"

All in all, deep in his psyche, the rebellious nine-year-old boy who risked his life by jumping off two-storey buildings to the delight of construction workers who'd paid him $1 to do so, still lived on as brave and foolhardy as in the past.

World-renowned Viennese-born New York psychoanalyst Dr. Erika Padan Freeman, who studied with Freud's pupil Theodore Reich, says that Patrick's self-confessed tendency to play with death may well be rooted in his birth.

"His difficult birth indicates an extremely strong personality being born. And it is not impossible that when he was a child, he overheard people around him talking a lot about how he almost died but survived. And after that, he may have unconsciously wanted to confirm that he could get away with it again—almost dying, then surviving. Proving that he really is invincible," she said.

But if Patrick was also spurred on to risk and danger because he believed he would impress his mother by jousting with death and surviving, he was sadly mistaken. Ironically, rather than being dazzled when hearing details of his increasingly more reckless than usual physical exploits on *Point Break*, Patsy was dismayed.

But even she knew that she was powerless to curb him and that nothing and no one could curtail his craving to fly far too close to the sun. "I know he's really suffered making all the physical scenes in his movies," she said. "But I can't say 'you can't do that,' because that will make him just go and do it!"

Of course, to paraphrase Freud, sometimes a cigar is just a cigar, and aside of any subliminal effect that his mother might have had on him, Patrick was clear about what he saw as the major reason for accepting the part. "To be honest, it gave me a chance to become a licensed skydiver and to fall off some of the biggest waves in the world," he said. "I've always played with death, like motorcycle stuff and diving off the cliffs in Acapulco without knowing the tides. I've loved walking the cliff's edge emotionally all my life. But rather than resist that tendency, I've tried to embrace it; to turn [it] into a power and an asset rather than something destructive."

He was brave and determined, and although at the start of shooting he was both a surfing novice and a skydiving novice, his goal was to master both skills to such a high degree that he didn't have to have a stunt double to perform them for him.

He received skydiving lessons from instructor Jim Wallace, who called him a natural. "He wanted to do free style right off the bat—flips, twirls, spins. I had to continually hold him down."

He flung himself into both skydiving and surfing with a vengeance. His costar, Keanu Reeves, wasn't so foolhardy. "I jumped once, just to kinda check it out, on a Saturday," he remembered. "But everybody kept jumping and eventually the company had to kind of say, 'We're going to sue you guys if you don't stop jumping out of airplanes.' I mean, during the course of filming I think Patrick jumped thirty times."

To the horror of the movie's producer, Peter Abrams, Patrick was so enamored of skydiving that he did it off-camera, on weekends, as well. "Once I got over the abject terror of jumping out of a perfectly good airplane and realized that you could truly fly, it was the most alive feeling that you ever felt," Patrick said, adding, "Once I got into seeing it as a ballet or as a tumbling routine, fear went out."

"Patrick started jumping on his own," Peter remembered, "and he used to come in and say, 'Look, Peter, look what I did this weekend,' and I would say, 'You can't do that. Insurance . . .' Ultimately we agreed that if he would stop jumping while we were filming he could ultimately jump out of the plane after everything was done and that's what he did."

"It's very funny," Patrick said afterward, "because I had to battle the universe to get to do the skydiving in the movie and I never came close to dying once, but they never said one word about me getting my brains pounded in by the biggest surf on this planet and I almost died six to ten times. I thought I was going to be outta here."

His surfing teacher, Dennis Jarvis, who acted as adviser on the movie, observed that he was eager to learn but felt that he wanted to improve at a rate faster than his ability. "Patrick was very meticulous," he said. "He wanted to succeed even farther than what he could do."

Given the often-treacherous, fast-paced action scenes he insisted on doing, Patrick suffered predictable injuries during the making of *Point Break*. His stunt double Scott Wilder, who was on hand for those scenes he was categorically banned from doing himself, recalled: "His knee blew up. His knee was giant. It was triple the size of a normal knee. He would have the doctor come down and drain it at the end of the night and the next morning he was there, charging."

He injured his sternum as well because, as he put it, "I was on much bigger waves than I had any business being on. So we had to groove out my surfboards, build up my wet suits to try to get me off that bone, but of course that's not possible because every time you turtle through a wave, it just slams you. All I cared about was getting good enough so that when they cut away from me to my stunt double, I wouldn't look like Bobby Darin on a sound stage in a fifties beach bunny movie," he said.

Kathryn Bigelow, the movie's director, was inordinately impressed by Patrick's dedication. "I find him remarkably genuine. Given all the eccentricities of this business, it's extremely rare. He gives five thousand percent of himself," she said, later comparing him to the late actor Steve McQueen.

Kathryn attributed much of his genuineness to the soul-searching he had undergone for many years. His commitment to New Age philosophies was in evidence during filming. He kept what he described as "my new magic wand" in his trailer and happily showed visitors to the set the foot-long braided silver scepter with embedded gems and an amethyst at its tip. Round his neck he wore a black tourmaline crystal with an opal set in the center. "It's supposed to dispel negative energy," he said.

Lisa believed in crystals just as passionately and said, "Patrick wears two special kinds of agate crystals, an Indian crystal around his neck to give him physical strength and a fire crystal in his belt buckle to increase stamina and endurance."

Audiences liked the movie; critics, as usual with Patrick's movies, did not. And although *Point Break* would ultimately attain cult status, the truth was that the majority of his fans really wanted to see Patrick Swayze only as the romantic hero and had very little time for him in action pictures. To his deep chagrin, by and large, it was his body in a wet suit that drew the most raves, not his performance.

ten

BREAKING POINT

On October 27, 1990, in a radical departure both from his action man and romantic hero persona, Patrick hosted *Saturday Night Live*, parodying his own image in a skit with Chris Farley in which they were both bare-chested but for a bow tie and competing at a Chippendales audition. "Once the producers saw that I was completely willing to make fun of myself and that I have no reverence about anything, then we went crazy from dirty square dancing to a love story with Hanz and Franz," Patrick said.

Staying true to his self-avowed desire to continually ring the changes in his career, when he read the script of *City of Joy*, adapted from the fact-based novel of the same name, he felt he had found his mirror image, his other self, in Dr. Max Lowe. Lowe, an American doctor who visited Calcutta in the sixties, was so shattered by the poverty he found that he remained there and treated lepers. "He was president of his class, captain of his football team; he's gonna be this and gonna be that. But he's never good enough," he said. "That was my point of view about why I should do this role and no one else: because it was about my life at the moment."

City of Joy's distinguished director, Roland Joffé, had no doubt whatsoever about Patrick's burning desire to star in the movie; his eagerness was so transparent that he had asked to see Joffé ahead of their scheduled meeting, since he couldn't endure the waiting. "I came as close to begging for a role as I ever have in my life," Patrick admitted, recalling that he had sworn to Roland Joffé that "I would work myself to the bone for him. It blew him away.

"I told him that I might not be the best actor on this planet, but that I would give him a hundred percent of my heart, soul, and mind and that I would become Max. Then I called my agent and told him that if he lost this role for me, he was a dead person. I told him I would do it for nothing." The part was his.

During the first week of February 1991, Patrick and Lisa flew to Calcutta, where he would be spending four months on location for *City of Joy*, and checked into the luxurious Oberoi Grand Hotel there. Within hours, Joffé—who clearly understood the caliber and depth of the Method actor he'd hired—called and informed Patrick that a car was waiting for him. Given that the movie began with Patrick's character, Max, feeling alienated and alone in Calcutta, from the outset Joffé wanted Patrick to experience what it was like to be a stranger in a strange land.

When Patrick's chauffeur-driven limo pulled out of the opulent hotel grounds, he was immediately confronted by the harrowing poverty that is the essence of Calcutta: beggars flinging themselves in front of his car, crying out for him to throw them a coin or a crust of bread, women with babies covered in flies, open sewers, a seething ocean of humanity.

"It's so horrifying that out of self-preservation you want to turn it off," he said. "But I couldn't turn it off because of Max. I had to experience it like Max was experiencing it. So the way you react to it is to have a great deal of shame and guilt for coming from a country with so much."

In the interests of exposing Patrick to yet more authenticity, Joffé later dispatched him to Mother Teresa's Home for Dying Destitutes—Nirmal Hriday. There a harried clinic nurse mistook him for a volunteer and immediately put him to work in the pharmacy, where he was charged with changing the bandage of a seven-year-old boy.

"The little boy, three months before, had third-degree burns from his shoulder to his fingertips. And when he finally came back, it was my job to get the bandage off him. But it had grown into his body," Patrick said. He cast around for surgical instruments to remove the bandage and found that there weren't any. He knew that his only resort was to use his Swiss army knife. First, though, he peeled off the bandages, then he bathed the boy's wounds in a saline solution.

"The only time this little boy whimpered was when I got halfway down to his biceps . . . Tears were streaming down my face trying to get this [bandage] off, but I couldn't believe the pain I knew he was going through. And he never whimpered but once.

"As time went on I realized that they [the people of Calcutta] don't need or desire my pity. They just want to look in my eyes and have a real person looking back," he said.

At the time of the shoot, political turmoil was raging through India. Bengal's Communist-dominated state government made *City of Joy* the excuse for attacks on the New Delhi government, which had permitted the movie to be filmed in Calcutta.

As the temperature rocketed to 105 degrees, protests that the movie, which accurately depicted Calcutta's vast poverty and corruption, was offensive to the city escalated. Six small bombs were thrown at the set during demonstrations against the movie, and the death of a local journalist was wrongly blamed on the crew.

Early on in the shoot, Lisa was scheduled to go back to America for a six-week stay. She was on the point of leaving when, during one of the first scenes shot in the streets of Calcutta, 1,500 protesters surged toward the cast and crew, hurling sticks and stones at them. Patrick and Lisa were rushed to safety, where she chain-smoked and he stayed close by her. "It was a frightening experience," an insider said.

Once the demonstration died down, Lisa left for America. However, before she did, in a misguided but innocent attempt to moti-

vate Patrick to give the best performance of his life, she harked back
to their Method training and urged him, "There's got to be a lot of
grief down there that you have not been willing to look at. If you allow yourself to go down and look at that pain and live in it for Max,
you'll be wonderful."

However, by delving into his character through Method, he
would be embarking on an exploration that would end up unnerving
him completely.

"Method acting requires a great deal of emotional stamina. It
can be very painful, very deep, and very dark, as the actor has to
wallow in his own pain and then get himself out of it afterward. It's a
dangerous journey and some actors become so identified with a character that they can't get out. And it takes a very courageous actor to
make that journey," psychoanalyst Dr. Erika Padan Freeman, who
specializes in treating creative personalities, said.

In order to experience the full depths of Lowe's despair at the
horrors he was witnessing in Calcutta, he stopped sleeping and began losing weight. "I'd lock myself in my room at night, pacing and
racked with sobs," he recalled. "My face was red and my lips were
swollen and I'd have to try and work. I had to find that place where
I'd be willing to kill myself. I didn't like that place.

"This is a role that I can't turn the light switch off . . . that's the
thing that is eating me up. At the end of the day, when they call
wrap, I'm all dressed up and nowhere to go. I have this massive emotion and what to do with it? I pace all night."

What Patrick didn't realize at the time was that he was suffering
the negative effects of his own Method acting techniques in very
much the same way as Marlon Brando had while making *Last Tango
in Paris* in 1973. As Paul, a middle-aged expatriate American lacer-
ated by the death of his wife, Brando improvised a monologue that
was autobiographical in that—in true Method style—much of it was
conjured up from his own painful feelings about the death of his
mother. Brando suffered to such an extent during the monologue
that in his autobiography he wrote: "When it was finished I decided

I wasn't ever again going to destroy myself emotionally to make a movie."

Patrick was obviously now employing similar Method techniques to his part as Brando had to his and suffering in the same way. However, unlike Brando, he was unprepared to stop destroying himself emotionally in the cause of making a movie.

Instead, in the dead of night, he would spend hours poring over the script, chain-smoking. The part affected him so deeply that he would sometimes have tears in his eyes even when it wasn't his scene.

Alone in Calcutta without Lisa to guide him through the dark labyrinth of his own emotions, he began to sink into the abyss of his own psyche. His costar Shabana Azmi remembered seeing him looking really lonely. "I have yet to see another human being so completely entwined with his partner as he is with Lisa," she observed, "and he was completely lost, he looked very pale. I sat with him and said, 'Are you all right?' "

Now, on *City of Joy*, that loneliness and longing for Lisa was overlaid with his visceral reaction to playing Max. And although cast and crew all liked him immensely, sometimes his intensity became too much for them to take. Some days, when filming had ended, his costars Pauline Collins and Shabana Azmi were relaxing by the Oberoi's spectacular pool when Patrick would suddenly materialize, his eyes wide, script in hand, eager to share his latest insight about his character. "I drove them crazy. They almost started running away from me after a while," he admitted.

"He's the most hardworking actor I have ever met in my life," Shabana Azmi—who has appeared in more than one hundred films—said diplomatically.

After the emotional trauma he'd experienced while making *City of Joy*, he decided to make an attempt at giving up smoking, a surprising decision considering how fragile he must still have been. Lisa also took the treatment—acupuncture in the ear. At the time he was sincere in his vow, "I want smoking out of my life," and smoked only

Carlton Lights, but in the end he didn't succeed in kicking the habit after all.

In contrast, he was not tempted by a series of lucrative financial offers that came his way around the same time, all of which were in conflict with his high principles.

He reportedly nixed a $1 million deal offered him by an under-wear manufacturer willing to pay that much just for him to put his signature on their line of bikini briefs. Another company offered him a fortune to name a cologne "Patrick" after him. As determined as ever not to allow himself to be identified as a sex symbol and nothing else, he turned them down flat.

He and Lisa had always believed that the crystals they always wore would protect them from harm. Those crystals may well have held him in good stead when, at the end of July 1991, he was in-volved in a serious accident. He was driving a six-hundred-pound horse-drawn buggy down a hill at Rancho Bizarro when a dog sud-denly barked and the petrified horse bolted.

The buggy's left front wheel got stuck in a hole in the ground and fell off, and the buggy flipped over. Patrick hit the ground, and—like a professional stuntman right at the top of his game—just managed to roll out of the way before the buggy fell on top of him and crushed him to death.

Miraculously, he suffered only minor cuts and bruises. He had always loved to duel with death but now, for the very first time in his life, he had been close to dying for real. His lucky escape served only to make him and those who loved him conclude that he really must be born under a lucky star, with at least nine lives left to live.

Then, on August 26, 1991, he was awarded *People* magazine's accolade as "Sexiest Man Alive." To other stars receiving the award might have been euphoric, but to Patrick it was the equivalent of Marilyn being feted for posing nude for Tom Kelly's calendar, and not for her performance as Grushenka in the movie of *Crime and Punishment* instead.

Rather than denigrate the award, he made it clear that he wasn't about to allow it to inflate his ego. "You just can't afford to get too wrapped up in yourself," he pointed out. "I don't deride the people who voted for me—I'm very flattered and I thank them very much—but imagine what kind of person I would be if I went round taking that kind of stuff seriously."

He was still battling hard to dodge typecasting as a romantic leading man, nor did he welcome all the fan mania either. Patsy weighed in on the subject: "He doesn't think that his job deserves all that idolatry. He knows he's just an ordinary, down-home Texas kid."

Lisa, too, was instrumental in keeping his feet firmly on the ground, and for that he was grateful. "Lisa and I have a very irreverent way with each other," he said. "She's always kept my ego in check. That's not to say that being voted the world's sexiest man doesn't make you feel king for a day, but I don't think I'm God's gift to women or some kind of walking aphrodisiac."

Although he had professed to have given up drinking a few years before—and Lisa attended Al-Anon so that she could understand and help him—that wasn't true. He was drinking again, more than ever.

Given his family history, his drinking could have been genetic or learned or both. Swayze Mania may well have accelerated it, along with the loneliness and lack of self-worth he experienced when Lisa wasn't with him.

And there is yet another possibility. Through the decades there has always been a tendency for the most macho of actors—Errol Flynn, Richard Burton, and Richard Harris are classic examples—to feel on a subliminal level that acting, dressing up, wearing makeup, and reciting other people's lines is not a particularly masculine profession, then drinking themselves into a stupor in order to trumpet their masculinity to the world and predominantly to themselves.

Moreover, he had put his heart and soul and every iota of acting talent at his disposal into *City of Joy*, but the advance word on it was disappointing.

He had always resolutely refused to allow negativity of any kind

of unnerve him, and, as was his wont, threw himself into promoting
the movie with gusto. During the French leg of the promotion tour
he and Lisa spent a week in Paris, where they looked up their close
friend, Patsy's old pupil, choreographer Rick Odums.

"They took private classes with one of my teachers to keep in
shape," Rick remembered. "And they invited me to dinner every
night for a week, often with Roland Joffé, the movie's director.
Lisa and Patrick don't forget people. They know where they came
from."

Spending so much time with Patrick and Lisa gave Rick a perspective on both of them and on their marriage. "They are equal
partners. Neither of them takes the lead in that couple. And Lisa has
a type of fortitude about her so that she can be laid back when she
needs to lay back, and she can stand up and be very strong and very
authoritative when she needs to be," he said.

She would need all her fortitude during the months to come,
particularly during what would transpire in the aftermath of Patrick's
abortive January 1993 Las Vegas location shoot for Disney's *Father
Hood*.

At the downtown Las Vegas location, his twenty-six-foot trailer
was parked in front of the famous Horseshoe Casino—in full view
of the public—and any of his besotted fans who wanted to catch a
closer glimpse of their idol.

The temperature was an inclement 46 degrees and many of the
scenes were shot in the street. Everywhere he went, female fans lay
in wait for him, virtually stalking him, and it seemed he had no way
of escaping them.

Anxiously waiting for the two days when Lisa would fly down to
spend time with him in Las Vegas, he turned to drink, carousing the
nights away at the Shark Club on the Strip. An eyewitness, clearly
keeping score, reported that he had downed as much as two gallons
of wine, twelve Budweisers, cocktails, and rum and Cokes, and by
three in the morning he was staggering on the dance floor. A week

later, seeking help for his alcoholism, he checked into Sierra Tucson Rehabilitation Center in Arizona for a thirty-seven-day stay.

After his five-week stay at the Sierra Tucson, he resolved never to drink again, but hard as he tried to free himself of his addiction, down the line he would break his vow—with almost fatal repercussions.

Meanwhile, he was continually being offered movie parts. There was talk of him reprising his role as Orry Main in another sequel to *North and South*, but he simply wasn't interested, preferring to move forward, not back.

Many of his fans, nostalgic for that romantic character, fervently wished that he would take another part like Orry Main and must have been more than slightly dismayed when, instead, he made another western, *Tall Tale: The Unbelievable Adventures of Pecos Bill*, which he began shooting in Colorado on September 12, 1993.

Meanwhile, Lisa was hired to replace the newly pregnant Marla Maples in the Broadway production of *The Will Rogers Follies*, and signed a $3,000-a-week contract to play the part of Florenz Ziegfeld's favorite—celebrated for her fabulous cartwheels.

"I think I'm too dumb to be nervous," she said with a laugh during rehearsals. "As some point I'll be hit with a lightning bolt of terror—it always happens. But I guess the stuff is there to do, I can do very well."

There were rumors that Patrick might even be joining the cast as well. Joking that he kept on talking about donning a feather headdress and doing an Indian dance, she allowed, "You know what? I wouldn't put it past him. Musical theater gets in your blood. I know he's going to want to get into the act."

She was wrong. He knew that this was Lisa's moment and he had no intention of overshadowing her. He was rooting for her with all his might, willing her to succeed, and at intermission on opening night he was so nervous on her behalf that he thought he was about to throw up.

Thankfully, disaster was averted and her performance—including a challenging series of cartwheels—was flawless.

In a felicitous coincidence, May 27-opening night—happened to be the day after her thirty-seventh birthday. During the final curtain call, her costar, country and western singer, Larry Gatlin, who was playing Will Rogers, began the chorus of "Happy Birthday" as Patrick walked out on stage, cake in hand, and surprised her.

Afterward, he and Lisa celebrated her birthday over dinner *a deux* at the Mulholland Drive Café. Soon after, he flew back to the west coast, where he was looping *Father Hood*.

Each time he returned to New York to join Lisa during the show's run, he did all he could to make her life easier. "I'm trying to be the best backstage husband I can and provide support. I shop for everything she needs from eyelash glue to feminine things," he said.

Then, in a touchingly loyal moment, "Lisa is having a great time, and all the kids in the show are real excited to have her in it because she's a wonderful dancer and a wonderful singer and actress," he said.

In contrast to Lisa's successful Broadway debut, *Father Hood*, released on August 27, 1993, could not, by any stretch of the imagination, be classified as a success.

Lisa's stint in *The Will Rogers Follies* ended on September 4, 1993. Throughout the run Patrick had been intensely proud of her performance. However, he was less than sanguine when he read many of her fan letters. "I see the letters she gets. There are men who are head over heels in love with her. She gets flowers saying, 'Oh, you're so beautiful,' and they know she's my wife. I'm going, 'Wait a minute, slow down, dude. That's not a stunt man you see in my movies. I will kick your butt.' "

But if any love-struck man had romantic designs on Lisa, or any love-struck woman on Patrick, on May 31, 1994, when the Swayzes' sensuous, romantic dance to an instrumental version of Whitney Houston's "All the Man That I Need" at the World Music Awards in Monte Carlo was transmitted on ABC-TV, just by observing the soaring passion they both exuded for each other, they would have been firmly disabused of that notion. Afterward, his voice overflowing with emotion, Patrick said, "It was a very special experience for me for the world to see what an absolutely beautiful miracle angel she is."

There was further happiness in the cards for him when in June 1994 he splashed out $3.7 million on a Lear Jet. When the eight-seater plane was delivered, Patrick's boyish enthusiasm came to the fore. He named the plane *Baby* (presumably *not* after Jennifer Grey's character in *Dirty Dancing*) and even carried a Polaroid of it in his wallet.

Lisa, forever the fearless Texan tomboy with five brothers, was also thrilled with the plane, and—with Patrick—took flying lessons. Once qualified, they loved inviting friends to fly with them in the plane, which also boasted a killer sound system on which they would play Bonnie Raitt, and, in particular when they were breaking through clouds, the theme to the movie *Out of Africa*.

They were both jocks, both strong willed, sometimes even pig headed. In the midst of one flight, they encountered a cloud bank in front of them. Lisa was all for sneaking below it, whereas Patrick was determined to climb above it. A massive argument ensued that ended only when they landed and asked the flying instructor to arbitrate, whereupon he informed them that they were both wrong. "You should have flown right through it," he explained.

They were brave enough to have done just that. And if anyone had doubted Patrick's courage for one moment, they only had to ponder the choice of his next movie role, drag queen Vida Boheme in *To Wong Foo, Thanks for Everything, Julie Newmar*, a role and a movie that would probably have stopped Johnny Castle dead in his macho tracks.

eleven

THANKS FOR EVERYTHING

*I*t was almost ten years since Patrick had played Johnny Castle, and now he was opting to play a part so radically different that even his biggest detractors must have felt a certain respect for the artistic risk he was taking.

Only Hollywood's most experimental, cutting-edge actors—Robin Williams, James Spader, and John Cusack—had even momentarily considered taking the part of Vida, or of Noxeema or Chi Chi, the two other drag queens in *To Wong Foo* (though it was rumored for a time that Mel Gibson was actually interested in playing Vida).

From the time that Patrick first became a professional dancer, all those years ago, alternative sexual mores had been a part of his life and he'd never exhibited an iota of homophobia. He had no misgivings about playing a drag queen. Quite the reverse—he took it as a challenge.

He flew the red-eye from New York to Los Angeles, where the audition was being held, "Try to be a drag queen on no sleep. It's hard enough on a good day, much less after a bad night. I auditioned completely made up and in a dress," he said.

Noting that most actors would have projected outrageousness in the audition, he felt that approach "would be a put-down to people who didn't deserve it." Instead, he jettisoned the script and launched into a forty-five-minute monologue he'd written himself and which drew on his painful boyhood memories of getting beaten up by redneck bullies for being a ballet dancer.

A tape of his audition was sent to the movie's producer, Steven Spielberg, who watched rapt, then, perplexed, demanded, "Who is that actor? *That's Patrick Swayze?* The guy with the large forearms?"

Patrick got the part but was not thrilled about breaking the news to the second most important person in his life. "My mother was horrified when I told her about it. There was a silence on the other end of the phone," he said. "Patsy didn't want him to play a drag queen," Zetta Alderman confirmed.

Undeterred by his mother's disapproval, he even went on to model his portrayal of Vida on her and her voice on Lauren Bacall and Demi Moore, then added a soupçon of Audrey Hepburn in *Breakfast at Tiffany's.*

Lisa tutored him on how to stand and walk like a woman. "I'd get the hips, but then Lisa would tell me I'd lost the shoulders," he said.

She had kidded him to stay away from her closet and pretended to be mollified when he informed her that he was only interested in her accessories. "Think of it this way, you're not losing a husband, you're gaining a girlfriend!" he said.

Apart from his initial difficulties learning to walk like a woman, Patrick also had other problems in transforming himself into Vida: "these big Swayze forearms and hands." However, his dilemma was solved the moment he donned false nails, which forced him to be delicate in eating or dialing the phone.

The problems of his masculine arms and fingers now overcome, he still had to cope with another, more delicate issue. "What do you do with your penis? You tuck it back under. You have these 'gender benders' that they actually make for this purpose, but I almost never had to wear one unless I was wearing tight pants or something," he said.

During the eighty-day shoot, where Lisa was often on the set, he was generally compelled to get up at four in the morning just so that he could be transformed into a woman in time for shooting to begin. Each morning he was waxed and plucked and even had to submit to being shaved five times a day. Wearing high heels turned out to be the worst ordeal for him. "No matter how much they say it's your size, it never feels like it's your size. Your back is killing you," he complained. But—as professional as always—he managed to endure the discomfort till the end of the day, when he could remove his clothes and, as he put it, let "the blood flow back where it should be flowing."

He set himself rigorous standards. "I wasn't going to be happy with myself as a woman until I reached the point where I thought I was good enough to sleep with," he said. "In the beginning, I was hopeful because I was actually light years prettier than anyone dreamed. But I seemed to go downhill from there. So I had to confess to myself, 'I'm not my type.' "

Patsy, it transpired, did not have a similar sense of humor, particularly when she visited him on location. "Out comes Buddy dressed as a woman and that threw Patsy for a loop," said Zetta Alderman. "She was livid that he was playing a part in drag and said, 'I can't even believe my son is doing this!' "

His mother's disapproval aside, he had always had an unshakable sense of his own masculinity, even as a teenager studying ballet, when he was taunted for being a sissy. "I don't have anything to prove," he declared. "I'm as heterosexual as a bull moose. That's what made me so comfortable as Vida."

Before shooting began, he, John Leguizamo (Chi Chi), Wesley Snipes (Noxeema), and director Beeban Kidron did a one-night tour of Manhattan's most fashionable drag clubs.

"We made a lot of nice drag-queen friends that night," Patrick said before revealing that—by employing Method-style research tactics, asking if they dressed in drag to cloak a private sorrow—he almost alienated them.

"They were like, 'Whoa. We don't go there.' At first I thought it was denial. Then I realized these guys who dress up like women have made a specific choice to do what makes them happy. They aren't sad creatures."

By rights, the making of *To Wong Foo* should have been fun for Patrick, Wesley, and John, but from the first it was pistols at dawn. "Sometimes the competitive edge was unbelievable," said director Kidron. "Mostly it took the form of joking—my tits are better than yours, my legs, my heels. I can walk on gravel and you can't, and so on."

"I'm proud to say that I was the only one in the bunch who didn't need to wear a corset!" said Patrick, as ever determined to win the first-place ribbon.

The competition flared yet further when he filmed a scene in which, as Vida, he says to John Leguizamo, as Chi Chi, "I think they're just going to eat me up." Instead of reading the line that came next in the script, John—still in character—cracked, "You better get over yourself . . . 'Cuz you're a dinosaur and the only love you're gonna get is from a paleontologist."

In his book *Pimps, Hos, Playa Hatas, and All the Rest of My Hollywood Friends*, John Leguizamo writes that Patrick yelled Cut! and growled at him, " 'Why don't you just say the line?"

" 'Make me,' " I say.

"And he says, 'I'll punch you in your face.' "

" 'You must be PMSing,' " I say, " 'beeyatch.' "

Whereupon Patrick took a swing at John and he swung back. Wesley Snipes egged them on and the crew yelled "bitch fight!" in the background before reluctantly pulling the two men apart.

Relations between Patrick and John soured further after John's memoirs detailing their spat were published in 2006, and Patrick let it be known that he was going to punch him in the head next time they met. Luckily for John, that meeting never happened.

However, Patrick did establish a good rapport with Wesley Snipes, although they did have a few joking bouts of macho one-upmanship between scenes.

"Wesley would say, 'Excuse me, Miss Swayze, I ain't the dance dude that had to swing his butt to make history.' And I said, 'Yeah, well, I'm not that dumb ass that fell off the plane in *Passenger 57* and then had to figure a way just to get back on so there would be a plot.' We were merciless with each other but we had a good time," Patrick said.

He had more fun when they were filming the cornfield scene outside Loma, Nebraska (population 23). Just before Sheriff Dollard (played by the late Chris Penn) pulled Patrick's car off the road and interrogated him, Patrick covertly slid a corncob into the front of his underwear. Consequently, when Penn put his hand up Patrick's skirt, his expression of shock at what he found there was real.

Heidi McGowen, *To Wong Foo*'s second assistant director, described working with Patrick as an enjoyable experience. "I was fairly new to the job and he went out of his way to help me. I was always making mistakes and he was just like, 'You're fine. You're doin' it.'"

She noted that he and Lisa always had their dogs with them on set, and was also extremely impressed by his kindness in offering the crew rides back to L.A. in his plane.

"One time the executive producer was asking me all these questions over the radio and I was nervous. Patrick was on the radio as well and he said to the producer, 'Give her a break and let her breathe a minute, so she can answer all your questions!'"

As always, Patrick was ever the gentleman. When Heidi lost her father two weeks into filming and flew home to help the family, Patrick and Lisa sent flowers to the funeral. "When I got back they brought me into his trailer, said they were so sorry, and asked if there was anything they could do. They had all these crystals in the trailer and they said that I should pick whichever one I wanted. I picked a beautiful clear rose quartz which I still have to this day. He and Lisa were both incredibly friendly to everyone and she's very supportive of him."

When shooting ended in August 1994, Patrick hosted the wrap party at Mulholland Drive Café, where his guests included a bevy of drag queens, including Miss Coco Peru (a.k.a. Clinton Leupp), who had coached Patrick for the role and had one line in the movie.

"Of course, he's Patrick Swayze and people want to be around him and take his photograph, but he made it clear by his actions that that was not what he was there for," remembered Coco before going on. "At one point he pulled me and my guest off to the side and said: 'Let's just sit down and talk. We don't need to deal with that.' And we sat down around a table and just chatted away. He made sure that we were having a good time and everyone treated us properly."

Sadly for everyone involved with *To Wong Foo*, after the movie was released on September 8, 1995, although it took in a respectable $9 million at the box office during the first week, the critics were lukewarm and tended to compare it unfavorably with *The Adventures of Priscilla, Queen of the Desert*, which had a similar storyline but was set in Australia.

However, audiences and fans alike still loved Patrick as Vida. "There's something about Vida that has turned people on," he said at the time. "Women seem to feel that I'm a sexier man because I can understand a woman's needs, and I can empathize with them. I've had a lot of fan mail as a result."

And when Lisa saw the movie, she was overcome by the poignancy of his performance, confessing, "He made me cry two or three times in the middle of this raucous, fun movie. He'd be great as a girlfriend!"

Patsy, too, was ultimately impressed by Patrick's performance. "She said she thought he did a wonderful job," Zetta Alderman reported.

Later that year, Patrick's acting in *To Wong Foo* garnered the recognition he so richly deserved when he was nominated for a Golden

Globe for the Best Performance by an Actor in a Motion Picture Musical and Comedy category. His fellow nominees were Michael Douglas in *The American President*, Steve Martin in *Father of the Bride Part II*, Harrison Ford in *Sabrina*, and John Travolta in *Get Shorty*. Travolta won the award.

On November 15, 1994, Patrick began shooting *Three Wishes*, which would take place over four months in and around Los Angeles. A romantic fantasy costarring Mary Elizabeth Mastrantonio, *Three Wishes* centered on a chance encounter between two unlikely protagonists who become soul mates.

According to director Martha Coolidge, Patrick was always the first choice for the part of the hero, Jack, a tramp who is hit by Mastrantonio's car, after which she nurses him to recovery and then falls in love with him. "Patrick is a uniquely sensitive person. He's a wonderful person to work with, good with people and children and animals," Martha said.

She knew, without a shadow of a doubt, that he would be perfect to play Jack because of his own strong spirituality, his "interest in spiritual matters, his physicality and the kind of probing intelligence and need to learn," she said.

"When we started talking about the character and the Zen philosophy, for every resource book we knew, Patrick mentioned four more!" producer Clifford Green said.

The movie's theme of two dramatically different people meeting and falling in love resonated deeply with Patrick. "The love story aspect of this film is about soul mates and that soul mates do exist in this world. I have long felt that my wife Lisa is my soul mate, that we have lived a life together before this one," he said.

Patrick's childhood friend Larry Ward had once characterized Patrick's parents' marriage in terms of Patsy being the fire and Big Buddy the rock. The identical dynamics were also apparent in Patrick and Lisa's marriage, except that he had always been the fire and Lisa the rock, and that was never more true than in the first week of December 1994.

Four-year-old Patrick, with his parents after swimming in an East Texas lake nearby the oil fields where Big Buddy was working that summer. (*Credit:* Michael Ochs Archives/ Getty Images)

Patrick at three, outside the Oak Forest house, already exuding self-confidence and star quality. (*Credit:* Michael Ochs Archives/ Getty Images)

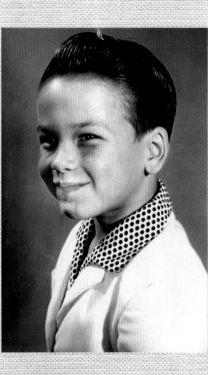

A portrait of Patrick at seven, beaming and ready to take on the world. (*Credit:* Michael Ochs Archives/Getty Images)

The class of '61, with nine-year-old Patrick spruce in collar and tie (back row, third from right) at St. Rose of Lima School, Houston. (*Credit:* Michael Ochs Archives/Getty Images)

The Swayze home in Candlelight Wood where Patrick lived until his early twenties. (*Credit:* Wendy Leigh, 2009)

Number 23 in the front row, just like his mother always told him to be. (*Credit:* Michael Ochs Archives/Getty Images)

Patrick dancing with his first love, Nikki D'Amico, at his mother's studio in 1969. She was succeeded by Terri Harsch, Sandra Perez, and, finally, Lisa. (Credit: Michael Ochs Archives/Getty Images)

Young love in bloom by the side of Lake Travis, the night after the prom, before which Patrick had tried to teach Terri to dance like the wind, but failed. (Credit: Terri Harsch Smith)

Patrick and Terri hiking in Huntsville State Park toward the end of their romance. (Credit: Terri Harsch Smith)

Lisa and Patrick on June 12, 1975, their wedding day, photographed during the reception at her home. She made her wedding dress and his tuxedo as they couldn't afford to buy them. (*Credit:* Michael Ochs Archives/ Getty Images)

Patrick demonstrates his classical ballet technique during rehearsal for a 1976 Harkness Ballet performance. (*Credit:* Michael Ochs Archives/ Getty Images)

Patsy supervises her "angel" and her "beautiful boy" rehearsing for his 1978 Broadway role in *Grease*. (*Credit:* Michael Ochs Archives/Getty Images)

Patsy, Patrick, and Lisa on the porch of the family home in Oak Forest in the summer of 1979, a few months before Patrick made his first movie, *Skate Town U.S.A.* (*Credit:* Michael Ochs Archives/Getty Images)

Patrick kissing Lisa at the October 1979 *Skate Town U.S.A.* premiere at Flippers Roller Rink in L.A. Although Lisa looks happy, Patrick didn't like the movie at all. (*Credit:* Fotos International/Hulton Archive/ Getty Images)

The last picture of the Swayze family taken by Lisa, just before Big Buddy's sudden death. The family had just finished playing ball in their backyard. Back row, l to r, Patrick, Donny, Sean, and front row, Patsy, Big Buddy, Bambi. (*Credit:* Michael Ochs Archives/Getty Images)

Patrick at his handsomest and most protective, with Lesley-Anne Down in a scene from *North and South*, the blockbuster mini-series which made him a star. (*Credit:* ABC/ Photofest)

Patrick and Jennifer Grey re-create their off-camera horsing around for a scene which ultimately ended up in *Dirty Dancing*. (*Credit:* Kobal/The Kobal Collection/Getty Images)

Patrick and Jennifer (or is it her stunt double?) in the celebrated lake scene during which Patrick injured his already fragile knee. (*Credit*: Kobal/The Kobal Collection/ Getty Images)

Patrick in a brooding Brando moment during a break while making *Dirty Dancing*. (*Credit*: Kobal/The Kobal Collection/Getty Images)

Patrick and Jennifer at the *Dirty Dancing* premiere after-party. (*Credit*: Time Life Pictures/ Time & Life Pictures/Getty Images)

Patrick at his home, Rancho Bizarro, with one of his beloved
poodles in 1987. (*Credit:* Michael Ochs Archives/Getty Images)

A suitably menacing Patrick tries out a karate move in readiness for one of the more violent fight scenes in *Road House*. (*Credit*: Kobal/The Kobal Collection/Getty Images)

A romantic moment from the notorious *Ghost* pottery scene in which Patrick got splashed with clay but said it turned him on. (*Credit:* Kobal/The Kobal Collection/Getty Images)

Patrick's passionate and touching last dance with Demi Moore in *Ghost*. (*Credit:* Kobal/The Kobal Collection/Getty Images)

Patrick and Keanu Reeves bonding during the filming of *Point Break*.
(*Credit:* Fotos International/Hulton Archive/Getty Images)

Patrick resplendent in drag, strutting his feminine stuff in *To Wong Foo*. (*Credit:* Kobal/The Kobal Collection/Getty Images)

Patrick in top-to-toe Chanel, along with Wesley Snipes (in braids), and John Leguizamo, not particularly happy after some of his scenes with Patrick. (*Credit:* Kobal/The Kobal Collection/Getty Images)

Patrick and Lisa during happy times at the 2000 *Vanity Fair* post–Oscar night party. (*Credit:* Sam Levi/WireImage/Getty Images)

February 25, 2006, at the Day of Dance for Heart Health. (*Credit:* Gary Gershoff/WireImage/ Getty Images)

"Buddy called me, distraught," Zetta Alderman remembered. "I thought something had happened to Patsy. He said, 'It's not Patsy, but I have very bad news. Are you okay to hear it?' I said I was, and he said, 'Vicky committed suicide.' I could tell that he was just about to break down. He had just seen his sister a few days before. He loved her a great deal and she thought he owned the moon and was a wonderful dancer.

"After her two marriages broke up and she began to have serious mental problems, Buddy made sure she had the best doctors. He bought her a car, paid for her apartment, and took care of all her medical bills. And after she committed suicide, none of the family wanted Patsy to see her dead body, so Buddy went in and identified her for the authorities. It was heartbreaking for him."

Vicky was buried next to their father, in the Simi Valley cemetery, under the shade of the Texas pine tree her mother had planted. The words "She dances on the wind" are etched on her headstone.

Patrick felt at the time that her death had changed his life. "It was hard not to feel responsible, that I could have done something to prevent it," he said despairingly. "The longer your life goes on, the more death you face. After my father, my manager, and then my sister died, I started to feel like I was cursed," he said.

"The only thing you can do in those circumstances is to find some kind of meaning. You have to take that moment and make a promise to yourself that you will honor the spirit of the person you have lost for as long as you live."

He tried to distract himself from the pain of Vicky's death by concentrating on his work in *Three Wishes*. However, the reception his current movie, *Tall Tale: The Unbelievable Adventures of Pecos Bill* (held back after filming was completed in the fall of 1993), received did not bode well for *Three Wishes* when it opened on March 21, 1995, either. "I did *Tall Tale* because I needed to inspire the little boy in me," he said. He had always been upfront that many of the parts he picked were merely vehicles for him to live out one fantasy or another: surfing, ice hockey, kickboxing, and now cowboys and Indians.

It was five years since *Ghost*, yet he seemed impervious to the reality that he hadn't had a hit in a long time and needed one if his career was to endure in cutthroat Hollywood. However, it increasingly became clear that he simply didn't care whether it did or it didn't. "If these movies are hits, then that's cool. If they're not hits, then wait until the next one," he declared defiantly.

"My agent hates me for saying this, but ten years ago I decided I'm gonna have a great time screwing up my career," he said in a startling confession made during an interview with *Gulf News*, finally offering his own explanation for his often-disastrous career choices.

He had often made those choices because he longed to escape from the celluloid straitjacket of his romantic idol fame, and to stretch his acting ability, but it also may well be that he never really felt that he deserved all that adulation and then unconsciously set about smashing it.

In June 1995 he and Lisa celebrated their twentieth wedding anniversary by throwing a party on the grounds of Rancho Bizarro for their closest friends and family. As a salsa band played under the stars, Lisa made a heartwarming but somewhat cryptic speech to Patrick, thanking him for "the best three years of my life."

"He was trying to figure out which three years she was talking about," Lisa and Patrick's personal assistant, Rosi Hygate, recalled in an interview with Margaret Howden, president of the Patrick Swayze International Fan Club, leaving the answer up in the air, perhaps because Lisa had chosen to keep it private between her and Patrick.

That same month, in circumstances which indicated that a taste for reckless adventuring simmered in the blood of both Swayze brothers, Don was involved in a near-fatal accident.

Like Patrick, Don was also an actor and a self-confessed adrenaline junkie, and whenever he could, he pursued his hobby of parachuting off tall buildings. After safely performing almost two thousand jumps from buildings as diverse as a nine hundred-foot Las

Vegas tower and practically every major building in L.A., he was both fearless and experienced.

However, on June 14, 1995, in the midst of a jump from a six hundred-foot San Diego navy tower, the special parachute he had strapped to his back failed to open. Don—who, earlier in his acting career had played a skydiving stuntman in the movie *Drop Zone*—bounced off the tower, slammed into the ground, and shattered forty bones in his left foot, his left hand, his pelvis, and his left thigh.

Doctors doubted that he would ever walk again, and Patrick paid all his hospital bills so that he would get the best treatment. But after a three-hour operation during which a steel rod was inserted into his left thigh and secured with two steel screws and the bones in his foot were also reset, he made somewhat of a recovery.

Thus it seemed that the Swayze brothers had yet another trait in common apart from being adrenaline junkies: Both of them had a tendency to look death in the face and then, in an eleventh-hour miracle, ultimately survive.

However, tragically for Patrick, no miracle could save his beloved eleven-year-old, 115-pound Rhodesian ridgeback, Cody, when—in the summer of 1995—Cody contracted cancer.

Patrick had always taken Cody with him on location, both as his bodyguard and his friend. "I could look at him across a room of three hundred drunken people, give him a command with my eyes to watch somebody, and he would do it," Patrick said.

He stayed with Cody in the hospital around the clock, refusing to leave him alone for even a second.

"When I saw them taking away his IV, I broke down and wept. Our animals are our children, so watching him die was the most difficult thing I've done in my life," he said.

"Cody dying was like my son dying. Cody and I went everywhere together. The night Cody died, all the animals on the ranch went into mourning. The cats, the peacocks, the horses, every single animal. Oh yeah, those guys knew. I went up to the hill where we'd made a grave and the only animal that came with me was the youngest poodle. That night, he sat on Cody's grave and just started to howl. He would not stop screaming and he didn't stop until I accepted the death, and went and sat on the grave with him. Then he was quiet. It was like Cody was there again. I had to leave for the set, but I couldn't leave his grave. I just sat there, and Lisa was telling me I had to go."

After the unexpected deaths of so many people close to him—his father, his sister, and Bob Le Mond, as well as Cody—the normally optimistic Patrick sank into a depression.

"I was so cut up about my dog, and all, that I had resolved to sell my ranch," he said afterward. "But Cody's spirit returned to me through another one of my dogs and made me realize I was about to screw up the rest of my life."

By some strange, almost mystical synchronicity, *Three Wishes*, which was released on October 27, 1995, just months after Cody's death, featured a magical dog with genie-like powers.

That same month, Mulholland Drive Café, the East Side restaurant Patrick and Bobby Ochs owned in Manhattan, filed for chapter 11 bankruptcy protection and closed down.

Patrick was philosophical about bad reviews and the closure of his restaurant, which, in comparison to the death of Cody and, of course, the suicide of his sister, hardly impacted him at all.

On May 9, 1997, while in the midst of shooting his next movie, the thriller *Letters from a Killer* in remote Yolo County, Sacramento, California, he came close to losing his own life as well. He was playing a scene in which he was driving a Bronco in a car chase with the police when the truck skidded and flipped over.

"Everything happened so fast," a shell-shocked Patrick said afterward. "The truck started crashing when we were upside down. I looked back and saw streams of gas leaking on everyone." The roof and the windshield caved in on him but, in yet another of the miracles that seemed to occur at regular intervals in his hitherto charmed life, he climbed out of the wreck with only a few bruises.

On October 12, 1997, during one of the lighter moments in

shooting, Patrick and the crew were in the midst of filming outside the American Legion Hall in St. Rose, Louisiana. Inside the hall, sixty relatives of the Schexnayder family were celebrating a family party when one of them, Kathy Louque, spotted a man outside getting out of a white Suburban.

"When we realized it was Patrick Swayze, we were so excited," said Kathy, "We couldn't believe our eyes. You see him in the movies, but to see him in person, Wow!"

She and some of the other family members began waving at him in delight. Ever friendly and kind to his fans, he instinctively waved back, and in the process unwittingly ruined the scene. "The production people told us if they could reshoot the scene with no problems, Patrick would come over and talk to us afterward," Kathy recalled. "We thought, 'Yeah, right.'"

Patrick finished the scene, then—ever a man of his word— walked over to the family, whereupon a stunned Kathy offered him a bowl of gumbo and a couple of Rice Krispies treats.

Instead of playing the big star and ignoring her, Patrick told her he loved gumbo, tried some, and took the Rice Krispies treats with him, promising to eat them later. Then he posed for several pictures with the family, signed autographs and, in answer to their solicitous inquiries about his recovery from the accident, told them that he had had a rod inserted in his right femur and was still healing but feeling much better.

He had survived his on-set accident, but fate obviously wasn't finished with him yet and, a few weeks later, he had a second brush with death. During one scene, shot while he was riding a quarter horse through the woods, the horse was suddenly spooked by a snake, bolted, and headed straight toward an oak tree.

They say that a drowning man sees his life flash in front of his eyes, and so perhaps does a rider on a runaway horse who is about to have his skull crushed to smithereens against the trunk of an oak tree.

But if that was the case for Patrick, with his gymnastic training, he didn't have time to notice. Instead, he grabbed two handfuls of the horse's mane and flipped his body around so his legs and not his skull smashed into the oak tree. "Thank God for reflexes, because I really should be dead," he said.

Fortunately, Lisa was on the set that day and came running to Patrick's side. As he lay on the ground in agony, all he could think of was maintaining eye contact with her. "I was using her as a barometer for myself. Am I going into shock? Am I talking stupid? I kept looking at her to tell me if I was going to be okay," he said.

He'd saved his own life by his quick thinking. Nonetheless, he had suffered grave injuries: breaks in both his legs (a broken fibula and a broken femur) and four detached tendons in his shoulder as well.

In the past he had always been brave, headstrong, and determined that the show must go on, no matter how severe the pain, no matter how dire the consequences to his health. In this instance, however, the doctor's advice prevailed over his own stubborn courage, and he agreed to take three months off and to walk with a cane till his legs had mended.

The cameras had been rolling at the time of the accident and—out of curiosity—he viewed the footage. Thereafter, he began to suffer a recurrent nightmare in which he died in the accident.

Much as the nightmares must have troubled him, in keeping with his positive thinking credo, he endeavored to learn something from the accident, and ultimately did. "One of the things I've come away from this experience with is an unwillingness to put off the things that are important to me. We're only here so long! Let's get on with it!" he said and then elaborated, "When you come close to dying like I did, it's really like a slap in the face. I had all those thoughts about how precious life is and how little time we all have, and I wanted to work nonstop."

twelve

DOWNWARD SPIRAL

*O*nce upon a time, as a young, aspiring actor without a single movie to his name, Patrick had made the pilgrimage to Hollywood Boulevard, gazed at star imprints outside Grauman's Chinese Theater, and dreamed that he would one day have his own there.

On August 18, 1997—his forty-fifth birthday and the day after the tenth anniversary of *Dirty Dancing*'s release—his dream at last came true when he received the belated tribute of having his own star on Hollywood Boulevard.

A crowd of five hundred fans gathered at the corner of Hollywood and Vine, listening rapt as he said, "I thought all last night what I'd say and still have no idea. This means more to me than you can imagine."

Overwrought by being in his proximity, one of his most ardent fans, Sandra Korner from Munich, Germany, fainted, but luckily was revived in time to join the crowd in a spirited rendition of "Happy Birthday."

The following month, on September 3, after the doctors had given him the go-ahead, he took up where he left off filming *Letters from a Killer*, and then, in December of that same year, went straight on to *Black Dog*, which was shot in Georgia, Texas, Nevada, and

Arizona and in which he played a truck driver who accidentally kills a man.

His costar Randy Travis was aware that Patrick had been in a serious accident the previous year and noted his courage. "He doesn't say much," he reported. "I think sometimes he's in pain. I'll ask him, 'Are you hurtin'? Is today a bad one?' But he just sort of shrugs it off and keeps going."

Patrick's bravery aside, the movie turned out to be one more in his catalogue of minor action movies, and after *Black Dog* was released on May 1, 1999, the movie sank without a trace.

That same month he began filming *Forever Lulu*, the story of a psychiatric patient in long-term treatment (played by Melanie Griffith) who tracks down her old college soul mate, played by Patrick.

During the shoot in Orange County, California, Patrick was his normal, genial self, happy in his camaraderie with cast and crew. "Sometimes at the end of the day, after I had wrapped the camera and come off the camera truck, Patrick was still around hanging out with the crew, just talking," remembered first assistant cameraman Glenn Deitell.

Patrick was kind and generous with his time, but sadly neither the critics nor the audience were as positive about *Lulu*. The movie did very little business at the box office, and he may well have been left pondering whether or not it might be preferable for him to stick to action pictures.

He was almost forty-seven now and—however good shape he was in—his time in action movies was probably winding down. Vicky's suicide and his last punishing accident had taken its toll. He was hitting the bottle again and giving free rein to what he termed the "wild man within," yet never allowed his demons to infringe on his performances.

In May 2000 he began filming his next movie, *Green Dragon*, set in the aftermath of the Vietnam War. He played the sergeant in charge of Camp Pendleton, then the temporary home of thousands of Vietnamese refugees.

As always, he was accessible to his fans, happy to pal around with the crew, and never insisted on any special treatment.

Then, just after 11 a.m. on the morning of June 1, 2000, his universe almost imploded when, while flying his twin engine Cessna 414A from Van Nuys airport to Las Vegas, New Mexico, he crash landed his plane on a building site in Prescott Valley, Arizona.

A few days later, he gave an interview to Phoenix KTVK-TV in which he claimed that he had crashed the plane simply because— as a smoker—he was so affected by the altitude that he fell unconscious.

"It was a scary thing landing a plane in hypoxia and with a small amount of carbon monoxide poisoning," he said. "The air wasn't pressurizing and smokers' body altitude is eight thousand feet higher than what you're really at. My body thought I was at twenty thousand feet and I fell unconscious, took half my wing off, but still kept flying. I now know there's an angel sitting on my shoulder because someone else helped me land that aircraft."

Interviewed by reporters about the crash, Patsy said, "There was an angel on my boy's shoulder and I believe it was my father—he was a World War I fighter pilot. I know it was him who saved Patrick.

"Pat has been flying a long time. I've been up in his plane. I was not worried one bit. He was very cautious, very careful, just like his beloved granddad. And that's shown by his landing well in an emergency," she said—whether knowingly or not—reinforcing his story.

He did indeed land well. However, the rest of Patrick's story was pure fantasy. And when the truth was made apparent in an excruciatingly detailed report, written by D. Miller of the Prescott Valley Police department, it made for extremely unpleasant reading. For while Patsy indignantly swore, "I just can't believe that my son would be dumb enough to get into a plane if he had been drinking," the police report makes it crystal clear that is exactly what he did.

On the day in question, he emerged from the plane with blood-shot eyes, unhurt but clearly intoxicated. As a group of construction workers who'd witnessed the crash gathered around him, he handed one of them a half-empty thirty pack of Miller Lite and, his speech slurred, asked him to get rid of it. Then he asked all of them for help. Flattered that a Hollywood star was asking for their assistance, the upshot was that some of them obscured the truth from the police that he had been flying under the influence of alcohol.

A construction worker took him to his house, from where he first made a call to his attorney, then his publicist, then Lisa, and where he remained for a time until—at 4:15 in the afternoon—he checked into a local Best Western, where he remained for another three and three-quarter hours, and only then did he respond to D. Miller's numerous telephone messages.

By the time Patrick presented himself at the police station and made a statement swearing that he had not ingested any alcohol, prescription drugs, and/or illicit drugs prior to or during the flight, almost twelve hours had passed since the crash. In accordance with Arizona's Revised Statutes, the time had passed in which it would have been legal to administer toxological tests to him in order to ascertain the level of alcohol in his blood.

Given the evidence in the police report, had Patrick submitted to those tests, he would have been in danger of arrest and imprisonment on the grounds of flying a plane while intoxicated and in the process endangering his own life and that of other pilots and their passengers, not to mention a number of people on the ground.

As it was, no charges were ever filed against him. But the fact remains that while Patrick has always been the people's Hollywood star, in the same way as Diana was the people's princess, it is easy to forget that with a battery of agents, attorneys, and spin doctors all at his disposal, he also has had the ability to shield himself from the normal vicissitudes of life. Despite all his open-hearted press interviews, his ability to be self-revelatory, sometimes to his own detriment, when the situation demands it, Patrick is capable of being as self-protective and as duplicitous as any anyone else, and as human.

• • •

On July 24, 2000, Patrick began filming *Donnie Darko*, the eighties saga of a schizophrenic teenager starring Jake Gyllenhaal as Darko. Patrick had eighth billing in the movie and can't have been happy when certain critics suggested that he—and Drew Barrymore—had been cast in it only because they evoked that decade.

He tried gamely to inject some life into his character, motivational speaker Jim Cunningham, and said, "It's a small part, but difficult. Jim's a terrible person and it was fun to play."

The truth was that he had arrived at the Norma Desmond chapter every major Hollywood star—from Robert Redford to Sylvester Stallone—has to reach when they still remain big in terms of their charisma and their fan base, but it's the pictures that got small.

And it was clear that casting agents were now relegating him to playing character parts, some minor. Under those circumstances, some might say that it would have served him better if he'd had a Garboesque epiphany and retired from acting altogether, leaving his devoted fans with the memory of Orry Main, Johnny Castle, and Sam Wheat to sustain them, but Patrick would have violently disagreed.

His next movie, *Waking up in Reno*—about two Arkansas couples who tried to enliven their stale marriages by a trip to Reno—didn't feature him in a major starring part either. Instead, he played Charlize Theron's somewhat dopey but soft-hearted husband, and Billy Bob Thornton and Natasha Richardson made up the foursome.

He and Billy Bob had long been friends, so the on-set chemistry was good, not merely among the leading actors but, thanks to Patrick, among the rest of the cast and the crew as well.

"On one particularly stressful day, an hour after he wrapped, Patrick rode up to the set on his electric scooter wearing a bathrobe, a long redneck wig, and buck teeth. He circled the crew a few times and then disappeared. His timing was perfect! We all had a laugh and were recharged to finish our work," remembered the movie's director Jordan Brady.

But no matter how much fun the movie might have been for Patrick to make, no matter how high-wattage the cast, not to mention the fact that the concept for the movie came from Billy Bob himself, who originally conceived it as a redneck *Bob & Carol & Ted & Alice*, when the movie was released on October 25, 2002, it still failed dismally at the box office.

At that inauspicious moment, Patrick made the surprising decision to reprise his role as Johnny Castle in a sequel to *Dirty Dancing*. In the past, no matter how many different production companies had begged him to play Johnny again and how often, he had always refused. As he said with considerable pride, "I've never taken a role for the money," and neither the various concepts nor the scripts had ever appealed to him. Now, though, he inexplicably agreed to do a brief cameo in *Dirty Dancing: Havana Nights*, in which he played— not Johnny Castle—but an unnamed dance class instructor.

The character wasn't Johnny, nor did the story have anything to do with him, and Patrick appeared in only two short scenes, during which he danced with the female lead, Romola Garai. "It's one of those moments where you stop yourself. Your brain goes, 'This isn't happening. This is too removed from my life,' " she said afterward.

She may have been transported by her dance with Patrick, but critics were not impressed by either his performance or his appearance in the movie.

Fortunately, the following year he and Lisa would finally achieve their cherished dream of adapting *Without a Word* into a movie entitled *One Last Dance*. The play had won six Drama Critics Circle awards, but it had taken them ten years to bring it to the screen— although it would end up being released only on dvd.

Lisa wrote and directed the movie and she and Patrick starred in it. Shot over thirty-one days in Winnipeg, Canada, *One Last Dance* told the story of three aging dancers who reunite to help keep a struggling dance company afloat.

The movie gave Lisa a chance to demonstrate her acting and dancing talents and showcase her incredibly long legs, her stellar dance technique, and her haunting beauty—a beauty so pristine that in many of the close-ups she is a dead ringer for Grace Kelly.

Afterward, Patrick jokingly said, "Most fun for me was to watch my wife, the director woman in a little scantily clad nymph costume on a dolly bossing big grips around. That's kind of a fantasy for me and kind of turned me on."

In all the scenes in which Patrick watches Lisa dance, his face is incandescent with joy at her talent and beauty. And in the scene where he realizes that her character's little girl is actually his daughter as well, he has tears in his eyes, and it seems highly likely that those tears were engendered by him imagining the child he and Lisa might have had together, had life unfolded differently.

The movie also gave him the opportunity to return to his roots. "I think this movie is going to surprise a lot of people because we wanted—for one moment in time—to do a film and get back to the level that we were when we were dancing with ballet companies in New York," he said.

As they anticipated, he and Lisa loved every minute they worked together. "We know each other best, we know each other's strengths and weaknesses," she said.

"It's amazing," Patrick said. "I feel like the picture of Dorian Gray . . . My body should be hurting. I've broken more things than you can imagine. I've torn muscles, pinched nerves, had back problems over and over again. But I've kept myself together as a dancer over all these years since Feld, and it feels better for me to dance now than at any time in my life."

Sadly, a shadow was cast over their happy time filming in Winnipeg after their fourteen-year-old poodle, Bohda, who (with Gabriel, Lisa's Rhodesian ridgeback) was on location with them, became ill and had to be put down.

In playing a dancer in *One Last Dance*, Patrick had returned to his roots. The following year he traveled back to another branch of them by contracting to star for two weeks as razzle-dazzle lawyer Billy Flynn in the Broadway production of *Chicago*.

"Even though it was unannounced, people caught me," he said. "The entire city seemed to know. Everywhere I went, from cab drivers to subways, people would say, 'Welcome back, Patrick. It's good to have you home. We missed you.'

"I figured it's time to put a fire under my tail. 'Crazy Swayze' on the comeback road. People are saying, 'He's back,' but I'm not sure I went anywhere."

Aware of all the heightened expectation surrounding his impromptu stage appearance, he was surprisingly nervous and described his first performance, on December 15, 2003, as "being shot out of a cannon." He then reprised the part again at Los Angeles's Pantages Theatre during a three-week run that started on January 8, 2004. His reviews were less than spectacular.

Then, turning the kaleidoscope of his career again, he contracted to spend four months in Africa starring as Allan Quatermain in *King Solomon's Mines*, a four-hour Hallmark Channel feature based on H. Rider Haggard's classic book of the same name, which he had read as a child and loved.

Executive producer Nick Lombardo was thrilled that *King Solomon's Mines*, marked Patrick's first TV role since *North and South*. "He has always portrayed characters of passion, he just has that ability to be impassioned about what they do. That is what shows on camera," he said.

Apart from the fact that Patrick could wear his own clothes in the movie and just swapped his cowboy hat for an African bush hat, here in Africa he was also able to indulge his thirst for adventure, his propensity for dueling with danger. As he later confessed, "I took big chances because I am a horseman and nobody could do the horse work like I could."

On the first day of shooting, the horses picked up the scent of a nearby lion and took off. Ever the hero, he charged after them on his own steed. While cast and crew watched, enthralled, he lassoed the horses and drove them home. Although he couldn't help bragging afterward, "That's when everyone said, 'Swayze can ride a horse,' " he allowed that the experience "was scary" and was later disappointed that the scenes shot of his dangerous escapades didn't make it into the final cut.

But he still relished being in Africa and in particular working with two fifteen-foot elephants named Harry and Sally. "I fell in love with Harry," he recalled. Then, in an admission that says a great deal about the ever-present little boy within him still yearning to be loved unconditionally, he recalled that when he was already sitting in his Land Rover, about to take off for the airport, "I wanted to see if this elephant really knew who I was. I yelled at him, and even though Harry had gone back with the herd, he ran to my vehicle and wrapped his trunk around my head. He didn't want me to go. It just broke my heart."

In retrospect, it seems as if he was determined to live each day as if it was his last, leaping from one movie role after another, just so that he could continue to work, to feel alive.

In 2004, he spent three months in Luxembourg filming *George and the Dragon*, working with Piper Perabo and stuntwoman Camilla Naprous.

"It was a great film to do, I really enjoyed it. We were filming in Europe, which I loved, and the cast were amazing," he said.

His next project, playing the lead role of former CIA spy Jason Monk in the TV movie adaptation of Frederick Forsyth's *Icon* took him to Moscow. "I've never played a superspy before, very reserved, very close to the vest. I'm usually, people say all the time, 'Mr. wear-your-heart-on your sleeve,' " he said wryly.

When *Icon* was broadcast on May 20, 2005, for once critics reviewed his performance positively. However, they wouldn't do the same for his next movie, a British black comedy called *Keeping Mum*, in which he played Lance, a sleazy, voyeuristic golf pro who has an affair with a bored wife played by Kristin Scott Thomas. Filming began on February 4, 2005, on the Isle of Man off the coast of Britain, and later in Cornwall.

"He is still Patrick Swayze, he is still the fabulous dancer and singer and all the women around the film set, in Cornwall and the Isle of Man, were so excited when they spotted him in the street," Scott Thomas remembered.

The scene in which Patrick is dressed in nothing but a red thong was far from romantic, nor, by any stretch of the imagination, was the grossly unappealing character of Lance. "The whole purpose of playing Lance was that he is a parody of some of those guys I used to play," Patrick said. "I loved playing him—although having to appear in one scene in nothing but a red thong was pretty intimidating. It was a really, really scary thing to do. It definitely tested my ability to laugh at myself."

"He's a very modest guy who is able to laugh at himself," Scott Thomas confirmed, enthusing, "He was fantastic because he really went for it, went all out for that kitschy, tacky look. Poor man, I don't think it was much fun for him because I got this dreadful cold hacking away as I was about to kiss him—eugh!

"We were filming in a cowshed on the Isle of Man and it was absolutely freezing. We just couldn't stop giggling. We had to do several reshoots because the director was laughing so much.

"But Patrick was great. Obviously he said he would do the scene so he just got on with it. I was so impressed. He's great fun."

When the movie opened in London on October 25, 2005, critics tended to make the crass mistake of assuming that Lance and Patrick were one and the same person.

Between May 15, 2006, and July 1, 2006, Patrick was in Austria filming *Jump!*, a biopic of legendary photographer Philippe Halsman that featured a kiss between him and young English actress Martine McCutcheon, who first came to fame in *East Enders*. "I was honored to kiss him," she enthused. "He's one of the few people that just had a real laugh and made me feel comfortable and did so much research and put so much hard work into when we were filming," she said.

When he spotted her in the canteen line, being shoved around by some of the crew pushing ahead to get their food, all his chivalrous, protective instincts kicked in and he came to her rescue, "Patrick stepped up, and everybody looked at him, and he said, 'Nobody puts Martine in a corner,' " Martine McCutcheon said.

She was young, pretty, and a rising star, but—true to form—Patrick didn't just restrict his good manners, camaraderie, and kindness to his peers.

When Lakewood, East Dallas, resident Suzanne Collins was selected to host him while he was promoting *Jump!* at the USA Film Festival there, she at first assumed that all she would be doing was taking him to and from the airport. "Well, it didn't turn out like that," she remembered. "We ended up going out to dinner and staying out until all hours of the night for three days straight."

Suzanne and her husband, Lang, took him to all the area's hotspots and he loved one of them, Campisi's, so much that "We couldn't get him out of there. And they loved him. In fact, at eleven o'clock when the restaurant closed, they locked the doors and wouldn't let him go."

As usual, he was mobbed wherever he went, but he signed autographs and joked with fans galore. "He didn't get a minute to himself," Suzanne said. And three days after he left town, he sent her and her husband a thank-you note.

He was courteous to his fans, loyal to his audience, kind to anyone who crossed his path. And he approached each part he played with creativity, energy, and commitment. But he still wasn't satisfied.

As he would say later, "There is probably that little bird that flies through your insides and says, 'I sure would like to make a mark in life.' I've made a pretty decent mark so far . . . nothing to scoff at. But it does make you think: Wait a minute. There's more I want to do. Lots more. Get on with it."

thirteen

FIGHTING BACK

By the end of July 2006, Patrick was not in the best of health. He had spent the summer in London living in an apartment in the Knightsbridge area while rehearsing his part as Nathan Detroit, which he would play for eight weeks in the West End production of the musical *Guys and Dolls* at the Piccadilly Theater.

His Liverpool-born costar, Claire Sweeney, had always been a great Patrick Swayze fan and she was apprehensive about meeting him in person, then appearing in the show with him. "The producers arranged dinner for us at the Savoy in London, and I was nervous when he walked over. But he took my hand and went, 'Just by looking in your eyes I know we're going to work well together and have a blast.' He disarmed me because he was so down to earth and normal—it was quite humbling to see how unaffected he was," she said.

He was originally slated to take his bow on July 10 and stay in the show until September 2 but was felled by a chest infection and lost his voice. "He came straight to rehearsals from doing a film and worked himself into the ground," Claire Sweeney explained. "His body packed up, he couldn't speak for a week."

"Sick as I was, I've not stopped working. I kept coming into rehearsals. I've been like Marcel Marceau, learning the choreography and the staging even though I couldn't speak," he said.

At the time, however, rumor had it that he was, in reality, suffering from stage fright. Stung by the suggestion, Patrick hit out in the press with "Stage fright? I've been doing this since I was born. I was raised and born into musical theater."

Claire Sweeney, however, remained enchanted by him. "Working with Patrick is so much fun. He's charming and so good at what he does. I knew I'd learn so much from him and I am—he's unpredictable and throws out random lines that make me react differently, so no show is the same. It keeps it exciting. That's his Hollywood star quality."

When he finally opened in the show on August 7, 2006, sadly critics were not bowled over by his performance.

After he returned to America, he performed a small role as the voice of Cash, dreaming of Grand Ole Opry stardom in *The Fox and the Hound 2*, which opened on November 7, 2006.

Then he was back in London again, where, on December 23, he performed in the presence of Prince Charles and the Duchess of Cornwall at the Royal Variety Performance at the London Coliseum.

Home in America once more, on December 27 he and Lisa were flying their twin-engine Cessna 414 from Van Nuys to New Mexico when their right engine lost power and they were forced to make a precautionary landing at Barstow-Daggett Airport in California. Lisa, who was piloting the plane at the time, miraculously succeeded in landing with only one engine.

"With a forty-six-knot crosswind, she greased it," Patrick said. "We stayed totally calm and professional, like a unit in the cockpit, and nailed it."

The following year, on April 23, 2007, he was back in Winnipeg again, filming *Christmas in Wonderland*, then, on August 6, 2007, he followed up by filming *Powder Blue* in Los Angeles with Kris Kristofferson, Ray Liotta, Jessica Biel, and Forest Whitaker.

In spite of its stellar cast, *Powder Blue* was not slated to set the world on fire, and Patrick's role—that of a seedy strip club owner for which he sported a long blond wig, dark, smoky eye makeup, leather trousers, and a leather waistcoat—was unlikely to garner him many critical accolades or to appeal to his fans much either.

Looking back, his brother Don, who was appearing in the movie with him at the time, reported, "He was healthy, tan. He was better than ever! You couldn't tell a thing." *Powder Blue* producer Bobby Schwartz concurred, "The guy looked very young, very healthy, very energetic," he said.

On November 6, 2007, Patrick made an unheralded appearance on *The Oprah Winfrey Show* as a surprise to Welsh couple James Derbyshire and Julia Boggio, who had performed a *Dirty Dancing* routine at their wedding and then made a YouTube video of it that attracted 2.5 million hits. After James and Julia chatted with Oprah for a while, they began their dirty dance together.

"We were halfway through when the audience started screaming," James remembered. "Julia stopped dancing and was frozen in my arms. I felt a tap on the shoulder and Patrick Swayze asked if he could cut in. I pretended I was jealous and sulking at the side. Then he looked at me and I shouted, 'Let's do the lift.'

"So I ran toward him and he put his arms out and he lifted me up. He said he loved what we had done and wanted to meet us. He's a fabulous bloke and is so nice."

In December 2007 Patrick flew to Chicago, where he began filming the pilot of A&E's *The Beast*, which would mark his return to television and in which he would be playing undercover FBI agent Charles Barker. Just after the filming was finished, he noticed that he had lost weight and that his face looked slightly yellow. Soon afterward, he began spitting up blood. Yet, stoic as always, he did nothing.

However, on New Year's Eve he realized that the champagne wasn't agreeing with him, was like "acid on an open wound." And it was then that—like the trained dancer he was—he took an objective look at his body and at last confronted the truth that he had inexplicably dropped twenty pounds without even trying.

He was accustomed to enduring physical pain, broken limbs, and suffering in silence, but by the end of January 2008, he knew he could no longer avoid facing up to his symptoms and underwent tests.

Lisa was given the news first that he had pancreatic cancer, one of the worst cancers there is, with only a 5 percent five-year survival rate. Aware that he was still dopey from the aftereffects of the exploratory procedure, and perhaps also remembering the nightmarish moment over two decades before when she'd been compelled to break the news of his father's sudden death to him, she decided to delay telling him the truth until the morning.

The next few weeks then became a nightmare from which he and Lisa knew they couldn't wake up. Not then, not ever.

The majority of human beings, upon receiving what is tantamount to a death sentence, might have cashed in their savings and embarked on a world cruise, a gambling binge in Las Vegas, or an adventurous voyage up the Amazon. Patrick could have done all the above and more. He could have thrown in the towel right then and there and instructed his agent to put out the word that he had retired from movies, that he wasn't accepting any more roles, but that wasn't his way.

"How do you nurture a positive attitude when all the statistics say you're a dead man? You go to work," he would say down the line.

Consequently, right after he received the news that he had pancreatic cancer, one of his first calls was to Sony executive Jamie Erlicht, whose company was coproducing *The Beast* with A&E.

"He told us, 'Guys, I have some horrible news. But if you can be patient and stand by me, I'm going to come back and do the show.' He said: 'I'm in great condition. I'm a cowboy. I'm a dancer. I'll beat this,' " Jamie Erlicht remembered.

His reason for not calling Patsy first, for keeping the news from her for the time being, eerily paralleled the plot of *Goodbye Lenin*, the 2003 Academy Award–nominated movie in which the mother—a committed Communist—falls into a coma and when she wakes up, her son is unable to tell her that the Berlin Wall has fallen, as doctors have told him that any shock will kill her.

"A few days before Buddy found out he had pancreatic cancer, Patsy had eye surgery," recalled Zetta Alderman. "Beforehand, the doctors told her that if she cried tears after the operation, she could become blind. So it was crucial that for a period of time after the operation, she wasn't upset in any way. That's why neither Buddy nor Lisa told her that he had pancreatic cancer. And when she found out anyway, she was livid that they hadn't told her themselves." As soon as Patsy had calmed down, however, she took refuge in the hope that he would survive because, "I'm sure he's got the best doctors."

He did, indeed, have access to the best doctors. He squared his shoulders and put himself under the care of the Stanford Cancer Center, where he began receiving chemotherapy along with the experimental drug Vatalanib, which operates by cutting off the tumor's blood supplies in the hope that it will shrink.

The weekly treatments—each lasting for as long as five hours—continued through much of February 2008. His brother Don was with him at the ranch when the doctors called to break the news to Patrick that his prognosis was not all they had hoped it would be. As Don told *People*, "I was looking in his eyes and I didn't see a flicker [of fear]. I saw him think about it for like five seconds, and then he moved right into, 'Well, we've got a battle ahead of us.'"

At that point, as forthright as ever and as courageous, Patrick asked his oncologist, Dr. George Fisher, to define his enemy for him. "I just want to see it and I want to confront it and I want to attack it head on," Patrick said.

After all the physical pain he'd suffered in his life, his bravery during this particular battle was never in question. Don, who was with him during chemotherapy, said that Patrick "spends the time coaching the doctors on how they ain't seen nothing yet, and saying,

'You just wait! I'm going to be the guy that five years from now we're all going to be talking about this day . . . ' And we realize he's had the chemo running for the last ten minutes. He's oblivious."

Throughout his life, right back to when he was a child bullied by rednecks who didn't understand his dedication to ballet, through all the painful injuries to his knee that would have felled a lesser man, he had always fought like the proverbial lion to overcome the pain, the obstacles.

Now, more than ever, both his courage and his positive thinking came to the fore. During his years of struggle as a dancer in New York, he had survived the lean and difficult times partly by adhering to the discipline of repeating a positive affirmation to himself day in and day out. Passionately positive in his approach to life, he had sometimes joked about his Pollyannaish tendencies, but now they would prove to be a lifeline for him.

So of course was Lisa, who was always by his side, giving him his medications, making him fresh juice, and pureeing his high-fat food, or flying him in their Beechcraft Super King Air 200 to Stanford for his chemotherapy treatments.

At times, the pain was so severe that he would end up on the bathroom floor railing out loud at the pain from colitis and inflamed bowels—all consequences of pancreatic cancer—and swore that he wouldn't let it beat him.

Ever since his early childhood, he had been in the limelight, already under the gaze of the public, adoring the applause, loving the attention. However, when the *National Enquirer* broke the news of his pancreatic cancer during the first week of March 2008, for the first time in his life the public exposure was hard for him to bear.

Finally, in recognition of the fact that the story could not be stopped, he issued a public statement through his publicist Annett Wolf that he was being treated for pancreatic cancer, adding, "Patrick is continuing his normal schedule during this time, which includes working on upcoming projects. The outpouring of support and concern he has already received from the public is deeply appreciated by Patrick and his family."

The official announcement that he had pancreatic cancer sent shock waves throughout the world, resulting in an outpouring of love and support from his friends, fans, and practically everyone who had ever worked with him, who had heard rumors of his illness but until then had hoped desperately that they were false.

From London, Claire Sweeney, his costar in Guys and Dolls, said, "Patrick is kind, gorgeous, and a close friend. He is the most beautiful man ever. My thoughts are with him and Lisa. God bless and be strong." Tom Cruise, his old friend from The Outsiders, sent him his good wishes, praising him as "a fighter." Jennifer Grey issued a statement saying, "I wish him all my love, and I have great faith that he is a fighter," and thousands of fans from all over the world expressed their encouragement to him via letters and the Internet.

Distressed by tabloid reports that he had only weeks to live, Patrick agreed that a statement from his oncologist Dr. George Fisher be included in the press release. "Patrick has a very limited amount of disease and he appears to be responding well to treatment thus far," Dr. Fisher said, adding, "All of the reports stating the time frame of his prognosis and his physical side-effects are absolutely untrue. We are considerably optimistic."

Patrick remained that way, but he was also defiant and determined not to give into the disease, nor to allow it to break his spirit or alter his lifestyle. In mid-March 2008, as he waited to board the plane after his latest round of chemotherapy at Stanford, he was photographed puffing on a cigarette. That picture was presumably taken without his knowledge. Throughout his career, he had never allowed himself to be photographed smoking, nor would he ever smoke in front of children, but—in true Marlboro man style—he still harbored the belief that smoking was the cool cowboy thing to do instead of accepting that it might well be a factor in the disease that could one day kill him.

He would finally admit the truth in December 2008, during an interview with Barbara Walters, that "probably smoking has something to do with my pancreatic cancer," and then went on to make the frank confession that while he had cut down his smoking, he had no intention of stopping, at least not then.

Nor did he turn to holistic or alternative methods of treatment, other than Chinese herbs, primarily because he believed, "There's one thing I'm not gonna do is chase . . . is chase . . . staying alive. You'll spend so much time chasing staying alive that you won't live."

Amid the ensuing public criticism from those who believed that he was being self-destructive in smoking, his family rallied round and spoke out in his defense and in his praise. "We're pioneer stock. I think if anyone can hang on and beat this, Patrick can," his aunt, Diana Latham, asserted, adding, "Because we're strong people."

The New Mexico ranch was now his refuge and there he went on cattle drives and spent as much time as possible with Lisa.

In the ultimate romantic gesture, he and Lisa renewed their marriage vows. "We did it very Prince Charming and Snow White. I rode in on a snorting steed, a white stallion," Patrick recalled to Barbara Walters.

At the beginning of April 2008, he underwent an experimental type of surgery using the CyberKnife, performed by a laser mounted on a robotic arm; it was designed to concentrate massive doses of radiation on the tumor while sparing surrounding healthy tissue. And while conventional treatment generally focuses radiation on a tumor from five or six different angles, the CyberKnife aimed two hundred beams of radiation at it.

By the end of the month, Dr. Fisher made the statement that Patrick continued to "respond well" to his chemotherapy and would be continuing on the same course of treatment at Stanford.

Somewhat heartened, Patrick and Lisa issued a statement to *People* magazine: "We're thrilled and grateful for the positive response

Patrick has shown towards his treatment. Also, we can't help but feel that all the prayers, meditations and good thoughts sent his way by everyone have made a difference. Thank you!"

On April 30, Patrick was photographed shopping at a convenience store in Lake View Terrace, California. And while rumor had it that part of his stomach had been surgically removed, he looked thinner but relatively unchanged by the disease.

Forever brave and positive, he did all he could to live a normal life and, at the end of May, he and Lisa attended a LA Lakers and San Antonio Spurs game. "He was still gaunt and pale, but compared with recent pictures it was a huge improvement," an eyewitness said, adding, "He was grinning all through, and kept cheering and clapping with the rest of the crowd. It was encouraging to see."

To emphasize his good spirits and determination to beat the disease, and to hearten all his fans, friends, and family, on May 27, he issued a statement to *People*: "Lisa and I have been back and forth from New Mexico enjoying the arrival of spring and new baby calves. This past weekend, we spent a fun time with friends in Reno for Lisa's birthday, where I took her jewelry shopping at Kenny G and Company and [we] were able to find her something really special and much deserved! In the meantime, I am continuing treatment at Stanford and the great news is I continue to respond."

During the first week of June, he learned that—based on reports from his doctors—the A&E and Sony executives overseeing *The Beast* had made the choice to put their faith in his resilience, his capacity to work, and his determination and decided to make the series with him in it.

"Patsy was worried about Buddy doing *The Beast*, but she knew she couldn't tell him no. If he really gets his mind on something, you can't tell him no," said Zetta Alderman.

Filming of *The Beast* was slated to begin in Chicago at the end of July and to last four months, during which time Patrick would continue his treatment at Stanford. On July 20, he boarded the flight from L.A. to Chicago. At O'Hare Airport, an eye witness couldn't believe what a great mood he was in. "He was so upbeat and friendly. I told him that he looked really good. With a smile he shot back and told me that not only has he gained twenty pounds but that 'he's a miracle. A f***** miracle!' "

His fellow cast members, too, marveled at Patrick's positive, optimistic attitude toward his disease. "In his mind, nothing was wrong. That's the kind of person he is—very positive," said actor Larry Gilliard Jr.

Still drinking as much fresh juice as possible—in particular, fresh pressed ginger root juice—he arranged to have all his meals delivered to his hotel from Whole Foods. Together, Patrick (in baseball cap and sunglasses) and Lisa dined together at the health food restaurant Grocer and Goddess. "He looks very good considering his condition and couldn't have been nicer," one of the staff who served him said.

He had taken control of his illness and felt stronger for having done so. On August 3 he, Lisa, and some friends went to Chicago's Rockit Bar and Grill and stayed there until he and Lisa took to the dance floor, where they danced together before leaving at 4:30 in the morning.

"Patrick has an incredible energy," *Beast* executive producer Steven Pearl said admiringly. "He's got a passion for life. It rubs off on the crew. People are there for him as a person and him as a character and what it is we are trying to accomplish as a show. It's a quiet leadership, and it's pervasive."

Throughout the months of shooting, cast and crew continued to be deeply impressed by Patrick's fortitude, by his insistence that the show must go on. On some cold and windy Chicago nights, he worked as long as twelve hours at a time.

But he never once collapsed on set. Nor did he whine or complain, even when he had to get up at three in the morning for a six o'clock call, because he had to prepare his body for the ordeal ahead.

Through it all, he steadfastly refused to take painkillers, not even one, afraid that they might dull his senses or, worse still, his brain. And so he suffered in silence. "I've always known Patrick's a really tough guy, but until all this illness came up in this past year, I had no idea really the depths of his toughness and the amount of fight in him," Lisa told Barbara Walters in admiration.

"He's fearless, an icon. I can't say enough good things about the guy. He's been an absolute inspiration, he's an amazing guy. He makes the little things seem not important," his *Beast* costar Travis Fimmel declared.

And the show's cocreator, Bill Rotko, said, "Although you forget sometimes that Patrick's going through treatment for cancer, it brings you very close together. There's a tremendous amount of respect going on."

By August 11, he was looking frail and appeared to have lost weight. Nonetheless, he soldiered on, determined to shoot all twelve episodes of the series. By his birthday, August 18, he'd rallied somewhat and—during a break in shooting—enjoyed lunch with Lisa in his trailer.

On August 29, 2008, at the Kodak Theater, Hollywood, he made his first major public appearance since his diagnosis. At the start of *America's Stand Up 2 Cancer Telethon*, to be aired simultaneously on ABC, NBC, and CBS, he stepped from behind a screen to a standing ovation.

All the stars present—Fran Drescher, Sidney Poitier, Keanu Reeves, Kirsten Dunst, Melissa Etheridge, Christina Ricci, Jodie Foster, Salma Hayek, and Jennifer Aniston—stood up to pay tribute to him.

Patrick, looking thin but handsome, moved forward and said, "I keep dreaming of a future, a future with a long and healthy life, a life not lived in the shadow of cancer, but in the light. I dream that everyone diagnosed will be fortunate enough to have hope that every human being lost to cancer isn't gone, but is standing here with us tonight. I see a future where all scientists come together with a unified agenda, and share their research and their brilliance. We can do anything, but the longer we do nothing, more people will die. Together we can make a world where cancer no longer means living with fear, without hope or worse."

Then, in a moment of supreme poignancy, he said, "Tonight I stand here, another individual living with cancer, who asks that we not wait any longer and I ask only one thing of you—please stand up with me."

His words met with tumultuous applause as the entire audience stood as one to salute him. "He looks amazing," basketball player Charles Barkley said. "For me, seeing Patrick Swayze, someone who is actually fighting this disease, was the best part of the show." And when Melissa Etheridge and Sugarland sang the last song, Patrick did a moment of solo air guitar to it.

After most of the crowd had left, he remained onstage, chatting with Fran Drescher and other cancer survivors. And then he held Lisa close and danced one final dance with her.

He was still flying to Stanford for painful and debilitating chemotherapy treatments and, in an October 29 *New York Times* interview, went public regarding how much he was suffering. "I'm still fine to work, I haven't changed." Then, hearing his own words, he stopped in his tracks, did a volte-face, and reverted to the truth. "Oh, I've changed, what am I saying? It's a battle zone I go through. Chemo, no matter how you cut it, it is hell on wheels."

Above all, he remained Patsy Swayze's son, forever true to the maxim she'd drilled into him. Work through the pain. Work through the suffering. Work, work. He had never worked merely for money, nor for praise or adulation. Deep down, he had always had a sense of mission, a feeling that he owed his audience more than just showing up. He once said, "I need to know that people are feeling better or lighter or understanding something more about their lives because of my work. The one thing you can take to your grave at the end of it all is that you gave something back."

• • •

He succeeded in completing every single one of the twelve *Beast* episodes, just as he intended. And when the show wrapped on November 21, he was left with an exhilarating sense of triumph, of hope for the future and for his survival.

On December 6, 2008—twenty years after she first interviewed Patrick—Barbara Walters visited the ranch again, where she interviewed him and Lisa for a special, "Patrick Swayze; The Truth."

After the interview, Barbara said, "Everything about him impresses me: his courage, his humor. There's something very valiant about him. Whether you've seen his films or not, you realize that he's a remarkable man."

When the special aired on January 7, 2009, many of Patrick's friends and fans were deeply shocked by Barbara asking him point blank how long he thought he had left to live. However, as Zetta Alderman explained, "Patsy said that Patrick asked Barbara to ask that question on camera."

Just days before *The Beast* was due to premiere on January 15, on A&E, Patrick checked himself into Cedars Sinai in Los Angeles. He had pneumonia, a serious development since his body was already weakened by the pancreatic cancer coupled with the chemotherapy. Lisa was by his side as he underwent high doses of intravenous medicine. He was released from the hospital a week later. Patsy, who saw him in *The Beast*, said, "He was brilliant in it. You couldn't see any signs at all that he is sick."

However, on January 28, 2009, she talked to Zetta Alderman, who reported, "She told me he has good days and bad days. I don't think I've ever heard her sound so bad as she did. I've never heard her sound so desperate. She sounded defeated," Zetta said.

If Patrick had any regrets about his life, they centered around his own recklessness. "My big regret is the physical damage I've done to my body," he said. "I can do almost anything physically and I used to believe I was invincible, breaking bones over and over, playing football, doing gymnastics, diving, ballet, doing my own stunts, kickboxing, staging fights . . . it all seems a little stupid to me now."

His daredevil streak, he once admitted, was partially derived from the deep-seated feeling that he would die before his time. Referring to Bodhi, the surfer he played in *Point Break*, he explained: "I think maybe somewhere Bodhi knows he's not long for this world. Romantically, he believes he'll go out in flames because he lives to ride the biggest waves in the world, to do anything that gives him that moment of rush. And I've lived that all my life."

Above all, he knew that he had lived out a life in which he was fortunate enough to have found his soul mate, his great love. As he once said, "Lisa has been a gift and a blessing, and someone worth falling in love with over and over again, like we've done. You could say I've got issues in my life. I've got so much passion. I'm like a team of horses. I'm an obsessive being, and I love it. I've been through the mill, and I wouldn't trade those years in my life, the dark moments. Life is a roller coaster, and I'm going to ride it where it takes me."

His mother, Patsy, was now eighty-one years old. She had borne him against all odds, loved him unreservedly, nurtured him, taught him, drilled him in the work ethic, put iron in his soul, knowing that he had talent and would flourish. At times his recklessness had horrified her; at other times his phoenix-like ability for survival had fortified her.

Now, though, he had been struck down by a virtually invincible foe and no matter how strong, how brave he might be, how heroic, she feared that there was little hope.

Fighting back her tears, she spoke out to the press, "It breaks my heart to know he's suffering. But he bears it and he's determined to beat this. He's hanging in there and getting the best treatment he can. And if anybody can be saved it is my son, as he is so strong and despite all he's going through remains positive.

"He doesn't deserve to get this! He just doesn't deserve it. He's got such a big heart. He's been such a good and generous and thoughtful person," she said.

She was right. For Patrick Swayze does have a big heart and has been good and generous and thoughtful and more. For almost thirty years, he has given joy and happiness to the millions of fans who have gloried in him in all his screen incarnations, from the noble Civil War hero Orry Main, a hero in every sense of the word, to the dashing bad-boy-turned-Prince-Charming Johnny Castle, and the celestial Wall Street executive Sam Wheat, the personification of eternal love and life everlasting.

And offscreen, in a world in which being a man has often meant never showing any emotion, being hard, impassive, even cruel, he has taught us that all that isn't necessarily the measure of a man, and that a man can be unafraid even to cry openly on national television, can be a loving and monogamous husband, and still remain a man.

Above all, throughout his struggle and suffering with pancreatic cancer, by being brave enough to make public the most intimate details of his battle against one of the worst diseases of our time, he has, by example, shown all of us all how to cope with our own tomorrows as well. For Patrick Swayze, the man who taught the whole world how to dance, has also taught all of us how to live, and for that, I, among millions, shall always be grateful.

EPILOGUE

*I*f you or a loved one is facing pancreatic cancer the following organizations can offer hope and support:

Pancreatic Cancer Action Network
Advance Research Support Patients Create Hope
www.pancan.org

Lustgarten Foundation
www.lustgarten.org

Michael Rolfe Pancreatic Cancer Foundation
www.rolfefoundation.org

Hirshberg Foundation
www.pancreatic.org

ACKNOWLEDGMENTS

*I*n 1967, Richard Branson assigned me to interview actor Robert Stephens for his *Student* Magazine. Since then I've interviewed hundreds of stars from Sylvester Stallone to Kate Winslet, Mae West to Mickey Rourke. Along the way, I've learned that the majority of Hollywood stars handle a press interview as if they belong to the Sopranos and are pledged to maintain *omerta* and reveal nothing. Or else they become the human equivalent of broken records, repeating tired anecdotes ad infinitum. In fact, when confronted by an interviewer, most stars become as closed-mouthed about their deepest thoughts and feelings as any hardy Guantanamo detainee under interrogation.

In advance of an interview with the star, copy approval is often demanded, countless areas are ruled inadmissible, certain questions banned, and often a PR flack hovers menacingly like some super-annuated KGB agent, ready to pounce if anything personal is even whispered.

Patrick Swayze is a rare exception to virtually every other star interviewee, and always has been. Due to Patrick's openness and honesty, in the literally thousands of interviews he has given the media over the past thirty years—quotations from some of which are reproduced in this biography—he has created a roadmap to his innermost emotions, his trials, tribulations, his very mind, heart, and soul.

So that while most biographers are faced with the uphill struggle of exploring the self behind the frontage, removing the mask to reveal the man, Patrick—like some starry Wizard of Oz emerging from behind the screen—has consistently stripped away his own frontage, invaded his own privacy by exposing and dissecting his own most profound, intimate emotions, openly informing the world exactly who he is.

Initially, I had planned to contact Patrick regarding him granting me an interview for this book, and to also contact the rest of his family, as well. However, by the time I arrived at the point in my research at which I intended to make those requests, the state of Patrick's health was such that I felt I should not. Further down the line, he announced that he is, in fact, writing his autobiography.

Although I didn't realize it at the time, my journey toward this biography of Patrick Swayze can be traced back to May 12, 2006, when—on behalf of *The Mail on Sunday*—I breakfasted at the London Covent Garden Hotel with Eleanor Bergstein, the writer and creator of *Dirty Dancing*, who gave me her perspective on the movie and on Patrick. And while I have not quoted anything she said during that meeting in this book, her story proved to be fascinating. All the more so when—just a week later—I saw Patrick in *Guys and Dolls* on the London stage.

Every biography begins with in-depth research. From the first, I was greatly indebted to my enthusiastic, gifted, and intelligent assistant, Michelle Ferrer, who worked on the book at every stage, researching, interviewing, fact-checking, and shepherding it through the writing and editing phases.

Countless libraries, individuals, websites, and institutions were consulted in the course of the research for this book, and I am grateful to all of them, including Edda Tasiemka of the Tasiemka Archives, Tom Freeman of Freeman News Services, the Margaret Herrick Library, the Academy of Motion Pictures Arts and Sciences, IMDb

(Internet Movie Database), Netflix, the American Society of Cinematographers, the Grammy Foundation, St. Rose of Lima Catholic School, Oak Forest Elementary, F. M. Black Junior High, Waltrip High School, St. Jacinto Junior College, Oak Forest Neighborhood Association, Key Biscayne Public Library, The British Library, The Biography Channel, The Lincoln Center Library for the Performing Arts, The New York Public Library, *the Houston Chronicle* Archives, News Library, Press Display, High Beam Library, among others.

I owe thanks to George Thwaites, editor of Section 2 of *The Mail on Sunday* for having initiated my meeting with Eleanor Bergstein in the first place, and to *The Daily Mail* Good Health editor, Justine Hawkins, who, in June 2007, assigned me to write a story on the ravages of pancreatic cancer as told by Maggie Suckley, whose husband, Nick died of the disease. Maggie's courage in detailing her husband's tragic struggle with pancreatic cancer not only led to the feature published in *The Daily Mail* on July 17, 2007, but also to my understanding of the disease as well.

My guiding light while researching, interviewing for, and writing this biography was, as always, the spirit of the legendary journalist and documentary producer, the late Desmond Wilcox, with whom I worked as a researcher at BBC TV at the start of my career, and again, at the very end of his life when I was associate producer on his last three documentaries, also for BBC TV.

In working with Desmond so early on in my career, I was following in the illustrious footsteps of Sir David Frost, who—at the very start of his career—was a trainee at the British television station at which Desmond was the star reporter. In another incarnation Desmond might well have been a great actor. He was also a masterly raconteur, and one of his favorite stories centered around the time when he was mounting an investigative documentary in Norfolk, England, and dispatched David ahead of him, exhorting him to "book me the best suite in the best hotel in town." On arrival there, David discovered that all the hotels were booked. Nonetheless, he succeeded in booking Desmond the best suite in the best hotel in town, as instructed. Asked by Desmond how he'd pulled off such a coup, David admitted that as Sandringham, the royal residence, was only a few miles away from the best hotel in town, he'd insinuated to the hotel manager that Desmond was expecting a midnight visit from a certain royal princess, and therefore needed the best suite in his hotel. An object lesson in Sir David's early resourcefulness, even then.

True to Desmond's maxim that any journalist worth his salt who wants to interview the best sources for his subject needs to book "the best suite in the best hotel in town," in Houston, I stayed at the glamorous Hotel ZaZa, where I entertained sources in the even more glamorous Black Label suite, overlooking the Houston skyline. In San Diego, the Four Seasons Aviara provided a serene and beautiful setting for some of my detailed conversations with Lois Zetter, Patrick's manager for eleven years, through *Dirty Dancing* and right up until *Ghost.*

In the same vein, The Polo Lounge at the incomparable Beverly Hills Hotel was the scene of one particular meeting crucial to this book. In London, interviewing at the fabulous Baglioni felt like being on location in a hip Oscar-winning movie, and The Royalton in Manhattan was an elegant environment in which to interview sources. And once the book went to press the ultra-cool and stunningly beautiful Shore Club in Miami and, in particular, its restaurant, Ago, were the perfect places in which to celebrate.

While researching and writing this and my five other biographies, I was helped by the encouragement and support of my fellow biographers, friends, and colleagues, and should like to thank Roger Alton, editor of *The Independent*; Sandy Williams-Martel, former commissioning editor of *The Daily Mail*'s Weekend Magazine; Peter Evans, author of *Nemesis*; Sian James, assistant editor, Features, *The Mail on Sunday*; Jim Gillespie, features editor of *The Daily Mail*; Anthony Summers and Robbyn Swann, authors of *Sinatra: The Life*; Steven Gaines, author of *Fool's Paradise*; and Gwen Robyns, the doyenne of us all.

Scores of people contributed to this book, which was greatly enriched by the in-depth cooperation of many of Patrick's closest family friends, his mother's long-term students, his schoolmates, his dance partners, his serious girlfriend, Terri Harsch, who was gracious enough to allow me to reproduce personal photographs of herself in this book, cast members of his movies, Lois Zetter, his first manager, and a number of confidential sources, some of whom who have known him since his childhood, and others who have worked with him on a long-term basis. I am immeasurably grateful to all of them.

With appreciation to Dr. Susan Horsewood-Lee, Maggie Suckley, Winston Quitasol, Charles Bukey, Heidi McGowen, Jeff Habberstad, Gray Frederickson, Paul Diekman, Eileen Eichenstein, David B. Lasater, Debbie Contreras-Williams, Brenda Kruemcke, Judy Britt, Terri Harsch, John Askins, Paula Abbott, Cookie Joe, Danny Ward, Judy Nichols, Roger Seward, Zetta Alderman, Sam Kwasman, Pam Brumfield [Miller], Daniel Epper, Terri Anne White, Rick Odums, Linda May-Randell, Walter Unterseher, Sandy and Nick Martel, Charlotte Mann, John Connolly, Rebecca Michael, Nina and Bill Judson, Dr. Erika Padan Freeman, Rosalind Clarke, Herb Gains, Fergus Greer, Chad Tauber, Dustin Blauvelt, Marty Elfalan, Glen Deitell, George Baetz, Mamie Scheidemantel, David Cliff, Stephanie MacLean, Joanne DiVitto, Ken Eiland, Beverly Allen, and John Townley, the brilliant astrologer who did Patrick's chart for me the moment the subject of my writing his biography was broached.

As always, I was blessed by having the support and help of my mother, Marion Charles, an author in her own right and my eternal inspiration, both in my work and in my life.

I am once more proud to be published by the dream team of Simon Spotlight Entertainment, Publisher Jennifer Bergstrom, Editorial Director Tricia Boczkowski, Editor Sarah Sper, Publicity Director Jennifer Robinson and Art Director Michael Nagin. I extend my deepest thanks to all of them.

And thanks to Dan Strone, CEO of the Trident Media Group, and the best agent on the planet, bar none.

SOURCE NOTES

Prologue **THE STAR**

1. Patrick's birth time: Mary Sit-DuVall, *Houston Chronicle*, March 17, 1999.
1. Patrick's birth: Roderick Barrand, *Hello!*, October 24, 1992, Frank Durham, *OK!*, April, 1994 and interviews with Paula Abbott and Zetta Alderman.
1. **St. Joseph Hospital:** Ralph Bivins, *Houston Chronicle*, October 31, 1995.
2. **Statistics on average baby length and placenta previa:** Dr. Susan Horsewood-Lee, M.B. B.S. MRCGP.
2. **Gladys Karnes:** Interview, Rick Odums; interview, Cookie Joe; and www.genealogy.com.
2. **"We think we've lost":** Frank Durham, *OK!*, April 1994.
3. **"I'll never forget the words":** Frank Durham, *OK!*, April 1994.
3. **the pediatrician was his great-aunt:** Frank Durham, *OK!*, April 1994.

One **DEEP IN THE HEART OF TEXAS**

6. Swayze genealogy: www.genealogy.com and the genealogy page of John Blythe Dobson.
7. **"sir":** *North and South: The Complete Collection*, directed by Kevin Connor and Larry Peerce.
7. **"There's a real power to Texans":** Kathryn Casey, *Ultra for Men* magazine, June 1990.
7. **Houston:** The Greater Houston Partnership.
8. **"By the time I got off":** Luaine Lee, *Howard News Service*, November 10, 1995.

8. **the Incarnate Word Academy of Houston:** www.iwacademy.org and www.tshaonline.org.

8. **"that there is no such thing as failure":** Caryl Bigenho, *Ventura County Star* (CA), October 22, 1998.

8. Buddy and Patsy's marriage: www.genealogy.com

8. **St. Joseph Hospital:** Ralph Bivins, *Houston Chronicle*, October 31, 1995.

9. **Candlelight Wood and Oak Forest:** The Oak Forest Neighborhood Association.

9. Author viewed exterior of house on Del Norte.

9. **Marcella Donovan Perry:** Kathryn Casey, *Ultra for Men* magazine, June 1990.

9. **"I kind of came out of the womb onstage":** *Patrick Swayze: All the Right Moves*. The Biography Channel, 2000.

10. **When he was only eight months:** Roderick Barrand, *Hello!*, October 24, 1992, Frank Durham, *OK!*, April 1994.

10. **his pictures from that time:** Roderick Barrand, *Hello!*, October 24, 1992.

10. **"Patrick was the most outgoing":** Helen Dorsey, *Family Circle*, April 4, 1989.

10. **Theater seats:** Jane F. Lane, *W*, June 12, 1989, and Alex Kadis, *YM*, September 1990.

Two **AN IMPRESSIONABLE AGE**

11. Malcolm Gladwell, *Outliers: The Story of Success*. New York: Little, Brown & Company, 2008.

11. Muriel Spark, *The Prime of Miss Jean Brodie*. New York: HarperCollins, 1999.

12. **"She reminded me of":** Cookie Joe, interview.

12. **Far from being a girlie girl:** Cookie Joe, Paula Abbott, Rick Odums, Zetta Alderman, interviews on Patsy's appearance.

12. **"He took care of":** Danny Ward, interview.

12. **"A dance studio is like":** Zetta Alderman, interview.

13. **"born and bred a redneck":** Lisa Birnbach, *Parade*, April 8, 1990.

13. ***New York Times* crossword:** Lester Middlehurst, *The Daily Mail*, November 29, 2005.

13. **"My father was the kind of man":** Lester Middlehurst, *The Daily Mail*, November 29, 2005.

13. **"Little Buddy really has a lot of his dad":** Zetta Alderman, interview.

14. **"His father was the rock":** Larry Ward, *Patrick Swayze: All the Right Moves*. The Biography Channel.

14. Music in Swayze household: Mike Hughes, *Chicago Sun-Times*, May 31, 1994.

14. **"I love to watch people develop strong bodies":** Robyn Loewenthal, *Los Angeles Times*, Ventura County Life Section, April 18, 1991.

14. **"Patsy wasn't a housekeeper":** Zetta Alderman, interview.

14. **"She was the most wonderful teacher:** Zetta Alderman, interview.

15. **Unlike most teachers:** Cookie Joe, interview.

15. **"Patsy was very much like Mama Rose":** Cookie Joe, interview.

15. **"She was very short tempered":** Zetta Alderman, interview.

15. **Paula Abbott:** www.apacdance.com.

15. **"Get in the front!"** Paula Abbott, interview.

16. **"Patsy was big on teaching us to kick the highest":** Cookie Joe, interview.

16. **"She instilled a competitive nature":** Cookie Joe, interview.

16. **"He was probably the most competitive person I've ever met":** Larry Ward, *Patrick Swayze: All the Right Moves* The Biography Channel.

16. **If he ever fell short:** Larry Ward, *Patrick Swayze: All the Right Moves*. The Biography Channel.

16. **"I wouldn't trade her for the world":** Sara Barrett, *The Daily Mail*, October 4, 1990.

16. **"All of us felt so challenged":** Zetta Alderman, interview.

16. **A classic Patsy vignette:** Cookie Joe, interview.

17. **Tommy Tune Awards:** Theatre Under the Stars website.

17. **"With the boys, you have to build a desire":** Sylvia L. Oliande, *Daily News* (Los Angeles), March 14, 1999.

17. **His daredevil propensity:** Frank Durham, *OK!*, April 1994.

17. **"One boy had already been killed":** Roderick Barrand, *Hello!* October 24, 1992.

18. **"He wanted to do everything":** Patsy Swayze, *Patrick Swayze: All the Right Moves*. The Biography Channel.

18. **"She wanted all of us to achieve the same levels":** *Patrick Swayze: All the Right Moves.* The Biography Channel.
18. **"My mother was so intense":** Sara Barrett, *The Daily Mail*, October 4, 1990.
18. **"Patrick was so open hearted":** Lois Zetter, interview.
19. **"I could see someone who is very rigorous":** Nancy Griffin, *Premiere*, March 1992.
19. **"On certain levels, I felt ripped apart as a kid":** Stephanie Mansfield, GQ, February 1992.
19. **"I can't remember Patsy missing dance class":** Paula Abbott interview.
19. **"an ability to work":** Sara Barrett, *The Daily Mail*, October 4, 1990.
19. **St. Rose of Lima:** www.stroselima.org.
19. **"You know, Mom":** Roderick Barrand, *Hello!* October 24, 1992.
19. **"convinced that he could do anything":** Sue Russell, *Sunday Express Magazine*, July 21, 1991.
19. **"He was never one to want help":** Frank Durham, *OK!*, April 1994.
20. **Ice cream carton and the bullfrog:** Cheryl Laird, *Houston Chronicle*, May 12, 1991.
20. **"Ever since I was a little boy":** Gill Pringle, *People*, November 26, 1995.
20. **"I've been an adventure king":** Patricia Sheridan, *Pittsburgh Post-Gazette*, June 9, 2004.
20. **Patrick and Tarzan:** Susan Schindehette, *People*, August 6, 1990.
20. **Big Buddy taught his eldest son:** Jim Jerome, *Us Magazine*, May 29, 1989.
21. **"He was as intent":** Larry Ward interview, *Patrick Swayze: All the Right Moves.* The Biography Channel.
21. **Waltrip High:** www.waltriphighschool.net.
21. **"Buddy was in the theater group":** Pam Brumfield, interview.
22. **"If you ever start a fight":** Wayne Miller, *Playgirl*, June 1992.
22. **Martial arts:** Lawrence Linderman, *Playboy*, June 1992.
22. **"I started walking around with a chip on my shoulder":** Susan Spillman, *USA Today*, August 26, 1987.
22. **Broken jaw:** Rick Fulton, *Daily Record*, June 8, 2004.

22. **"beat the snuff out of them"**: *Patrick Swayze: All the Right Moves.* The Biography Channel.

22. **"He issued them a challenge"**: Zetta Alderman, interview.

23. **"To his face"**: Cookie Joe, interview.

23. **"Little Buddy volunteered"**: Zetta Alderman, interview.

23. **"We got done early"**: Cookie Joe, interview.

24. **"He was a strong, strong character"**: Danny Ward, interview.

24. **"He was kind of shy"**: Debbie Contreras, interview.

24. **Donald Duck**: Brenda Kruemcke, interview.

24. **"In my yearbook"**: Judy Britt, interview.

25. **"Buddy was very handsome"**: Mamie Scheidemantel, interview.

25. **"I had a crush on him"**: Pam Brumfield, interview.

25. **"Patsy loved Nikki"**: Cookie Joe, interview.

25. **"Whoever he dated"**: Mamie Scheidemantel, interview.

25. **Jaclyn Smith**: Andrew Goldman, *Elle*, February 2004.

26. **However, by the time he was fifteen**: Larry Ward, interview, *Patrick Swayze: All the Right Moves.* The Biography Channel.

26. **"One thing you didn't do was cross Patsy"**: Larry Ward, interview, *Patrick Swayze: All the Right Moves.* The Biography Channel.

26. **"He inherited Patsy's quick temper"**: Cookie Joe, interview.

26. **"Patsy would tell us"**: Zetta Alderman, interview.

26. **"None of us would"**: Zetta Alderman, interview.

27. **"The Pied Piper of Astro World"**: Interview with source.

27. **"She believed that every child"**: Rick Odums, interview.

28. **Christian Children's Fund**: www.christianchildrensfund.org.

28. **Patsy always brought them into the studio**: Cookie Joe, interview.

28. **Deeply touched**: Henrietta Knight, *Hello!*, August 28, 1993, and *Woman's Own*, November 11, 1993.

29. **"I saw this little girl coming down the plane stairs"**: Cookie Joe, interview.

29. **"The Swayzes practically saved my life"**: Henrietta Knight, *Hello!*, August 28, 1993, and *Woman's Own*, November 11, 1993.

30. **"I remember watching Patrick dance"**: Henrietta Knight, *Hello!*, August 28, 1993, and *Woman's Own*, November 11, 1993.

31. **"He took my husband into a room"**: Zetta Alderman, interview.

31. **"It's bred into male dancers"**: Rick Odums, interview.

31. **He was so badly injured**: Cookie Joe, Zetta Alderman, Paula Abbott, Rick Odums, interviews.

32. **"You just turn yourself into a master and commander":** Cindy Pearlman, *Chicago Sun-Times*, February 24, 2004.

32. **"My mother wanted me to be everything":** Nancy Griffin, *Premiere*, March 1992.

three **PRINCE CHARMING**

33. **"Buddy was a masculine dancer":** Rick Odums, interview.

33. **"At least ten women":** Paula Abbott, interview.

33. **"One of my first memories of Patrick":** Kathryn Casey, *Ultra for Men* magazine, June 1990.

34. **"Patsy used to brag":** Cookie Joe, interview.

34. **"I was shocked because we never talked before":** Terri Harsch, interview.

35. **"He was amazed that I couldn't lift my leg":** Terri Harsch, interview.

35. **"We'd end up":** Terri Harsch, interview.

36. **"One of my happiest memories":** Terri Harsch, interview.

37. **"He came to my door":** Terri Harsch, interview.

37. **"I stood in front of the railing":** Terri Harsch, interview.

38. **"We were all trained in ballet":** Sam Kwasman, interview.

39. **"I met Buddy again in 1989":** Roger Seward, interview.

39. **"All that squatting and turning":** Mitchell Krugel, *Patrick Swayze*. New York: St. Martin's Press, 1988.

40. **"I don't ever want to get satisfied":** Barry Koltnow, *The Orange County Register*, April 15, 1992.

Four **MY ANGEL**

41. **Tom Jones:** Martin Townsend interview on September 18, 1988.

42. **"all the dancers were fussing over Patrick":** Karin Haapaniemi, *Patrick Swayze Fan Club Magazine*, December 1996.

43. **"The very first time Lisa walked into the studio":** Zetta Alderman, interview.

43. **"Patsy called Lisa":** Paula Abbott, interview.

43. **Lisa Anne Haapaniemi:** Karin Haapaniemi, *Patrick Swayze Fan Club Magazine*, December 1996.

43. **"I think being raised in a family of boys"**: Karin Haapaniemi, *Patrick Swayze Fan Club Magazine*, December 1996.

44. **She was also knowledgeable about football**: Karin Haapaniemi, *Patrick Swayze Fan Club Magazine*, December 1996.

44. **Her ability to focus**: Karin Haapaniemi, *Patrick Swayze Fan Club Magazine*, December 1996.

44. **"I started out again to locate the Drama Department"**: Karin Haapaniemi, *Patrick Swayze Fan Club Magazine*, December 1996.

45. **"Buddy was so great"**: Zetta Alderman, interview.

45. **"Buddy and I were still committed"**: Terri Harsch, interview.

46. **He spent three months dancing**: Jessica Sommer, *Blake Beat—James Hubert Blake High School*, March 17, 2005.

46. **"He was very romantic with writing poetry"**: Jessica Sommer, *Blake Beat—James Hubert Blake High School*, March 17, 2005.

47. **"He made a lot of plans"**: Terri Harsch, interview.

47. **"We met outside the studio"**: Terri Harsch, interview.

48. **"Lisa had a very wise head on her shoulders"**: Lester Middlehurst, *The Daily Mail*, November 29, 2005.

48. **"I wasn't sure I liked Patrick"**: Karin Haapaniemi, *Patrick Swayze Fan Club Magazine*, December 1996.

48. **"Love is supposed to start with"**: Susan Schindehette, *People* August 6, 1990.

48. **"She didn't buy any of my nonsense"**: Wayne Miller, *Playgirl*, June 1992.

49. **"I never met a girl like her"**: Wayne Miller, *Playgirl*, June 1992.

49. **"I was not the cheerleader type"**: Wayne Miller, *Playgirl*, June 1992.

49. **"I wasn't interested in his accomplishments"** Melina Gerosa, *Ladies' Home Journal*, May 1998.

49. **"We were both kind of misunderstood"**: Susan Schindehette, *People*, August 6, 1990.

49. **"She was so proud of him"**: Cookie Joe, interview.

50. **"In Houston I was Mr. Kingpin "**: Jay Carr, *The Boston Globe*, May 14, 1989.

50. **"I'll always be a classical ballet dancer"**: Susan Schindehette, *People*, August 6, 1990.

50. **"He made a big impression on me"**: Linda May-Randell, interview.

51. **"I did the est training":** Jerry Lazar, "Leader of the Pack," *Us Magazine*, November 12, 1990.
51. **"We were very excited for Buddy":** Cookie Joe, interview.
51. **"She talked constantly":** Interview with source.
52. **"When I found out Lisa was coming":** Wayne Miller, *Playgirl*, June 1992.
52. **"I think it was perfect for Patsy":** Cookie Joe, interview.
52. **"Patsy was very strong":** Zetta Alderman, interview.
52. **"Lisa does have Patsy's character":** Rick Odums, interview.
53. **"I tried to make Lisa my mother":** GQ, February 1992.
53. **"I mistrusted women":** Sara Barrett, *The Daily Mail*, October 4, 1990.
53. **"I just felt at the time":** Michelle Tauber, *People*, March 24, 2008.
53. **"I thought all I was":** Wayne Miller, *Playgirl*, June 1992.
53. **"I didn't know if there was anything inside":** Jim Jerome, *Us Magazine*, May 29, 1989.
53. **"Every bit of validation he'd gotten":** Bill Zehme, GQ, February 1989.
53. **"He gave me a hard time":** Mitchell Krugel, *Patrick Swayze*. New York: St. Martin's Press, 1988.
54. **"I grew up with a lot of sexual hang-ups":** Stephanie Mansfield, GQ, February 1992.
54. **"My father walked in":** Lydia Slater, *The Daily Mail Weekend*, November 25, 1995.
54. **"I couldn't sleep around":** Lydia Slater, *The Daily Mail Weekend*, November 25, 1995.
54. **"Lisa and I lived with each other":** Lydia Slater, *The Daily Mail Weekend*, November 25, 1995.
54. **Propose he did:** Melina Gerosa, *Ladies' Home Journal*, May 1998.
54. **Beforehand, Lisa sewed:** Melina Gerosa, *Ladies' Home Journal*, May 1998.
54. **Founded by:** Melina Gerosa, *Ladies' Home Journal*, May 1998.
55. **self-taught carpenters:** Rick Odums, interview.
55. **"Lisa—who had started sewing:** Karin Haapaniemi, *Patrick Swayze Fan Club Magazine*, December 1996.
55. **Consequently, Patrick also worked:** Rick Odums, interview.
55. **Underwear photograph:** Interview with source.

55. **"As heterosexual as a bull moose"**: Steve Daly, *Entertainment Weekly*, September 22, 1995.

55. **Life in Manhattan:** Rick Odums, interview.

56. **"I went insane"**: Dan Yakir, *The San Francisco Chronicle*, May 14, 1989.

56. **"They held her up"**: Rick Odums, interview.

56. **"I was the Godzilla of ballet"**: Mitchell Krugel, *Patrick Swayze*. New York: St. Martin's Press, 1988.

56. **"He was a tough guy"**: Elliott Feld, *Patrick Swayze: All the Right Moves*. The Biography Channel.

56. **"a genius"**: Eirik Knutzen, *The Toronto Star*, April 28, 1991.

56. **"He was this motorcycle freak"**: Rick Odums, interview.

57. **Patrick was poised to leave:** Mitchell Krugel, *Patrick Swayze*. New York: St. Martin's Press, 1988.

57. **"Patsy was devastated"**: Paula Abbott, interview.

57. **"All of us were terrified"**: Cookie Joe, interview.

58. **"Pitted against what he just innately had"**: Lisa Niemi, *Patrick Swayze: All the Right Moves*. The Biography Channel.

58. **"It was always touching"**: Tom Moore, *Patrick Swayze: All the Right Moves*. The Biography Channel.

59. **"To me, he was more Danny Zuko"**: Zetta Alderman, interview.

59. **"I think sex appeal comes from who you are"**: Nancy Mills, *Cosmopolitan*, April 1988.

59. **"She taught me [life] ain't about coasting"**: Barbara Walters interview, May 11, 1988.

59. **"People would lose it"**: Stephanie Mansfield, *GQ*, February 1992.

60. **"the actor creates with his own flesh and blood"**: Lee Strasberg.

60. **"Patrick's a tough guy"**: Stephanie Mansfield, *GQ*, February 1992.

60. **"They were like Tristan and Iseult"**: Stephanie Mansfield, *GQ*, February 1992.

60. **"Most people come to Hollywood"**: Mitchell Krugel, *Patrick Swayze*. New York: St. Martin's Press, 1988.

Five **EMERALD CITY**

61. **Back home in Houston:** Zetta Alderman, interview.

63. **"His performance in *Skatetown USA*"**: Lois Zetter, interview.

63. **But like Patsy:** Paula Abbott, interview.

63. **"I nearly starved after *Skatetown*":** Jerry Buck, *The Record* (New Jersey), November 3, 1985.

63. **"He wanted to work with Lisa":** Lois Zetter, interview.

63. **"It used to screw me up":** Garth Pearce, *Sunday Magazine* (London), September 30, 1990.

64. **"People couldn't understand":** Martin Townsend interview on September 18, 1988.

64. **Lisa was a natural at carpentry:** Melina Gerosa, *Ladies' Home Journal*, May 1998.

65. **"I tried to talk him out of doing his own stunts":** Lois Zetter, interview.

66. **From the first, Patrick and the veteran director:** Mitchell Krugel, *Patrick Swayze*. New York: St. Martin's Press, 1988.

66. **Looking back:** Mitchell Krugel, *Patrick Swayze*.

67. **"That film was a lot of young kids":** Grey Frederickson, interview.

68. **"I've always known Patrick to be a good man":** Tom Cruise, *People*.

68. **"I still feel all the guys":** Wayne Miller, *Playgirl*, June 1992.

69. **"I thought that Patrick did wonderful work":** Lois Zetter, interview.

69. **"I felt good about it":** Scott Cain, *The Atlanta Journal-Constitution*, February 8, 1986.

69. **On the morning of November 9:** Susan Schindehette, *People*, August 6, 1990.

70. **"If anybody ever died again":** Bill Zehme, *GQ*, February 1989.

70. **Grief-stricken in the extreme:** Barry McIlheney, *Empire*, November 1990, and interview with Zetta Alderman, who was told the news of his death by the family.

70. **"But every time I tried to touch his body":** Barry McIlheney, *Empire*, November 1990.

71. **"I inherited my father's knife":** Bill Zehme. *GQ*, February 1989

71. **"I found his grief continued on":** Patsy Swayze, *Patrick Swayze: All the Right Moves*. The Biography Channel.

71. **"Every time my life got to a place":** Wayne Miller, *Playgirl*, June 1992.

71. **Drinking:** source who witnessed it.
72. **During his drinking bouts:** Susan Schindehette. *People*, August 6, 1990.
72. **Other times his rage:** Lawrence Linderman, *Playboy*, June 1992.
72. **"I turned into a lunatic":** *The Globe and Mail*, October 27, 1990.
72. **"His pain was so severe":** Patsy Swayze, *Patrick Swayze: All the Right Moves*. The Biography Channel.

Six **TOP OF THE WORLD**

73. **Apart from seeing the world:** Jim Jerome, *Us Magazine*, May 29, 1989.
74. **"You could have fainted":** Lois Zetter, interview.
75. **"The only hope I had":** Lawrence Linderman, *Playboy*, June 1992.
75. Patrick's desire to work with A list: Lawrence Linderman, *Playboy*, June 1992.
76. **"This time Patrick":** Lisa Birnbach, *Parade*, April 8, 1990.
76. **"I hated myself":** Sharon Feinstein, *Sunday Magazine* (London), October 18, 1987.
77. **"I did something silly":** Scott Cain, *The Atlanta Journal-Constitution*, February 8, 1986.
79. **"During the early years":** Lois Zetter, interview.
79. **"We were looking for a strong":** Mitchell Krugel, *Patrick Swayze*, New York: St. Martin's Press, 1988.
79. **"He has an uncanny natural ability":** Paul Freeman, *Patrick Swayze: All the Right Moves*, The Biography Channel.
80. **Boone Hall:** Lee Winfrey, *Lexington Herald-Leader* (KY), May 4, 1986.
81. **"Just the opportunity to get":** Sharon Kerr, *Woman's Own*, October 17, 1987.
82. **"The next thing I knew":** Judy Watts, *The Post and Courier* (Charleston, SC), March 13, 2003.
82. **"He's either sleeping":** Fred Robbins, *The Newfoundland Herald*, May 3–9, 1986.
82. **"It's a very, very scary thing to do":** Sharon Feinstein, *Sunday Magazine*, October 18, 1987.

82. **"I never realized how scared I would be":** Jay Carr, *The Boston Globe*, May 14, 1989.

83. **"I poured all my sexual energy":** Sharon Feinstein, *Sunday Magazine* (London), October 18, 1987.

83. **"I'm so terrified":** Sharon Feinstein, *Sunday Magazine* (London), October 18, 1987.

83. **"Though once I do":** Sharon Feinstein, *Sunday Magazine* (London), October 18, 1987.

83. **"When it really started cooking":** Jeannie Park, *People*, August 26, 1991.

83. **"I believe there was":** Lois Zetter, interview.

84. **"because it's bizarre":** Jay Carr, *The Boston Globe*, May 14, 1989.

86. **"Living outside L.A.":** Melina Gerosa, *Ladies' Home Journal*, May 1998.

86. **Rancho Bizarro:** Mark Morrison, *Hello!*, December 3, 1994.

86. **Lake Arrowhead:** *Milwaukee Journal Sentinel*, September 28, 1997.

87. **"Finally, I turned around":** Susan White, *Lexington Herald-Leader* (KY), June 6, 1986.

Seven **DIRTY DANCING**

88. **it had always been his dearest wish:** Interview with confidential source.

89. ***Tiger Warsaw* is the most hardcore, emotionally demanding film":** Bob Strauss, *Chicago Sun-Times*, August 30, 1987.

89. **"While I'm making films":** Sharon Feinstein, *Sunday Magazine* (London), October 18, 1987.

90. Patrick's alcoholism: Interviews with two sources who witnessed it at the time.

90. **It was John Wayne's:** Barry Koltnow, *The Orange County Register*, March 23, 1995.

91. **Like Baby:** Eleanor Bergstein interview for *The Mail on Sunday*, conducted by author on May 12, 2006, at the Covent Garden Hotel.

91. **Linda Gottlieb:** Cindy Pearlman, *Chicago Sun-Times*, August 17, 1997, and Linda Gottlieb, *Premiere*, May 1988.

91. **"Johnny to have love-me eyes like Travolta":** Lisa Birnbach, *Parade*, April 8, 1990.

92. **Despite the intensity of her pitch:** *Dirty Dancing* dvd, added features.

92. **"Patrick pointed his finger at me":** Kenny Ortega, *Dirty Dancing* dvd.

93. **"Let's just get on the plane":** Eleanor Bergstein, *Dirty Dancing* dvd.

93. **"One of those women pushed forward":** Eleanor Bergstein, *Dirty Dancing* dvd.

94. **"I pretended it was the seventies":** Jennifer Grey, *Dirty Dancing* dvd.

94. **"When Jennifer heard":** Linda Gottlieb, *Access Hollywood* interview, 2007.

94. **"She really jumped into this stuff":** *People*, September 14, 1987.

95. **"I still get chills":** Bob Strauss, *Chicago Sun-Times*, August 30, 1987.

95. **Cynthia Rhodes:** Bob Strauss, *Chicago Sun-Times*, August 30, 1987.

95. **"He's a great leader":** Ernest Tucker, *Chicago Sun-Times*, August 28, 1987.

95. **"Everybody kept telling me to tone it down":** Bob Strauss, *Chicago Sun-Times*, August 30, 1987.

95. **"I refused to shoot it unless they did it my way":** Bob Strauss, *Chicago Sun-Times*, August 30, 1987.

96. **As Linda Gottlieb remembered:** Linda Gottlieb, *Premiere*, May 1988.

96. **"all his usual charm and energy":** Linda Gottlieb, *Premiere*, May 1988.

96. **The following day:** Linda Gottlieb, *Premiere*, May 1988.

97. **"I remember Patrick":** Cindy Pearlman, *Chicago Sun-Times*, August 17, 1997.

98. **"They got on well":** Lois Zetter, interview.

98. **"I remember he was very thoughtful":** George Baetz, interview.

98. **"I really enjoyed working with him":** Eileen Eichenstein, interview.

98. **"one of the hardest lines":** Sharon Feinstein, *Sunday Magazine*, October 18, 1987.

99. **"That's the one time":** Bob Strauss, *Chicago Sun-Times*, August 30, 1987.

99. **"Fighting my ego":** Bob Strauss, *Chicago Sun-Times*, August 30, 1987.

99. **Patrick's jump:** Chris Osher, *The Atlanta Journal-Constitution*, August 21, 1988.

99. **"I had a feeling":** Sharon Feinstein, *Sunday Magazine* (London), October 18, 1987.

101. **"I'd like to go back to the hotel":** *USA Today*, August 19, 1987.

102. **"My mom called me up":** Cindy Pearlman, *San Francisco Chronicle*, May 29, 1988.

102. **"I guess I'm just this catalyst":** *The New York Times*, January 13, 1988.

103. London and Berlin dates: Lois Zetter's date book.

103. **"I'd seen the fans":** Lois Zetter, interview.

104. **"all kinds of things":** Martin Townsend interview on September 18, 1988.

104. **"There have been times":** Kathryn Casey, *Ultra for Men* magazine, June 1990.

104. **"All these people would lean over me":** Claudia Dreifus, *Woman's Own*, August 24, 1992.

104. **"When we go places the little girls go crazy":** Bruce Westbrook, *Houston Chronicle*, November 3, 1987.

105. **Kristy Harvey:** Hank Gallo, *Daily News*, July 12, 1990.

105. **"I used to have nightmares":** Dan Yakir, *The San Francisco Chronicle*, May 14, 1989.

106. **"I don't feel famous":** Sue Russell, "Hollywood's Prime Mover," *Sunday Express Magazine*, July 21, 1991.

106. **"Even if it's a cool place":** Bill Ervolino, *New York Post*, May 14, 1989.

106. **"You deal with the fact that the way you zip up your zipper":** Bill Ervolino, *New York Post*, May 14, 1989.

106. **"I'd go out, and sure enough":** Tom O'Neil, *Us Magazine*, September 1995.

107. **I think he's one the most:** Barbara Walters, interview, May 11, 1988.

107. **"Lisa literally is my creative partner":** Barbara Walters interview, May 11, 1988.

107. **"There's an intense passion between us":** Melina Gerosa, *Ladies' Home Journal*, May 1998.

107. **"I loved that man":** Barbara Walters interview, May 11, 1988.

Eight SWAYZE MANIA

109. **"He opted for some terrible movies":** Lois Zetter, interview.

109. **"I would come up to him":** Bill Zehme, Bill Zehme, *GQ*, February 1989.

109. **"Word didn't get to the maids fast enough":** Bill Zehme, *GQ*, February 1989.

109. **"I was buck naked in the bathroom":** Wayne Miller, *Playgirl*, June 1992.

110. **"It blew me away, man":** Bill Zehme, *GQ*, February 1989.

110. **"A few times, Patrick and Lisa would be chatting":** Michelle Tauber, *People*, March 24, 2008.

110. Hazard, Kentucky filming: Ginger Lundy, *The Spartanburg Herald-Journal*, September 2, 1988.

111. **"He was wearing a gray sweatshirt":** Ginger Lundy, *The Spartanburg Herald-Journal*, September 2, 1988.

111. **"The boys adore him":** Sylvia L. Oliande, *Daily News* (Los Angeles), March 14, 1999.

112. **As a valentine from Lois Zetter:** Lois Zetter, interview.

112. **"Swayze Dancing":** Author viewed *Swayze Dancing* dvd.

112. Lois Zetter, interview.

112. Walter Unterseher, interview.

112. **"I've got all these martial-arts skills":** Louis B. Parks, *Houston Chronicle*, October 1, 1995.

112. **"Since his father's death":** Lois Zetter, interview.

113. **"Patrick was a nice young boy":** Walter Unterseher, interview.

113. **"They love each other and it's apparent":** Michelle Tauber, *People*, March 24, 2008.

113. **"I wish it could have been in a little bit better taste":** Dan Yakir, *The San Francisco Chronicle*, May 14, 1989.

114. **"He's strong, but he has grace and agility":** Jeannie Park, *People*, August 26, 1991.

114. **"I loved Patrick, and I respect him as an actor":** Joan E. Vadeboncoeur, *Syracuse Herald American*, May 14, 1989.

115. **Perhaps because of the pain:** Interview with source who witnessed it.

116. **"I can't believe all the screaming women":** Cindy Pearlman, *The San Francisco Chronicle*, May 29, 1988.

116. **"She couldn't take her eyes off of Patrick":** Barry Koltnow, *The Orange County Register*, June 9, 1988.

116. **moonlit riverside fight:** Hal Lipper, *St. Petersburg Times*, May 19, 1989.

116. **a raft sailed by:** Bill Ervolino, *New York Post*, May 14, 1989.

116. **"It was actually messin' with my insides":** Jay Carr, *The Boston Globe*, May 14, 1989.

117. **"If I'd stayed in that room, I'd probably be dead by now":** Sharon Feinstein, *Sunday Magazine*, October 18, 1987.

117. Fresno shoot: *The Fresno Bee*, May 12, 1988.

117. **"I've been in everything":** Tom O'Neil, *Us Magazine*, September 1995.

117. **"A real emptiness went through me after *Dirty Dancing*:** Barry Koltnow, *St. Louis Post-Dispatch*, August 9, 1989.

117. **"He comes by doing 110":** Bruce Westbrook, *Houston Chronicle*, June 18, 1989.

118. **hit the bottle even harder:** Interview with source who saw this.

118. **"Everyone was grabbing me":** Wayne Miller, *Playgirl*, June 1992, and Jerry Lazar, *Us Magazine*, November 12, 1990.

119. **"Cocaine put me into a living hell":** Lawrence Linderman, *Playboy*, June 1992.

119. **"I'd lock":** Stephanie Mansfield, *GQ*, February 1992.

119. **"One time I got so angry":** Melina Gerosa, *Ladies' Home Journal*, May 1998.

119. **"I was running away":** Melina Gerosa, *Ladies' Home Journal*, May 1998.

122. Jerry Zucker quotes from *Ghost* dvd.

Nine **GHOST**

120. *It's a Wonderful Life*: Barry Koltnow, *Knight Ridder/Tribune News Service*, October 27, 1995.

120. **"It made me cry":** Susan Schindehette, *People*, August 6, 1990.

121. **"*Ghost* was about living your life for the moment":** Susan Schindehette, *People*, August 6, 1990.

121. **"The reason I did *Ghost*":** Henrietta Knight, *Woman's Own*, November 11, 1991

121. **"There's a sense of foreboding":** Stephanie Mansfield, *GQ*, February 1992.

121. **"I am convinced that people who are dead":** Gill Pringle, *People*, November 26, 1995.

122. **"I took it as a challenge":** Gregg Kilday, *Entertainment Weekly*, August 3, 1990.

123. **"I saw a side of Patrick":** Jerry Zucker, *Ghost* dvd special features.

123. **"There's no one who can deliver a heartfelt line like Patrick":** Jeannie Park, *People*, August 26, 1991.

123. **"Patrick said, 'I'm not doing it unless she does it' ":** Tom O'Neil, *Us Magazine*, September 1995.

123. Casting of Whoopi Goldberg: Lawrence Linderman, *Playboy*, June 1992, and James Robert Parish, *Whoopi Goldberg*. New Jersey: Carol Publishing Group, 1997.

123. **"I love being with Patrick":** Karen Thomas, *USA Today*, July 12, 1991.

124. **"That was so far from the truth":** Sue Russell, *Woman Magazine*, April 30, 1990.

124. **"He's sensitive and has a vulnerability that's right out there":** Susan Schindehette, *People*, August 6, 1990.

125. **"He has a very sweet, gentle, kind heart, and those Southern manners":** Jeannie Park, *People*, August 26, 1991.

125. **"One of my jobs":** Winston Quitasol, interview.

125. **"He was very prepared":** Charles Bukey, interview.

125. **"We had a policy":** Lois Zetter, interview.

126. **"It's weird to know that some people":** Anthony Cotton and Scott Haller, *The America's Intelligence Wire*, April 2, 2003.

126. **"Patrick's face turned bright red":** Barry McIlheney, *Empire*, November 1990.

126. **"It was exciting":** Eirik Knutzen, *The Toronto Star*, April 28, 1991.

127. **"The electricity between them":** Bruce Joel Rubin, *Ghost* dvd.

127. **"that core feeling about the person":** Susan Schindehette, *People*, August 6, 1990.

127. **"When they're together":** Susan Schindehette, *People*, August 6, 1990

127. **"It's a movie I'm proud of":** Richard Freedman, *Chicago Sun-Times*, July 10, 1990.

128. Miscarriage: Jeannie Park, *People*, August 26, 1991, and Stephanie Mansfield. *GQ*, February 1992.

128. Lisa and baby: Interview with source who talked to Patsy about this.

128. **"I felt like I had lost a person":** Claudia Dreifus, *Woman's Own*, August 24, 1992.

128. **"He told me he and Lisa had their own little ritual":** Stephanie Mansfield, *GQ*, February 1992.

128. *Super Force:* Ana Maria Bahiana, *Hello!* January 19, 1991.

128. **"No matter where we are in the world":** Claudia Dreifus, *Woman's Own*, August 24, 1992.

129. Patsy's eating habits: Zetta Alderman.

129. Patrick's breakfast: Margaret Howden, fan club magazine interview with Rosi Hygate.

130. **"When he is in town":** Bernadette Wheeler, *Newsday* (Melville, NY), August 17, 1988.

130. **"I would tell him why":** Lois Zetter, interview.

130. **"I think one of the reasons he left":** Lois Zetter, interview.

131. **"His difficult birth":** Dr. Erika Padan Freeman.

131. **"To be honest":** Lawrence Linderman, *Playboy*, June 1992.

131. **"I've always played with death":** Sue Russell, *Sunday Express Magazine*, July 21, 1991.

132. **He was brave and determined:** Jeff Habberstad, interview.

132. **"He wanted to do free style right off the bat":** Jeannie Park, *People*, August 26, 1991.

132. **"But everybody kept jumping":** Betsy Pickle, *Scripps Howard News Service*, July 25, 1991.

132. **"Once I got over the abject terror of jumping":** Paul Willistein, *Austin American-Statesman*, July 17, 1991.

133. **"Patrick was very meticulous":** Kim Frick, *Daily Breeze* (Torrance, CA), July 12, 1991.

133. **"I find him remarkably":** *Point Break* dvd additional material.

133. **He kept what he described:** Jerry Lazar, *Us Magazine*, November 12, 1990.

133. Crystals: Sheila Johnston, *The Independent* (London) November 13, 1995.

Ten BREAKING POINT

135. **"Once the producers saw":** Anthony Cotton and Scott Haller, *Daily Pennsylvanian* (University of Pennsylvania), April 3, 2003.

135. *City of Joy:* Nancy Griffin, *Premiere*, March 1992.

136. *City of Joy* shoot: Bill Higgins, *Us Magazine*, June 13, 1991.

136. **"I told him that":** Barry Koltnow, *The Orange County Register*, April 15, 1992.

136. Oberoi Grand Hotel: Nancy Griffin, *Premiere*, March 1992.

136. **Nirmal Hriday:** Parvathi Menon, *Frontline, India's National Magazine*, September 20–October 3, 1997.

137. **"The little boy":** Martin Booe, *Entertainment Weekly*, April 24, 1992, and Luaine Lee, *Scripps Howard News Service*, April 8, 1992.

138. **"There's got to be a lot of grief":** Nancy Griffin, *Premiere*, March 1992.

138. **"Method acting requires":** Dr. Erika Padan Freeman, interview.

138. **"This is a role that I can't turn the light switch off":** Bill Higgins, *Us Magazine*, June 13, 1991.

138. **"When it was finished I decided":** Marlon Brando with Robert Lindsey, *Brando: Songs My Mother Taught Me*. Random House, 1994.

139. Patrick's Method acting: Nancy Griffin, *Premiere*, March 1992.

139. **"I have yet to see another human":** Shabana Azmir, Nancy Griffin, *Premiere*, March 1992.

139. **"I drove them crazy":** Nancy Griffin, *Premiere*, March 1992.

140. **involved in a serious accident:** *Sunday Mercury*, June 18, 2000.

140. **"I want smoking out of my life":** Karen Thomas, *USA Today*, June 19, 1991.

140. **to name a cologne "Patrick":** Stacy Jenel Smith, *The Times Union* (Albany, NY), August 28, 1988.

141. **"You just can't afford to get too wrapped up":** Henrietta Knight, *Woman's Own*, November 11, 1991.

141. **"He doesn't think":** Jeannie Park, Kristina Johnson, Nancy Matsumoto, *People*, August 26, 1991.

141. **"Lisa and I have a very irreverent way with each other":** Lester Middlehurst, *The Daily Mail*, November 29, 2005.

141. **He was drinking:** Interview with source.

141. **Richard Burton:** author interviewed, 1974.

141. **Richard Harris:** author interviewed, 1981.

142. **"They took private classes":** Rick Odums, interview.
143. **Sierra Tucson:** Melina Gerosa, *Ladies' Home Journal*, May 1998.
143. **"You know what?":** Ann Trebbe, *USA Today*, May 20, 1993.
144. **"I see the letters she gets":** *People*, July 26, 1993.
145. **"It was a very special experience":** World Music Awards: Mike Hughes, *Chicago Sun-Times*, May 31, 1994.
145. **When the eight-seater plane was delivered:** Bill Zwecker, *Chicago Sun-Times*, June 10, 1994.

Eleven THANKS FOR EVERYTHING

147. **"My mother was horrified":** Tom O'Neil, *Us Magazine*, September 1995.
147. **"these big Swayze forearms and hands":** Tom O'Neil, *Us Magazine*, September 1995.
147. **"What do you do with your penis?":** Tom O'Neil, *Us Magazine*, September 1995.
148. **Each morning he was waxed and plucked:** Andrew Stephen, *Sunday Times* (London), October 29, 1995.
148. **Patsy, it transpired:** Zetta Alderman, interview.
148. **"I don't have anything to prove":** Steve Daly, *Entertainment Weekly*, September 22, 1995.
148. **"No matter how much they say":** Andrew Stephen, *Sunday Times* (London), October 29, 1995
148. **"I wasn't going to be happy with myself as a woman":** Gill Pringle, *The Daily Mirror*, November 9, 1995.
149. Patrick during *To Wong Foo:* Interview with Fergus Greer on his photo shoot with Patrick for the *Sunday Times* (London).
149. Patrick to punch Leguizamo: *World Entertainment News Network*, July 31, 2007.
150. **"Wesley would say":** Jeanne Wolf, *Sunday Mirror*, October 22, 1995.
150. **Just before Sheriff Dollard:** Janet Weeks, *The Times of Trenton*, September 11, 1995.
150. **"I was fairly new":** Interview, Heidi McGowen.
151. **"Of course, he's Patrick Swayze":** Tom O'Neil, *Us Magazine*, September 1995.
151. **"She said she thought":** Zetta Alderman, interview.

152. **"Patrick is a uniquely sensitive person":** Louis B. Parks, *Houston Chronicle*, October 1, 1995.

152. **"The love story aspect of this film":** Gill Pringle, *People*, November 26, 1995.

153. **"Buddy called me, distraught":** Zetta Alderman, interview.

153. **"It was hard not to feel responsible":** Lester Middlehurst, *The Daily Mail*, November 29, 2005.

153. **"The only thing you can do":** Lester Middlehurst, *The Daily Mail*, November 29, 2005.

153. Vickie's death: Tom O'Neil, *Us Magazine*, September 1995.

153. **"I did *Tall Tale* because":** Barry Koltnow, *The Orange County Register*, March 23, 1995.

154. Anniversary party: Margaret Howden, *Patrick Swayze Fan Club Magazine* November 1995.

154. Don Swayze's jumps: Daniel Berger, *Daily News* (Los Angeles), March 15, 1998, and Jeanne Wolf, *Sunday Mirror*, October 22, 1995.

155. **"When I saw them taking away his IV":** Tom O'Neil, *Us Magazine*, September 1995.

155. **"The night Cody died":** Gabrielle Donnelly, *OK!*, December 25, 1995.

156. **"But Cody's spirit returned to me":** Gill Pringle, *The Daily Mirror*, November 9, 1995.

156. **"I had to leave for the set":** Joan Vadeboncoeur, *The Post-Standard* (Syracuse, NY), October 15, 1995.

157. **Schexnayder family:** Angel Thompson, *The Times-Picayune* (New Orleans, LA), October 26, 1997.

157. **second brush with death:** Melina Gerosa, *Ladies' Home Journal*, May 1998.

158. **"I was using her":** Melina Gerosa, *Ladies' Home Journal*, May 1998.

Twelve **DOWNWARD SPIRAL**

160. **"Sometimes at the end of the day":** Glenn Deitell, interview.

161. Prescott Valley police report.

163. **"On one particularly stressful day":** Featured article from official Patrick Swayze International Fan Club site.

164. **"It's one of those moments"**: Cindy Pearlman, *Chicago Sun-Times*, July 17, 2003.
165. **"Most fun for me was to watch"**: Patrick Swayze, *One Last Dance* dvd, special features.
165. **"I think this movie is going to surprise"**: *AP Worldstream*, August 26, 2005.
166. *Chicago*: Evan Henerson, *Daily News* (Los Angeles, CA), January 1, 2004.
166. **"He has always portrayed characters of passion"**: Kathy Blumenstock, *The Kansas City Star* (MO), June 12, 2004.
166. **"I took big chances"**: *The Cincinnati Post*, June 12, 2004.
167. **"I fell in love with Harry"**: Kathy Blumenstock, *The Kansas City Star* (MO), June 12, 2004.
167. **"It was a great film to do"**: Alun Palmer, Europe Intelligence Wire, October 25, 2002.
167. **"I've never played a superspy before"**: Luaine Lee, *Knight Ridder/Tribune*, May 16, 2005.
168. **"The whole purpose of playing Lance"**: Lester Middlehurst, *The Daily Mail*, November 29, 2005.
168. **"It definitely tested my ability to laugh at myself"**: Lesley O'Toole, *Sunday Express*, November 27, 2005.
168. **"I was honored to kiss him"**: Martine McCutcheon, *The Paul O'Grady Show*, 2008.
169. **"Nobody puts Martine in a corner"**: Oliver Duff, *The Independent*, October 19, 2006.

Thirteen **FIGHTING BACK**

170. *Guys and Dolls*: Alison Roberts, *Evening Standard*, July 17, 2006.
170. **"The producers arranged dinner for us"**: *Daily Express Saturday Magazine*, August 12, 2006.
171. Author was present at a performance of *Guys and Dolls* later that year.
171. **"Stage fright?"**: *World Entertainment News Network*, July 17, 2006.
171. **"With a forty-six-knot crosswind"**: Melina Gerosa, *Ladies' Home Journal*, May 1998.
172. **"He was healthy, tan"**: Michelle Tauber, *People*, March 24, 2008.

172. YouTube video, James Derbyshire and Julia Boggio.

172. **"acid on an open wound":** Barbara Walters interview, January 7, 2009.

174. Aware that he: Barbara Walters interview.

174. Author saw *Goodbye Lenin!*

174. **"A few days before Buddy found out":** Zetta Alderman, interview.

174. **"I was looking in his eyes":** Michelle Tauber, *People*, March 24, 2008.

175. **At times, the pain was so severe:** Barbara Walters interview, January 7, 2009.

176. **Tom Cruise:** Michelle Tauber, *People*, March 24, 2008.

177. **"probably smoking":** Barbara Walters interview, January 7, 2009.

177. **"We're pioneer stock":** Diana Latham, Alexis Patterson, *CBS 42 News* Austin.

178. **"Patsy was worried about Buddy":** Zetta Alderman, interview.

180. **"I've always known":** Barbara Walters interview, 2009.

181. **"I'm still fine to work":** *The New York Times*, October 29, 2008.

181. **"I need to know that people are feeling better":** Cindy Pearlman, YM, April 1988.

182. **"Patsy said that Patrick":** Zetta Alderman, interview.

182. **"My big regret is the physical damage I've done to my body":** Lesley Salisbury, *Sunday Mirror*, April 3, 1990.

183. **I think maybe somewhere Bodhi knows":** Sue Russell, *Sunday Express Magazine*, July 21, 1991.

183. **"Lisa has been a gift and a blessing":** Mary Riddell, *The Daily Mail*, July 29, 2006.

183. **"He doesn't deserve to get this":** Georgina Dickinson, *The News of the World*, February 2, 2009.